No Faith in t

A Search fo

NO FAITH

IN THE

SYSTEM

A SEARCH FOR JUSTICE

SISTER SARAH CLARKE

MERCIER PRESS

MERCIER PRESS
PO Box 5, 5 French Church Street, Cork, Ireland
    and
16 Hume Street, Dublin 2, Ireland

© Sr Sarah Clarke, 1995

ISBN 1 85635 128 9

10 9 8 7 6 5 4 3 2

Royalties for this book will be given to charity.
A CIP record is available for this book from the British Library.

ACKNOWLEDGEMENTS
I would like to thank Sr Christopher Callan for allowing me to
begin my work and Sr Helen Ryder and her council for permission to write this book.

I would like to thank the following people who read the man-
uscript and gave valuable advice: Fr Raymond Murray, Ronan
Bennett, James Chesterman, Pegeen O'Sullivan and Nollaig Ó
Gadhra; thanks also to Sr Miriam Corcoran, SCN, and Melanie
McFadyean for their help in getting this book to see the light of
day.

Printed in Ireland by Colour Books Ltd.

To Giuseppe Conlon
AND THE COURAGEOUS, LOYAL, FAMILIES WHO WERE AN
INSPIRATION TO ME AND OTHERS

CONTENTS

FOREWORD

This is an important book by one of the most significant and heroic women involved in the Anglo-Irish situation over the past generation. In time to come it will form an important chapter in the social, political and human rights history of Ireland and Britain. It will also prick various consciences, especially those of Church leaders and politicians of all colours. Politicians, Irish and British, do not emerge with much credit from this story, and in stating that, I am not confining the criticism to any one party, group or government.

I have no personal knowledge of Sr Sarah but I am reasonably familiar with the La Sainte Union order of nuns because my five daughters were educated by that order in Banaher, Co. Offaly. Great credit is due to Sr Sarah's superiors for allowing her to work for justice when many were too afraid or too politically correct to get involved. Credit is also due to the legal teams, her fellow campaigners and the brave clergymen, such as Fr Denis Faul, Fr Raymond Murray, the late Fr Brian Brady, as well as the late Cardinal Tomás Ó Fiaich for pursuing cases at a time when many people did not want to know.

Sr Sarah's story also concerns the plight of the Irish in Britain, especially the less well-off members, as well as the big cases that are now so sad a chapter of British legal history. The difficulties faced by sectors of the Irish community in integrating into British society are clearly seen in the way that they are treated by practically every level of the British political and legal establishments. There is also the geographical reality that Irish people in British prisons tend to be more isolated than most other groups. The costs and difficulties of visiting prisoners in Britain are also matters that have been fraught with problems. It is this extra dimension of punishment against Irish families that Sr Sarah focuses upon most forcibly and in a way that makes us all face up to the moral responsibility that rests on any authority which separates members of families.

One of the most terrible legacies of the past 25 years of violence has been that of long-term prisoners, jailed for various crimes for which many, but not all, were guilty. Many of the crimes would probably never have been committed had not a whole generation been sucked into a conflict of wrong-doing. But we must, as Sr Sarah reminds us, not abandon the sinners, and we, who are all sinners in various ways, must try to do what we can to end the causes of such terrible deeds, by breaking the cycle of violence, and the context in which it takes root. That is why those of us who set out on the Peace Process in the early 1990s worked so hard, in spite of all the difficulties. Political prisoners, Republicans and Loyalists, played crucial roles in negotiating the ceasefires that brought about that 'cessation of military activity' in the autumn of 1994. Since leaving office I continue to receive communications from parents of families or prisoners themselves, still languishing in prison, including many to my certain knowledge who helped to broker the idea of a Peace Process and a new departure, based on democracy, fairness and parity of esteem. I am glad that during my period as Taoiseach, we finally ratified the long talked-about European Convention on Prisoners that enables people convicted in any part of Europe to be transferred back home to serve their sentences nearer their families.

Sr Sarah is brave, consistent and principled, the moral good Samaritan, working at the coal-face, where she continues to play a pivotal role, in spite of a car accident a few years ago, in spite of advancing years and in spite of the fact that her eyesight has deteriorated in recent times. Sr Sarah has done a wonderful job in helping us to focus on the moral implications of the entire prison and justice system.

Now is the time for dealing with more urgent legacies of the previous political freeze-over, of which the issue of prisoners is one of the most crucial. Sr Sarah has put us all in her debt, by placing on record the horrors of the legacy we are seeking to undo. *Treise le do láimh, a Shiúir! Guím rath ar do chuid oibre agus gabhaim buíochas leat as ucht muid ar fad a chur ar an eolas faoin ghné den saol inár measc nár thug duine ar bith againn, b'fhéidir, aird a dhóthain air, san am atá caite.*

ALBERT REYNOLDS

1

GROWING UP

Deny yourself. Take up your cross and follow me.

I was born on 17 November 1919 to Brigid Claffey and Michael Clarke in the village of Eyrecourt in Co. Galway. My brother Michael was a year older. My father was injured from a fall off a horse, became an invalid and then developed TB. As far back as I can remember he was confined to a wheelchair. My mother Brigid had to take charge of not only the farm but also her own family pub and shop. She was small and stout, kind but wouldn't take any nonsense. I don't remember ever being smacked but I recall often running up the front stairs and down the backstairs and my mother couldn't catch me. I would cry and take refuge between the wheels of my father's chair where nobody could get me.

Although I would never consider myself rebellious I recall with pride that I am named after my maternal grandmother, Sarah Horseman Clarke. I think she must have been wonderful, a real rebel. She climbed out of a window and ran away to elope with my grandfather who was a Catholic, whilst she was Protestant. Her family emigrated to Australia in protest. My mother was very devoted to the Stations of the Cross as I am. Perhaps it's because of her that we didn't grow up bigoted, except now and again when we had rows with the Protestant kids in the village. They'd call us papal candlesticks and we'd call them 'prods'.

Many years later when I was in my seventies, I met my cousin, James Horseman, who was visiting Ireland from Australia for the first time in his life. It was the first meeting with the Protestant side of my family. His father had told him that they all had to get up body and bones and go to Australia after my grandmother became a Catholic. He told me things I didn't know – how his family were mill-owners and during the famine gave flour to starving people. I found it fascinating. He was very friendly.

Michael and I grew up as many do in Ireland. I loved being outside, climbing trees, jumping drains and hunting and fishing with Michael. Our mornings comprised rising at 7.30, Mass at 8, rush home to feed the animals, eat breakfast and be at school by 9 a.m.

When I was eight my ailing father's condition worsened. I remember he was dying for a long time and we weren't allowed in to see him when he got really bad. My mother used enter and leave his room, usually crying. I was at school when he died. We had two women who worked for us – a common thing in those days – and they came for us. I realised my father had died when I saw all the houses and shops on the street had their shutters drawn as was the custom. Then my mother took me to see my father laid out. It was not strange and I don't think I cried. They told us he'd gone to heaven, to God, and I was quite happy with that explanation.

A few years after my father's death my mother married again. Tim Cosgrave was a very rich man having inherited wealth, and he was also very kind. I remember the wedding; it was the first time I tasted champagne and I didn't like it at all. Tim's brother James had represented Galway at the Dáil and in the British parliament before 1922. After the wedding Tim moved into the Clarke family home. He bred horses and sold them to the British Army.

As a young girl I was almost unaware of the political upheavals in Ireland. But I have a vague sense of fearing soldiers as a child that must have come from the recent battle for independence. The barracks had been blown up and there were bullet holes in the gable ends of our house that were left there for years and years. My family was never involved at all – anything but. They were opposed to war. My mother, I remember, was very afraid of war because she believed my brother might be called up to fight for the army. I was terrified of police and courts. I re-member my stepfather going to court to get his licence renewed and I was hysterical because I thought they were going to take him away. There was a doctor in the village, Dr Annie Mason, whose brother Fr Michael Griffith had been taken out by the Black and Tans. We knew the story of how they had tortured him and pulled out his fingernails because they wanted him to tell them what people had told him in confession.

I remember being taken to see a bridge that had been blown up during the civil war. I went in the pony and trap with a woman who looked after us – she must have wanted to see Banagher Bridge for herself. I remember looking down into the black water and feeling frightened.

12

Although I didn't come from a Republican or political family, I had an early sense of the injustice meted out to the Irish by the British over the centuries. I spoke Irish from an early age as it was taught in the primary school in Eyrecourt, and steeped myself in the myths, legends, poetry and history of Ireland. There was a strict head mistress who used a cane. I was a good pupil but got the cane a couple of times across the palm of my hand, once for going off on a political parade, not out of any political consciousness but because it seemed like fun, and once for climbing the walls of Eyrecourt Castle and stealing flowers for the altar of the school chapel.

When I was eleven I went to board at St Raphael Convent, Loughrea, Co. Galway. For a child used to running free the strict régime came as a shock. There were no secondary schools nearby so I had to board. The thought of it was exciting at first, getting new clothes, going away; I thought I was going to heaven. When I got there I nearly died! It was very strict. It was a beautiful huge house and everything was very clean, polished floors, beautiful wooden cubicles but it wasn't home and I was homesick. I found it awful. Edna O'Brien went to the same school and she felt the same way about it. She wrote about it in *The Country Girls*. I have met her a few times and asked her how on earth did we stick it! But it was normal for a school in those days.

There was no talking after 7 p.m., we were in bed by 8.45 and up at 5.30 for Mass. After Mass we had to run over a mile around the grounds. We studied hard. You were fined sixpence if anyone heard you speaking English instead of Irish and you had to go and confess and say, *'Bhí mé ag caint Béarla'*. It was very frugal with no treats. We studied science, maths, Irish, English, Latin, French, geography, history and art. Standards were very high. I failed an exam in the first term and the sense of shame, the humiliation is still as vivid now as it was then.

The pay for teachers was very low and there was no free secondary education so the nuns supplied teachers and they took a large number of people in without charging them fees – Irish education owes a lot to the nuns. My school was run by the Sisters of Mercy who were very aloof – they taught classes and then they left. We had great respect for them. Only one frightened us – the head mistress. If we were talking and she came to the door she would stand there and say nothing and everyone would fall silent. On Sundays she sent us out for a walk and she would tell us to put on two coats, a coat and a rain coat, and galoshes over our shoes. By the time we had all that on we were barely able to walk! We used to take off the rain coats and galoshes and leave them at the gatehouse at the bottom of the drive where Matty, the gate-keeper, lived. But one day Sister Gertrude who was very friendly with the headmistress found all the coats and galoshes!

We went on walks in crocodile fashion, two by two holding hands and always unaccompanied, left to walk by ourselves on our honour. Only once do I remember that we strayed – we saw a lime-kiln and some of us went into it because we were intrigued. We'd never seen one before. Someone told the head mistress and we were punished.

I remember one or two of those Mercy nuns with that special fondness reserved for teachers who inspire lasting admiration in their pupils. One was Mother Aquinas. We didn't know what it was really but there was a mystique about her. She taught us Irish. She was gentle and kind and a great friend of Éamonn de Valera. He would come to visit her in the convent but we never met him. I was very fond of her and had great admiration for her. She used to talk about *Gone with the Wind* and say we should read it, that there was nothing wrong with it; she was very liberal – at the time there was talk of banning it. There were all sorts of whispering about her when she was a young girl. One story went that she had rowed a boatload of guns into Galway for Liam Mellows. We knew what he had done and we also thought he was a hero.

Another nun who made a lasting impression was Sister Kostka Duignan. She awoke in us a love of poetry and English literature at a very young age. She was a great Republican who often said: 'This is called the Free State. But this is not a free state. We still have a governor-general in Dublin'. Her brother was Bishop Duignan from our diocese, a great man, the only bishop to back Noel Browne and the Mother and Child Act. I loved Sister Kostka and kept friends with her until the day she died.

World politics were transmitted through a highly selective lens. The pupils prayed daily for the conversion of Russian Communists and Franco's victory in the Spanish Civil War. The head mistress, Sister Theresa, used to take us to the top study on Saturday evenings and read us bits of that week's papers about Franco's war. We had maps and followed the progress of it. Franco was the 'goodie', everyone else was the 'baddy'. Franco was a Fascist but then there was no such thing as talking badly about

14

Fascism: Hitler was good for the German economy and Franco was a good man, the defender of the Church. The Communists were the great menace. It was only many years later when I read Frank Ryan's autobiography and spoke to other people that I realised that Franco was a real villain and got a totally different picture. Frank Ryan was in the International Brigade and fought against Franco. The nuns described Soviet repression in a way that left a profound impression on me. I remember them talking about the secret police and the knock at the door in the middle of the night, and about the show trials. We were told what Communists did to people who practised their faith and of children being made to inform on their parents. Little did I know that I, too, would encounter the knock at the door and the police!

I WANTED TO BE A NUN for as long as I can remember. I was with the nuns all my life. I remember as a little child dressing up as a nun and saying the Rosary walking up and down the garden as the nuns did. I always wanted to be a nun but I'm not so sure I knew what it meant. I think as very young children we liked the nuns we knew. I have a photo of myself and a little friend dressed up as nuns.

My desire to take vows didn't lessen when I became a teenager. We were idealists; I think all youngsters are. I was not entering the convent for an easy life; I was knowingly entering a life of sacrifice – to serve God and other human beings. In the way you give up sugar for Lent, I was giving up the comfortable life. I didn't expect it to be easy. It was the ideal of doing things for others, of giving yourself to God, to work for God in others – but my heart was as concerned as any young girl's with the romance of adolescence. I had plenty of boyfriends and used to go to dances. I never had a serious love affair; I just used to go dancing, fishing and shooting. In fact I was a bit wild but at the same time as going to the dances I knew there must be more to life. Half my class at school entered convents. I don't know why it doesn't happen now. I think it's because we've grown more materialistic. It was a kind of dedication with us, sacrifice. The word *sacrifice* sounds negative but we were doing something positive by giving up everything to bring a blessing down on those around us and on the world.

It was very hard to give up the freedom I experienced as a child, to face all that my decision implied for the future, to take vows and enter into silence, celibacy and self-sacrifice, but in those days our heroes weren't pop stars; they were the saints. We had pictures of them on our walls. Damian the Leper was my hero but my mother wouldn't hear of me going to work with the lepers. Nobody tried to talk me out of taking my vows, but when I look back on it I understand my mother's pain at losing a daughter.

I used to take her out for drives on Sundays. One Sunday when I was eighteen and had just left school we drove near the La Sainte Union order's convent in Banagher. My mother suggested we call in to visit a friend. This was my first meeting with the La Sainte Union nuns and I was impressed. They were delightfully simple, very friendly, very nice, quite different from the Sisters of Mercy who had educated me and whom I found remote. Obedience, charity, simplicity and silence are the marks of the La Sainte Union order. The simplicity struck me; it was fascinating.

I visited the convent at Banagher several times with a friend Bridie Mulkern, a niece of the parish priest, and the two of us decided to enter the order. My mother had accepted my wishes but on the 3 September 1939 war broke out and my mother was anxious that I should not go to England. Perhaps she was playing for time. I was too young to know how she felt about losing her daughter, fired up as I was with conviction and enthusiasm. On 5 September, a few days before we were due to go to the La Sainte Union's Highgate convent in London, we went to Killashee. We were to travel from there accompanied by some of the Killashee nuns. Since we were now unable to go to London, the nuns at Killashee asked us if we wanted to make our novitiate there and we agreed. So, unexpectedly, I was not to return home – convent life started sooner than anticipated. My mother returned to the convent to collect the family car and to say goodbye. At the time I did not think about how sad my mother must have felt. I was her only girl – it must have been dreadful.

My days as a nun had begun but in those first hours at Killashee I was tormented with anxiety about the contents of my handbag. It was full of make-up. My mother didn't like it. That's why I kept it in the handbag and that's why I had to bring the bag with me so that my mother wouldn't find it after I'd gone. So there was I about to enter the convent with a bag full of make-up.

The convent was set in beautiful grounds with woodlands nearby. I went into the woods with the handbag and threw away the last vestiges of my adolescence and my material freedom. It was my private ceremony brought about not so much by any sense of drama as by sheer panic. I threw the Elizabeth Arden make-up about the woods and went back indoors.

We were unprepared for the noviciate. We didn't have anything to put over our heads so we went into the town and bought black berets. I wore mine until as a postulant they gave me the black lace. I never regretted leaving worldly comforts behind me but I still love lavender perfume.

As a young novice I immersed myself in the novitiate, ever the avid student, steeping myself in history, art and music. We studied the Holy Rule book and the history of the Church. We learned how to open and close doors without making a sound, never appearing to hurry no matter what. I chose the name Sister Mary Auxilius. I was the first novice in Killashee and Killashee is the Church of Auxilius, a very historic church in Irish Church history. It was there that the first synod of Irish bishops was held, presided over by St Brigid. That's why I took the name Auxilius. Although I loved the name other people had great difficulty with it and so I reverted to my baptismal name in 1970.

Entering orders isn't easy for anyone and I was no exception. I soon realised how hard it was. We were completely cut off from family and friends; we were not even allowed to write letters. I think that instilled in me from then an affinity with the prisoners I was later to come into contact with. There was no more privacy; if we received letters they were read. We slept in dormitories. In some convents they were ten or twelve cubicles to a dormitory; at Killashee it was three to a room. We never went home; even though I lived nearby I wasn't allowed to visit. Eventually we were allowed out, after many years, but not home – we had to go to another convent. We had to keep silent except in the course of duty and strict silence from nine at night until five the next morning when we got up for Mass. It was like that for the first twenty years of my life as a nun. It was hard, but I thought in some ways it would be harder. In those days you had to get a trousseau and a dowry. When you saw those old black dresses you knew what was ahead. I was dreading wearing big woollen stockings because I couldn't wear wool next to my skin; I dreaded that and the itchy black serge dresses – the regulation clothing for novices. We were not allowed anything personal, not even a photograph. Before I entered I had a trunk in my room at home and I had to put all the things I might need into it. I had the feeling all the time of turning away from family life. When I got to the convent the trunk was taken from me and kept somewhere. I wasn't free to take things from it. I've taken it home now, back to our family house where my niece lives, where the trunk belongs. It belonged to my maternal granduncle, Fr Michael L'Estrange Cummings. It had accompanied him around the world in his missionary work.

About three months after I entered the convent, the novice mistress called me out and produced a big pair of scissors. 'Now I'm going to cut your hair', she said and she chopped it so badly I was ashamed. I went up the stairs and I cried and cried. A few days later another novice suffered the same fate and I didn't feel so bad. I had thought it was just me. She made a mess of it and you could see our hair because we wore these tiny French veils.

There was a junior boys school attached to the convent where the novices worked. We had to wash the boys' dishes. They had bone china that breaks easily and breakages were viewed seriously. I kept finding bits of bone china floating in the washing-up water as I did the dishes and I always confessed to these breakages. The broken china became a test of my dedication. I was always in trouble over those old cups. I said to myself, the next cup I break I'm going home. I was determined, just as when I was a child and I used to run away when I did something wrong. I never broke another cup. We also had to wash the boys' socks and Reverend Mother made us pray in French, *'Je vous salue, Marie'*, I always associate that with those old socks. I used to wear stockings out in a week but in the convent you always had to wash and mend and darn. Everything was recycled, string had to be unravelled and brown paper flattened and uncreased. It was a great training in economics. Young couples before they get married should take a similar course!

In the summer of 1940 I was given my habit. It consisted of a large petticoat with a pair of big pockets – which were great, you could put the world and his mother into them – a large woollen dress and a woollen shawl. I wore a cap and a band that protruded and a big veil which we had to wear over our faces going up and down to communion. It was terrible to get all these heavy clothes in the middle of summer. Then we were sent out to dig the garden. We had to turn up the veil and push it round and pin back the shawl and dig. I thought then I'd never stick it.

Two years later, my novitiate complete, I was sent to Carysfort Training College in Dublin. I was terrified, twenty-one years old, and really lonely. I've always felt a kind of inferiority complex all my life. I was homesick and isolated at Carysfort for the first few months. I was the first and only sister from my order to go to this college but had visited Dublin several times for the Horse Show. I was terrified and lonely until after Christmas – anxious that I would fail the first year exams. Passing them cheered me and as the new year began I found friends amongst my fellow students. I came out after two years with a First Division Honours and a bilingual certificate so I could teach in Irish or in English. It wasn't only the academic learning that made an impression on me. There for the first time I met people from Northern Ireland. They told me about the big drums the Loyalists banged outside the homes of the Nationalists, about the anti-Catholic songs and tunes and how Nationalist homes were attacked especially during the marching season of July and August. It was completely new to me and the images stayed with me.

MY FIRST TEACHING JOB WAS at Our Lady's Bower, the order's boarding school in Athlone where I went in 1941. My arrival at the Athlone convent was inauspicious. It was a dark, foggy, wet night, so I took a taxi from the station to the convent. Sister Mary Rosa opened the door an inch and peered out, 'Who are you?' she asked.

'I am Sister Mary Auxilius.'

'Who told you to come here?'

'Reverend Mother,' I answered.

'Well, nobody's expecting you,' she said.

I was standing outside all the while with my suitcase. Eventually she let me in. Someone showed me to my bed and said I was not to have airs and graces because I had been at training college. The next day I was told I was to do the cleaning. I spent the whole of the Christmas holidays cleaning the dormitories, scrubbing the toilets and polishing the floors although I did get Christmas Day off and was allowed to listen to the radio. I thought it was a very peculiar place and the first test of my vocation.

I was to spend sixteen years teaching there. It was tough. There was strict observance of silence – we were not allowed to speak. We were the gardeners, the cleaners, the cooks, the doorkeepers, etc. – as well as teaching and running the schools. I was also teaching in Fairgreen infant school. We were in the chapel at 6.30 a.m. for prayers. At 7.10 a.m. I had to open the back gates. Cleaning duties followed. Open the shutters and building. Clean the corridors. Breakfast – walk fifteen minutes to school – teach from 9.30 a.m. until 3.30 p.m. Close school, clean classroom and garden. Return to convent at 4 p.m. Tea – church – vespers – extra classes (art). 6.30 p.m. Matin room – supper at 7 p.m. Washup and close windows, gates, back and front. Recreation – spiritual reading, needlework. It was bed at 9 p.m. and lights out.

I came across a book about child art by some Austrian artists and it made a big impression on me. Although the head mistress wasn't keen on my art teaching methods, a presenter from Radio Éireann, Marion King, encouraged me to enter the children's work in international exhibitions. My pupils were very successful and I showed their work in competitions in East and West Germany, India, South America, the USA and Ireland. The Indian prize was a statue of St George and one of my pupils won first prize. Pandit Nehru was going to present the prize and it was a big honour. Luckily on the day he gave the child a beautiful silver tray with lotus flowers engraved on it. I met Nehru in Dublin at the Department of Foreign Affairs. The children were having tea and he came in and shook hands. We had a little chat. I had him all to myself. We talked about India and I said how honoured I was that we had won the prize. He was very restless, eyes watching everywhere. I asked for his autograph and he gave it to me. I gave it to my grandnephew and I'm sure he has lost it.

I recall another visitor to the convent. I answered a ring at the door to find Seán MacBride standing there. He had given one of the pupils a lift to the school. I opened the door and said you look like Seán MacBride and he said, 'I am Seán MacBride,' so I invited him in. The MacBride family had been pupils at the Athlone school. I gave him tea and showed him the children's art. Seán MacBride was the son of Maud Gonne and John MacBride, executed after the Easter Rising. A lifelong radical Republican, Seán had been IRA Chief of Staff in the 1930s and in later years leader of the Republican party, Clann na Poblachta, and a Dáil member. In 1974, having served as Assistant UN Commissioner in Namibia, he won the Nobel Peace Prize and in 1977 was awarded the Lenin Peace Prize. He was a lawyer by profession and advocated the rights of prisoners. I met him on two other occasions during my work with prisoners. He also allowed Fr Brian Brady of Belfast to use his name to launch the MacBride Principles.

In 1957, after sixteen years at the convent in Athlone, I asked to be moved out of Athlone because I had such a huge work load.

This was partly due to my incapacity to say no to work that needed to be done. It wasn't usual to ask to be moved in those days so they weren't too pleased with me. I was given a week to pack and told to go to England and report to the mother provincial at the Highgate convent.

Just before leaving for England I went home to see my mother. I was allowed back into our family house. I had been home before – for one day – when my stepfather was dying but I wasn't allowed to sleep there. I wandered through the house. My room was as I had left it, all my books and things still there. I did feel odd. I had become so institutionalised. Now my mother was very ill, lying in her bed. I prayed with her and sat by her.

When I left Ireland in 1957, I remember going to the Dublin docks and getting the night boat. I felt very frightened and lonely. I stayed in my berth and went to sleep. I was so miserable and very worried that I wasn't near my mother who was ill, and I couldn't go home to her.

Life in England was better than it had been in Athlone because Athlone was a house of strict observance. In the early days in England I was sent to teach in the La Sainte Union convent high school in Southampton. The hardship I encountered there was of a different nature. The whole culture in England was so different. I felt like Kipling's Kim, always being told that this, that or the other wasn't done here. I felt everything I did was wrong. I realised much later that the education system we had in Ireland was much superior to the one in England. It's strange. I've spoken to other teachers since who felt the same. I didn't know anybody in England and to me it seemed a less friendly society and a different culture than in Ireland where everyone seemed to know everyone. The English class system was very evident. I felt insecure and had to learn what was done there. I prayed all the time because that was my way of dealing with the difficulties.

I wanted to visit my mother again at the end of the summer holidays in 1960. I had had a letter from my mother's doctor saying she was very frail and unwell. I thought I wouldn't be allowed to ask go back so soon, but I told the Reverend Mother that my mother might die. At last she said to me, 'I have good news and bad; you can go back to see your mother but you're being moved from here to Herne Bay.'

I returned to Ireland to visit my mother who was very ill. Still not allowed to sleep at home I stayed in the Eyrecourt convent and visited her at home every day. I would sit by her bed all night watching over her. She looked lovely, really young, pink cheeks and bright eyes. People came to see her and when she'd waken and sit up it seemed there was nothing wrong with her but then she'd fall back with weakness. She died one morning while I was at Mass. It was terrible: you have to experience a mother's death to understand it – you feel so awful. I wanted her to be out of pain but I didn't want her to die because I loved her so much. I was in a kind of dream afterwards.

The dream was a depression into which I slipped, traumatised by my mother's death, by the hostile environment of England to which I returned and exhausted by years of hard work. It was cumulative – my mother's death, this sense that everything I did was wrong. And I am by nature very direct and straight, not diplomatic. I did not ask for sympathy or help: I kept going. With hindsight I regard this as a useful and illuminating phase of my life; it gave me some intimation of what it was to be down and out, to be marginalised, to exist on the edges of society where life is lonely.

THEN THINGS CHANGED. In the mid 1960s, by which time I was living in the convent in Highgate, my health was not good. I was not teaching so I asked for permission from the Reverend Mother to enrol at Chelsea Art School. I felt, by taking the course, I would familiarise myself with the English education system and culture – I was thrilled when permission was granted. It was, I may say, unusual for a nun to go full-time to art school but not impossible.

Chelsea Art School was far removed in cultural, religious and social terms from the years of silent devotion in La Sainte Union convents. This was the heyday of the Beatles, the Rolling Stones, free love and marijuana, particularly amongst students, and especially amongst art students. Into this milieu I walked, dressed in my habit. But things had changed in convent life as well: I had my own room, a little attic under the eaves overlooking Highgate Fields and Hampstead Heath. I also had personal possessions by then: a radio, books and pictures. Nuns had begun to receive letters and we were given our own money, £5 a month, the first I had had since taking my vows.

When I appeared in the Chelsea Art School studios, I was not perceived as a swinging nun. Some of the students were afraid of me at first, I think, and me of them. There was I surrounded by flower power and miniskirts. I expected to be totally alienated but on the contrary I was fully accepted by the students after a very short while. There was a student whom I really thought was a prostitute because she was heavily made up and dressed in black and one day she said, 'I'm so glad you're here and that there is someone who believes in God. Since you arrived at the college they haven't stopped talking about God'. I did everything they did. They insisted! Not mini skirts and pot! But I listened to the Beatles and Elvis Presley and I enjoyed them. I also liked Johnny Cash because he used to sing about gaols; he had been there himself. I was in a queue for tickets for a Johnny Cash concert once and a woman in the queue was criticising him. I defended him. I went to the show. He wore black in solidarity with the poor and the deprived of the world and he will wear all white when injustice is wiped out. The sound of his deep rich voice was wonderful. I liked Mohammed Ali as well although I didn't like boxing. I liked the way he said, 'I'm the greatest!'

I adapted happily to my new life as an art student in Chelsea, opening my eyes and mind to the very different thoughts and lifestyles of the students around me. I still have friends from my time there. There was one, Nancy Fouts, an American student – now a reputable designer in London – who hired a nun's habit and wore it down the King's Road smoking a cigarette. She said, 'How can you bear to wear such clothes?' The students insisted I go to their parties. I'd go and stay for half an hour before slipping away. It became quite fashionable to have 'the nun' about – if I wasn't there someone would dress up as one. It may have been the swinging 1960s, but I never saw any of the students doing anything wrong.

I admired my fellow students with their energy, their 'wackiness', their rebelliousness, even though I have always been cautious and obedient – but I do not put up with foolishness, hypocrisy or injustice.

I made a life long friend at Chelsea in my graphics tutor, Edward Wright. I met Mr Wright when I went there for my interview. He tried to make me feel relaxed, being very friendly and kind. He was from South America and was a very warm-hearted man. He told me that his wife was from Galway and I felt I had an immediate rapport with him. As time went on I grew very fond of him and he always looked on me as family. I am godmother to his grandson. He was a Socialist and a Catholic, having been brought up by the Jesuits. Maurice Goldring was another tutor who became a great friend and when he became ill I did my best to help his family. I was also friends with another tutor, the late Paul Piech and I have a picture on my wall of Mr Wright done by Paul Piech and a design of Mr Wright's as well which his daughter gave me.

Edward Wright contracted cancer at the same time as I had a hysterectomy due to ovarian cancer. I recovered, Mr Wright didn't. On 2 October 1988, Ronan Bennett drove me to see him. He looked very weak but his mind was very clear. I was pleased I had gone to see him though I dreaded going and feared I would weep. He died on 16 October and I wrote in my diary:

> Patsy Wright rang to say Edward died at 8.30 this morning. A wonderful light has gone out. A great man has died and I have lost a great friend. May he rest in peace. I only hope that he will not desert us now in Heaven. I feel very sad.

My Chelsea years had been wonderful partly thanks to him. Chelsea was all the talk at the time – the scandals, the Chelsea set. The students asked me to write to the papers saying what it was really like so their mothers would stop worrying! When I left, the students sent me a farewell letter that said:

> Dear Sister
> Now that you have left us after three long torture-filled years, the school has settled down to real normality once again. We would like to say briefly (in spite of you driving us all mad) we enjoyed your company, your serenity, your generosity, and we wish you God speed in all future ventures. As a special request from Tom, would you desist from singing and dancing with wild abandon in the King's Road as the fines are quite heavy now.
> God bless.

The punks arrived on the scene. While most people were busy condemning them I loved them. One of them got on a bus one day wearing one red stocking and one green and her face painted; it made everyone smile. Anything that makes people smile must be good.

I met a punk another day on the tube – she was on the way to a CND march and I to Westminster Cathedral. Punks usually sit with me; they are very friendly. She was young with red hair frizzed to stand up on her head and a brown-red outline round her eyes with a curled V-shape at the outer corners. She had a gold lustre dress, orange stockings and looked smart. On her face she had a white balloon (as in a comic) outlined in black with an anti-nuclear message on it. It was artistic and ingenious. I did not join the march but stood on the side looking at the banners and twice defended the marchers against critics heckling from the pavement.

My art school days coincided not only with the cultural and social upheavals of the time but with the more serious upsurge of rebellion that characterised the swinging 1960s. Daniel Cohn-Bendit, the vibrant young revolutionary student leader from Germany known as 'Danny the Red', visited London in 1968. Some Chelsea students were invited to attend his training sessions at the London School of Economics and returned to the college full of ideas of strikes, the abolition of exams and other such revolutionary ideas. But I, whilst not being against Daniel Cohn-Bendit, was against the strikes because I thought they would achieve nothing and that if exams were boycotted the students would be the losers.

These were not only times of great political, educational, social and sexual upheaval, they were also years marked by radical religious changes in the Catholic Church. 1965, the year I enrolled at Chelsea, coincided with the completion of the Catholic Church's Second Vatican Council and the publication of its landmark documents. The council's decree on religious life recommends that:

> Communities should promote among their members a suitable awareness of contemporary human conditions ... If their members can combine the burning zeal of an apostle with wise judgements ... concerning the circumstances of the modern world, they will come to the aid of others more effectively. [Second Vatican Council *Decree on Appropriate Renewal of Religious Life.*]

Chelsea had given me back my sense of worth as a person. The Second Vatican Council gave me the licence to begin the work I chose to do.

BEFORE THE SECOND VATICAN COUNCIL convent life was difficult in many ways. It was very restrictive; for example, I could not play the piano or organ when I felt like it even though there were several pianos in the convent. Slowly patterns of life changed in the active orders and reforms began to take place – some of which I did not myself wish to embrace -- like changing my habit for modern clothes. For many years I lived a very strict and disciplined life and there are times when I long for the peace that silence brings. Silence is very soothing, very helpful. I like to have it at certain times. I suppose some people would say I am old-fashioned.

For many years I lived in the enclosed world of convent life; we were not allowed watch television or even have radios or newspapers. I remember the first time I saw a television programme. It was in Highgate Road and involved the arrest of a number of people in a small street. It graphically portrayed the fear and horror the people felt during that raid. Little did I know that I would come very close to knowing that fear. Those images never left me. The second time was when I lived briefly in a convent in Grayes in Essex. One night the head mistress said there was a good programme on the television, *Your Life in their Hands*. There was always silence after 9 o'clock in the evening and this programme was on at 9.30. The television was in a schoolroom lined with bookcases with glass panes in the doors. No matter where you looked there was the reflection of the television. I sat behind the other sister and watched the programme that was about a surgical operation. When the blood started running I tried to look away but it was reflected in all the glass panes. I faint if I see blood and I groaned (we weren't allowed to speak). She thought I was saying how good the programme was and said, 'Yes! Yes!' and I ended up fainting on the floor. At the end of the programme she had to lift me up and get me upstairs. We didn't have permission to watch it but the incident was so funny we told everyone what we had done.

We did not have permission to watch the moon-landing either. I was in the convent in Herne Bay in 1969 when it happened. The geography teacher and I watched it. At the crucial moment the Reverend Mother opened the door. 'What's this! What's this!' she said, and all we could do was turn it off and leave the room. In time the rules relaxed and we were allowed to watch certain designated programmes. That's all changed now.

Doubtless there are those who would consider my allegiance to some of the traditions of religious life old-fashioned. I'm like an old crow dressed in black and white! But I wasn't shocked by those new young nuns. I just hold that nuns should wear the habit because people like to know what you are and that is a silent witness to God on the streets reminding people of another kind of life. We as nuns should be identifiable to people in trouble so that they can come to us and we can try to help them. When we go out the sick and the poor come up to us as they did to Christ and the apostles. We should be the people to listen to the sad and the poor, to say a kind word. I don't mean this to sound patronising but it is the job of a nun to be accessible to people in need whom others might barely notice.

Many times I have been approached by people asking for my help. They identified me by my habit – relatives in visitors' queues in gaols, young people in the visiting-rooms, beggars on the street, distressed passers-by. I think that nuns are very useful at times of family crisis because they don't have families themselves.

Nuns are generally conventional, conservative and traditional – they maintain the status quo. I'm sure I was very conservative myself when I was in the convent in Athlone. We were all very right-wing partly because we didn't get newspapers or see the television news. Nuns didn't even have the vote in those days in Ireland. Later we changed. Chelsea Art School was to give me the boost I needed. I made lifelong friends of both tutors and fellow students and, perhaps most importantly of all, found my self-confidence again after it had been knocked out of me by the old style Reverend Mothers. I felt inadequate until I went to Chelsea but being there made me realise I wasn't the moron I was told I was!

The late 1960s and early 1970s were the years when civil rights movements flourished all over the world. As I listened to the music of the Beatles and the speeches of Cohn-Bendit, the Nationalist community in Northern Ireland rose up again against centuries of oppression in non-violent mass protest. For once I was in tune with the times and was inspired by the licence that the enlightened attitudes of the Second Vatican Council offered me. 'Aid humanity effectively', it said and that is exactly what I set out to do.

2

CIVIL RIGHTS

No one living in Britain today needs the work of social historians to understand that there exists an ingrained suspicion of the Irish.
RONAN BENNETT, *DOUBLE JEOPARDY: THE RETRIAL OF THE GUILDFORD FOUR*

While I was at Chelsea, the Nationalist community in the six counties was simmering. Discrimination was embedded at every political and social level. It began with the colonisation of Ireland by British planters in the seventeenth century. The subjugation of the Irish to the settlers marked the beginning of a long process of discrimination by which the Nationalist population was denied power, property and prosperity while the British and later the Unionist population controlled everything.

Discrimination existed, and still exists, at all levels as did, and still does, poverty. All over the six counties, and especially in Derry, a city with a majority of Nationalists, gerrymandering was practised. Many Nationalists did not have a vote because they hadn't houses and their right to vote in local elections was restricted. The fixing of boundaries ensured massive Unionist returns and supremacy in the highly influential local councils. A survey conducted by the British Labour government in 1968 concluded there was a 'very clear case of sectarian political discrimination.'

WHEN THE RESISTANCE THAT turned into the war of the last twenty-five years began, I was completing my degree in graphics at Chelsea Art School. When this course ended I was offered a place at Reading University, so I happily enrolled to do a post-graduate degree in typography and ergonomics. Three days a week I commuted from London to Reading for my studies. Although I was at art school I still led a sheltered existence. But little by little I was becoming more aware of what was happening in my native Ireland. It was in the newspapers – we used to get the *Daily Telegraph* at the convent.

In January 1970 I was on my way back from Reading. A man on the train began to speak to me. Like many Irish men and women he assumed that, being an Irish nun, I would be sympathetic to what he was saying. He had been on the Burntollet march in January. He told me what had happened. It was shocking.

The Burntollet march was organised by the People's Democracy, forty of whose members went on a four-day civil rights march from Belfast to Derry. They were ambushed at Burntollet four miles outside Derry by a mob of Loyalists, some of them armed with spiked cudgels and led by a vociferous Loyalist opponent of civil rights, Major Ronnie Bunting, then working with the Rev. Ian Paisley. Many of the marchers were forced into the nearby fields and beaten, some severely. Amongst the mob were many off-duty B-Specials. News coverage showed RUC men doing nothing to protect the marchers as their attackers waded in. Those marchers who got through to Derry were met with further violence as they entered the city. That night the RUC went into the Bogside where, in the words of the subsequent British government Cameron Commission, they were 'guilty of misconduct which involved assault and battery, malicious damage ... and the use of provocative sectarian and political slogans'. The next day in protest, the Derry citizens' army was formed and barricades went up. To this day in Derry's Bogside, a wall slogan says, 'You are now entering Free Derry'.

I listened as he told me the story. As he finished his account of the Burntollet march – having been attacked himself – I asked him how did he feel being over here working while all that was happening. He said, 'Oh don't worry, we're all prepared to go home to protect our families'. It made a big impression on me.

Immediately after this meeting on the train I went to the Mother Provincial and asked if I could join the civil rights movement. I felt I needed to do more than just pray for peace. The Mother Provincial suggested I seek the confessor's advice. He suggested I join the Northern Ireland Civil Rights Movement (NICRA), because it was not affiliated to any political party and it was a secular peaceful movement. Founded in 1967 by both Catholics and Protestants it was a hotchpotch of all kinds of people – Moderates, Republicans, Communists, young Unionists. They demanded 'one man one vote', an end to gerrymandering and discriminatory local government laws, the repeal of the Special Powers Act (the precursor to the Prevention of Terrorism Act), the disbandment of the B-Specials and reforms in housing allocation.

I was aged fifty-two when I went to my first meeting and,

despite my years, I was very, very naive. I heard that protesters were being told to sew up their pockets so the police could not plant 'offensive' weapons on them. I thought the government was there to do the right thing and that it would do it if it knew what it should do. I felt it was our business to go out and tell people what was happening, tell them about the oppression of the Nationalist people living in fear, having no jobs, no houses, all the discrimination they suffered. One of the sisters, a historian, wrote to Norman St John Stevas, at the time MP for Colchester. He was a Catholic, so she thought he would be sympathetic. She was disappointed with the reply which she thought was very patronising. I think politicians had the idea that nuns know nothing. I lost faith in him.

I picked another Catholic MP, John Biggs-Davison, and made the first of many subsequent trips to the Houses of Parliament to try and inspire support for Irish nationalists by lobbying MPs. It was an alarming experience. John Biggs-Davison ground me into powder! I was protesting that the Nationalists had no jobs, no houses, that they were discriminated against, I said it wasn't right or just for any section of any community to be treated like that. He asked me what I was doing over here, why was I over here, I should be back in Ireland. He was vicious! I expected he would be telling the cardinal about me and have me chopped up. I rarely show the anger I feel, many times forcing myself to repress it so that it becomes a kind of prickly irritation, something that has foiled people responding to me with bigotry and arrogance. No matter how disgusted or furious I may inwardly be, I am habitually courteous. It has often disarmed those opponents I sought to enlist to help me, including John Biggs-Davison as we became good friends even though we continually disagreed about events in the six counties. He was one of the first people of note to speak out about Giuseppe Conlon.

However, that first encounter left me feeling terrible. I went away feeling very bad. I was sure I shocked him and I thought that man will go to the cardinal and I'll be excommunicated. Instead of that he sent me some of his writings on Northern Ireland. The writings didn't impress me, expressing such sentiments as, 'The demand for Civil Rights in America or Ulster, the cry of one man one vote, in Ulster or Africa, have been used as fronts by ruthless men not concerned for social justice or social revolution. The grievances of negroes, or of Roman Catholics, are magnified and exploited to spread anarchy and bloodshed through countries vital to Europe and the west.' I thought of the man on the train who had been at Burntollet and I knew Biggs-Davison was wrong.

My first NICRA meeting was held in a room over a pub in Archway, not very far from the Highgate convent, but light years away from my life of the previous thirty years. It was so different from anything I'd been doing. I hadn't been in a pub since before I entered the order. I knew a little bit about the police from Chelsea students who had battered old cars but who had friends with Rolls Royces. In their battered old cars the police would stop them and search them for drugs but when they were in the Rolls Royces the police would doff their caps. I knew the police harassed the poor before civil rights came along.

My first great ally as I began my new working life was an Irish woman in her thirties called Eileen Finnegan who was married to the NICRA chairman. I sat beside Eileen and she would kick me and whisper, 'I'll tell you later,' when I made naive comments. I was shocked by so many things. What did I know after all those years in the convent where everyone was good and everything was bright and shiny. Suddenly I realised things weren't as they'd seemed to me.

I swiftly overcame my initial naïveté and within weeks was elected secretary of NICRA in London. At my second meeting in my new post, only two people showed up. I blamed myself that nobody was there. I thought it was because I wasn't doing the job properly. Then we started getting telephone calls that the Special Branch had visited the members' homes and were keeping them under house arrest. I returned to the convent in Highgate in some trepidation and went to see the Reverend Mother to ask had the Special Branch been there looking for me. To my relief, the Reverend Mother said, 'No, but what harm if they come? You're doing no wrong.'

When Bernadette Devlin was elected to the British parliament she articulated the anger and frustration of the Nationalists who were under attack from security forces and Loyalists. The IRA, recently reborn after many years of dormancy, dug out their old rifles and tried to protect the Nationalist community who were under siege. Bernadette asked Prime Minister Harold Wilson to call a constitutional conference to settle the Irish question once and for all. Harold Wilson, heedless of Bernadette's call, sent in the troops. The war had begun. Over 3000 have died since then and countless lives are ruined. Only now, more than twenty-five years later, has the British government agreed to take the Irish Nationalists seriously enough to enter into peace talks with them.

From the start I had assured Reverend Mother that I had no intention of going on marches. I knew that I wasn't an activist in the street sense. I'd always rather be in the background.

Just before 12 July 1971, NICRA sponsored a march in Trafalgar Square. A few days before, in one of the bloody incidents that were becoming sickeningly familiar on the streets of the six counties, two unarmed Nationalist men were shot dead in Derry by the British army. As a gesture of protest, remembrance and mourning I decided to mark the occasion with the carrying of traditional black flags. With a little ingenuity I contrived to make flags out of the old black habits other sisters at the convent were discarding in favour of more modern clothes. An elderly nun, Sister Anna, was in charge of the stores where the old clothes were piling up and, delighted to be rid of it all, helped me to turn the old clothes into flags. I painted some old broomsticks white and stapled the black cloth to them. The marchers carried the flags and the following day a photograph appeared in the *Daily Telegraph* showing a group of people standing around the lions carrying the nuns' old skirts. Startled and amused, I showed this picture to Sister Anna. Neither of us breathed a word, enjoying our secret.

In 1971 I first visited a gaol. A priest from Ardoyne Monastery in Belfast who served as chaplain at Crumlin Road gaol contacted me, asking me to visit some of his parishioners held at Brixton gaol. I had a booklet, published by Jesuits, that a chaplain at Brixton had written about his work – to keep families together and assist visitors. So I rang the Brixton chaplain, thinking I had to go through him to get in. I told him I wanted to visit four people from Ardoyne. He was very unco-operative and abusive – asking why I wanted to see these thugs – but I quoted what he had written in the booklet and he asked how I had got hold of it. I did not tell him.

I went with Eileen Finnegan who was used to visiting prisons. I was surprised to see only two of the four people we intended to see. I don't know where the others were. Eventually I was taken to the chaplain's room and there were these two very young men. The Anglican chaplain gave them the parcels and left. That was the first time I was ever in a gaol, a terrible place: the awful greyness, stone, cement, grey, harsh. I came out and did what I have often seen families doing since. I hung my head and cried standing under the big high grey walls, the old dirty windows, and I could hear the banging and clashing of doors.

The young men were from Ardoyne in Belfast and had come to London and opened a small corner shop in which the police had found weapons. They were later released without charge.

Events in the six counties came to prominence in London soon after 9 August– the infamous Internment Day. That night 342 people were interned, all of them men, all of them Nationalists, all of them held without charge for an indefinite period. It was a fore-taste of the succession of measures taken by one British adminis-tration after another to attempt to quell civil unrest. The subse-quent rioting over two days left twenty-two dead, 240 houses burned out in Ardoyne, and many families from both communi-ties forced out of their homes. Wives and mothers of men held came to London from NICRA's Belfast branch with accounts of abuses suffered by internees in gaol. The stories they told remind-ed me of the history lessons at school when we were taught about repression in the Soviet Union.

We called a big NICRA meeting in the Irish Club in Eaton Square. Fr Denis Faul and Paddy Joe McClean came. Paddy Joe McClean had been one of the 'hooded men' who had suffered the sensory deprivation torture and had been interned. I invited Arch-bishop Roberts and people from the Irish embassy in London. It was a good meeting, they gave us details of the excesses of intern-ment – men forced to run barefoot over broken glass pursued by dogs, being forced to go without sleep and made to stand for pro-longed periods of time, mock executions while they were hooded, standing against walls for hours in the search position, subjected to high-pitched noises and, while blindfolded, dropped from low-flying helicopters. Paddy Joe McClean said they wanted a confes-sor and a priest was brought in but no one would talk to him as they did not trust their captors to bring them a real priest. As the meeting continued it seemed that several disruptive elements were in the hall, determined to stop the proceedings. Later at a similar meeting in Hyde Park these same disruptive people were present. Then it became clear they were planted by the Special Branch. That explained a lot.

I was so appalled that after the visit to London of some NICRA mothers and wives, I documented their accounts of the arrest and imprisonment without trial, the torture and inhumane treatment of the internees. I distributed my notes amongst the Reverend Mothers in as many convents as I could in London and Reading, asking them to contact local MPs and ask if these things were happening. Several months later when I was lobbying in the House of Commons, I found out that none of the Reverend Mothers had acted on the documentation. 'For evil to triumph, it is sufficient that good people remain silent' – the phrase came to life for me then.

But I blamed myself. If I were more important, people would have listened. It made me angry – but what's the good of being angry! I met with a reluctance to talk about the question of the six counties elsewhere in the Irish community. I went to the heads of the Irish associations for help and was immediately treated like a leper. Not that they were rude, but they just turned and walked away. It gave me an terrible feeling. It happened again and again. Perhaps people would have taken a bit of notice of these injustices if they had occurred 2,000 miles away in Russia. There are thousands who, although professing the Christian faith, display apparent indifference to injustice in Ireland. Of the 342 men who were interned, twelve took their cases to the European Commission on Human Rights in Strasbourg. This commission determined in 1976 that their treatment constituted torture and inhuman and degrading treatment.

Two events brought my NICRA membership to an end: Eileen Finnegan's need to return to Dublin and my concern about the disruption of meetings and failure to accomplish work. There was also the fear of infiltration by the Special Branch. Although I left NICRA I retained important friendships formed there.

A few months later I was invited to join the newly formed Irish Civil Rights Association (ICRA) and was elected treasurer. Soon I was to meet a different kind of trouble – from the Church itself. My Provincial Superior, Mother Christopher Callan, told me of a recent conversation she had had with the vicar for religious of the archdiocese of Westminster. The vicar had been contacted by Cardinal Heenan who had asked him to inform the Mother Provincial that I should not be involved in such organisations. As far as Mother Callan was concerned my work had her blessing and I had permission to pursue my work in civil rights. I called on the vicar. He was very nice and said I should get on with my work so I went on working with ICRA for about two years but, just like NICRA, it became subject to internal divisions. It was almost impossible to get on with the work for justice, so I left. When I look back I wonder whether that group had also been infiltrated to subvert any power it might have had.

I am grateful for what I learned during my membership of NICRA and ICRA – how to lobby MPs, organisation skills, and most significantly, the subversion of my own innocence. My fears about another kind of subversion – that of state forces against activists such as myself and groups such as ICRA and NICRA were not unfounded. This spirit of suspicion was based on reality.

There were many times when, expecting commitment and co-operation from other Irish people, I encountered fear, feebleness, disengagement. In those early years Irish people had good reason to fear the activities of paid informers and infiltrators and I consequently found it easier to operate with one or two trusted people. In a way it was easier for me. Although undoubtedly aware of my activities and, as time went on ludicrously paranoid about my intentions as the security forces were, it was more effective and easier for a nun to work openly for civil rights.

IN DERRY ON SUNDAY 30 January 1972, British soldiers opened fire on a peaceful demonstration killing 13 people, seven of them under 19. Everyone was very shocked. We were looking at the news that evening and I remember seeing dead bodies. I was shocked. We saw Fr Edward Daly in the middle of the road with a white handkerchief crawling over to where a boy lay on the ground. Fr Edward Daly was a priest from the Bogside who described what he had witnessed that day:

An armoured car kept coming on. It suddenly dawned on people that this was something different. I remember a young boy laughing at me, I'm not a very graceful runner, that was the only reason he was laughing. He was very cheery ... the next thing he suddenly gasped and threw his hands up in the air and fell on his face. There was a terrible lot of blood. We pulled up his jersey and there was a massive bloody hole. He asked me, 'Am I going to die?' and I said no but I administered the last rites. The gunfire started up again and a bullet struck quite close to me. I lay flat and remember trying to talk to the wounded lad and calm him. He was getting confused and I can remember him holding my hand and squeezing it. We all wept ... we got him to the top of the street. I knelt beside him and told him, 'Look son, we've got you out'. But he was dead. He was seventeen but he looked about twelve. He had a baby face.

After Bloody Sunday I went on my first march. It was the only one I ever went on. Some of the other nuns were going on it and I went to the Reverend Mother and said I wanted to go on this march and she said I could. I went because I was profoundly shocked by the shooting dead of thirteen innocent people. I recall meeting Jock Stallard, MP, on the march, a man I had already lobbied with some success. He was wonderful at the beginning but, like so many others as the situation became increasingly repressive, particularly with the passing of the PTA, they were unwilling to associate too much with the Irish cause. Mr Stallard became privy councillor and to my mind became ineffective regarding Irish civil rights.

As the death toll in Ireland rose in the first years of the war, the after-shocks of bombing and gun battles began to reach Britain. The Irish population in British cities found themselves under attack by formerly friendly neighbours and an increasingly repressive and sophisticated police force. With the rising death toll came the rapid expansion of numbers of people imprisoned in Ireland. In 1969 the Bogside police station was closed due to lack of business, and there were only 750 people in gaol in Northern Ireland. Ten years later, by which time I was fully engaged in my work with prisoners and their families, there were 2,500 prisoners, the vast majority of them locked up for political offences.

3

THE EARLY 1970s

Whenever you listen to someone who is suffering, you hear Christ's voice. And whenever you meet someone suffering, you meet him in person.
DOM HELDER CAMARA

I was to find a natural ally in three Irish priests, Fr Denis Faul of Dungannon, County Tyrone, Fr Raymond Murray of Armagh and the late Fr Brian Brady of Belfast. I have worked closely with these priests for many years. Fr Faul asked me to help Irish people finding themselves caught up with the police and gaols on coming to England so I began my years of ministry to those arrested or imprisoned and their families.

In March 1971 Fr Brady, Clara Reilly, Frances Murray and Seán McCann started up the Association of Legal Justice (ALJ). The ALJ documented the growing number of abuses of Nationalist people attacked, homes raided and people arrested, held, imprisoned, often on flimsy or non-existent evidence, as the British state responded to the upsurge of revolt amongst Nationalists with increasingly re-pressive measures.

My work for prisoners and their families began in those early blood-soaked years as all sides in the war immersed themselves in a violent means to an end. Internment had hardened Nationalist resolve, successive measures to contain, suppress and silence the Nationalists led only to greater resistance – and more suffering. From the start I felt for those families – the families of prisoners.

It has been a war in which sides were easily taken and prejudices easily confirmed, by bombings in which many civilians were maimed or killed and which invited a natural and heartfelt anger and disgust. The Churches, whether Catholic or Protestant, blamed the 'hard men' on either side. In a joint statement in January 1973, the four main Churches of the six counties joined to condemn the violence. 'We appeal to the whole community to root out this evil – tell the murderers and assassins they are on their own. These sectarian and political murders, whether of civilians or security personnel, have brought shame and tragedy to countless homes. They are a crime before God and a disgrace to our common Christian heritage.'

The majority of clerics of all denominations spoke in such terms denouncing evil, blaming the IRA (and to a lesser extent the Loyalist UFF and UVF) but never the security forces or the absence of justice. Irish people in Britain became pariahs as far as the British general public was concerned – they were shunned, feared, reviled. People picked up and questioned were frequently denied basic human and legal rights. Irish people who lived in Britain for years found themselves arrested and treated as though guilty. To their families, the prisoners were not hard men or women, they were the boys and girls they had given birth to, brought up, or the men and women they had married and borne children with, drawn into a war that had its origins in colonialism dating back 800 years.

Anyone suspected of being associated with even the fringes of the Nationalist and Republican movement, let alone those thought or known to be connected to the IRA, could expect harsh and frightening treatment, reaching its zenith in the dubious convictions of the Guildford Four and Giuseppe Conlon, the Birmingham Six, the Maguire family, Judith Ward and many others all of whom have since been proved innocent, all of whom I was to work for and get to know.

Fr Faul, Fr Brady, Fr Murray and myself, unlike almost all other Church people, never judged the prisoners. Our motives were humanitarian and religious – not political. Christ never condemned the sinner – only the sin. To us the question of what bought them to gaol was not asked. To me the cause of conviction is irrelevant no matter what a prisoner has been involved in. Christ said, 'I was in prison and you visited me'. He did not say 'I was innocent and in prison and you visited me'. I don't judge prisoners according to their guilt or innocence, to me whether they are Loyalist or Nationalist, criminal or political, if they ask for help, I help them. My mission has never been political but humanitarian – to ease the suffering and hardship of prisoners and especially their families. That I had a special sympathy for Republican prisoners stems from the belief that had it not been for the political situation they would never have been in gaol, nor would their families have suffered or seen the inside of a gaol.

I spend much of my time in prayer and read the gospels every day drawing strength from them, as I also do from reading liberation theologians such as Gustavo Gutierrez and Dom Helder Camara. I love these and Leonardo Boff's book on the gospels. He was a liberation theologist who had been a Catholic priest; Dom Helder Camara was a Brazilian bishop. These were a great consolation to me because I felt strange when chaplains told prisoners not to go near me saying I was bringing the Catholic Church into disrepute.

No sooner had I begun my gaol work when the war came to London in a big way with the Old Bailey bombing on 8 March 1973. On the day of the bombing, car bombs were placed at four London locations, including the Old Bailey and Scotland Yard. There were 180 injuries, none of them serious, but one man who had been evacuated died a few days later of a heart attack. About 11.00 a.m. that day ten young people en route to Northern Ireland were arrested at Heathrow airport and charged with causing explosions.

I heard the names of those arrested on the radio news, names which meant nothing to me but were to become very familiar: Marian and Dolours Price, Hugh Feeney, Gerry Kelly, Roy Walsh, Paul Holmes, Billy Armstrong, Róisín McNearney, Martin Brady and Liam MacLarnon. I got a phone call claiming the sisters were being held in a police cell, their clothes had been taken from them for forensic testing. The refused to wear the police issue clothes and so had only a blanket to cover them. This was the first of many times I'd come across prisoners being forced to strip naked. I was appalled. Without your clothes you're depersonalised and extremely vulnerable. Some prisoners have told me the clothes usually are comical and ill-fitting. Often when I meditate on Christ's passion I am astounded at how little man's inhumanity to man has changed in two thousand years. In spite of science and technology, the gaolers still revert to the most degrading punishment available – stripped naked, paraded in ill-fitting garments, jeered and mocked, the prisoners' lot has not changed.

From the start these young Irish people were determined to serve their sentences in their own country, near to their families. At the time of writing there are still twenty-four Irish prisoners in gaols in England, hundreds of miles from their families. While Home Office policy is to 'make very effort to locate prisoners as close as possible to their own communities' this seems not to apply to Irish prisoners. William Whitelaw, the Home Secretary wrote a letter to a Labour MP in 1981, 'Where a prisoner has been convicted of a terrorist offence [committed in Britain], the balance is heavily weighed against a transfer [to Northern Ireland]. The return of a terrorist to a prison system where he might be regarded a hero by a substantial proportion of his fellow inmates might well diminish, and be seen to do so, the deterrent value of the punishment imposed for the offences.' Many of the Irish prisoners in gaol in England have been there for over twenty years. I have noticed that Loyalists convicted here of political offences are either sent home or serve their sentences in Liverpool – only a boat trip away from Northern Ireland.

But so determined have Irish prisoners been to serve their sentences in gaols in Ireland, that they have gone on prolonged hunger-strikes. Four of those young people arrested in 1973 for the Old Bailey bombing became household names when they went on a hunger-strike after their conviction in November that year. That hunger-strike lasted 207 days, during which time they were force-fed.

When the ten were first arrested and remanded, ICRA held a meeting. We got details from their distraught families who came over but in those days we didn't have to worry so much about the families as there were plenty of people who would meet them and accommodate them. When the Old Bailey people were in Brixton gaol, some of the Irish community rented a house where families could stay. They were also provided with food and transport. I went down to Brixton gaol with parcels. I was scared and very worried that they were in that horrible place. I asked to see all of them. There was no problem. I saw them one by one in the visiting-room. I was amazed as were their lawyers that they did not grumble or complain; they had accepted what had happened.

After Easter, only weeks after their arrest, I received a letter from Róisín McNearney. I read something that appalled me. She claimed a chaplain in his Easter Sunday sermon had told the gaol community attending the Mass that the Irish had the audacity to stage their rising on the day of Christ's resurrection. He also attacked the Irish for choosing the beautiful Easter lily as a symbol of the rising. This was substantiated by other prisoners. To me this was an example of an anti-Irish feeling embedded in every institution of British society, the Church being no exception.

All the Irish prisoners refused to attend Mass after this. Their refusal was of great concern to their families. It was bad enough being in gaol without the double blow of not being able to go to Mass. I rang Fr Brady and told him what was happening and he said, 'Sister, you have an obligation to go and tell each one of them they have no obligation to go to Mass'. I did this – no wonder I'm banned from gaols.

Fr Brian Brady recommended that I contact Monsignor Cunningham, then the head Catholic prison chaplain in England and request a new priest for Irish prisoners in Brixton. He received me courteously and I asked for another priest for them, explaining that if enclosed nuns need an extraordinary confessor, how much more do prisoners need someone to whom they could relate? Monsignor Cunningham promised to send in another priest although it would not be an Irish priest. I said I had not requested an Irish priest. Then I mentioned that Brixton gaol – that grey awful place, that depressing blur – needed a woman's touch. The poor man nearly died of shock! He said you could not possibly have a woman working with rapists and other criminals. However, today many nuns and deaconesses work with prisoners very successfully. He asked me did I want any other favours for them and I said no, I was only concerned with the spiritual side. I think he was suspicious of me even though he was very gracious and kind. It wouldn't surprise me if someone had been speaking to him.

Chaplains who are perceived to be too kind to the prisoners don't last long in the system. I know of two, one in Leeds who refused to go into the control unit in protest at the way the prisoners were treated, he said it was inhuman – he was transferred out of the prison service immediately. Then there was one in Wormwood Scrubs who was very good to the Irish prisoners and he got such a tough time that he had to leave the prison service immediately. The prison chaplain in Britain carries keys like a prison officer and sits on punishment boards. He has the power of veto over correspondence to prisoners and power of veto over visits to prisoners. In other words, to the prisoner he is part of the establishment. Nuns who are now part of the chaplaincy have no such power and do not carry keys. They're much more acceptable to the prisoners. The Old Bailey people did get another priest who went into the gaol to say Mass for them every Friday.

Every week during the period of their remand, I took ten parcels to Brixton gaol for the Old Bailey suspects. I scraped the money together for the parcels. People I knew – even though they had little money – would put money in my hand which would buy the food for the parcels. I had an old van then and it was always breaking down. It made the prisoners laugh because I'd always arrive with blackened hands from poking at it to make it go on the many occasions when it would just stop. For years Hugh Feeney and Gerry Kelly used to joke about that van.

During my visits to Brixton gaol I grew fond of the Old Bailey defendants and when they were moved to Winchester gaol a month before the trial began, I continued to visit every Sunday. Unknown to me until afterwards, Special Branch officers had come to the convent and the school asking questions. They had not specifically asked for me or about me. But it was odd. When I asked Mother Superior for permission to attend the trial, I was shocked by her response which was, 'I am warning you that you had better mind yourself'. When the trial began I went to it for several days. My actions did not go unnoticed. Later that year I went on holiday to Ireland to visit a cousin and her husband. My cousin was married to a northern Protestant who converted to Catholicism when they got married. This man, an educated, interesting man, was a Unionist in spite of the fact that he worked for the Irish government. He showed me a newspaper report which was critical of me because I'd attended the trial. I said it's a matter of justice and I was in Civil Rights. He replied if you give Catholics an inch they'll take a mile. It was no use arguing with him. It was an example of the entrenched hostility and suspicion shown towards the Republican prisoners and their families.

I also had to get used to the world of the British courts. It was my first experience of courts and of the security measures. I was always mending things and my handbag was like a toolman's bag – scissors, screwdrivers: you name it, it was there. They'd take my bag and put everything out of it in front of everybody and it was mortifying. I was searched and frisked, under the arms, between the legs and while some of the searchers were very courteous, others were very strange. Oh it was horrible. As I came away I felt dirty. I didn't object to being searched but you did get these very strange women.

On the last day of the trial when they were sentenced, I was struck by the attitude of the defendants. They weren't a bit cowed. They waved at me. I was mesmerised by it all. They made speeches from the dock and it bought me back to history lessons in the classroom when I was a girl with Emmet's speech from the dock.

The trial ended on 15 November 1973. Marian and Dolours Price, Gerry Kelly, Hugh Feeney, Billy Armstrong, Paul Holmes, Roy Walsh and Martin Brady got life sentences. Liam MacLarnon got fifteen years. Róisín McNearney was acquitted. The lifers immediately applied to serve their sentences in Ireland and announced that unless the request was met, they would go on an indefinite hunger-strike. After they were convicted I was stopped from visiting gaols. Marian and Dolours Price, Hugh Feeney, Gerry Kelly, Roy Walsh, Paul Holmes, Billy Armstrong, Martin Brady and Róisín McNearney are amongst the only Irish prisoners I have been able to visit.

After the trial the families went back to the house in Brixton where I met them. I was feeling very low and Mr Kelly tried to cheer me up by saying that they would be transferred soon. At 9 p.m. we watched the television news. Greece, Middle East, USA, everything but at last the Winchester trial. The families were very angry at the way the case was reported. They tried to ring the number of the BBC but were left hanging on so long that they gave up. After the trial a group of relatives had waited for the prisoners' possessions – as they had been found guilty, the family were obliged to collect their possessions and take them away. They packed them into their car and set off for London. Within minutes they were surrounded by police on motor-bikes and in cars. They were ordered out of the cars in the pouring rain. They were told to accompany the police to the police station and driven there under escort. No reason or explanation was given. At the police station, one of the relatives asked again why they were been treated like this. 'Orders from the top', they were told. Although told they were not under arrest, they were not allowed to go for a walk. Eventually, the bags were bought in and the contents taken out. The police removed things from all the properties. They did, however, overlook one set of depositions.

I wasn't allowed to visit the Old Bailey prisoners, or to write to them. Nobody was allowed any contact with them who had not known them before they were arrested. This was to isolate them. I wrote letters but they were sent back. The prisoners were bought to different gaols all over the country and all of them went on hunger-strike. Some came off after a short time, a week or fortnight, but Marian and Dolours Price, Hugh Feeney and Gerry Kelly stayed on it for 207 days.

The hunger-strikes were gruesome. Marian Price wrote in a letter to her family describing a force-feeding session on Friday 1 February:

> I was pulled from my bed and carried bodily by the arms and legs from my cell to the room where it takes place. I was put in a chair, my legs were held and my arms forced up my back and held tightly. My head was held and my nostrils blocked in an attempt to open my mouth for air. I opened my lips to breathe but kept my teeth tightly clenched together. Pressure was then put on my chin several times to make me open my teeth apart, but I held on. At this stage I was blindfolded and a metal clamp was used to prise my teeth apart, the wooden gag was then placed in my mouth and the plastic tube shoved down my stomach. After the liquid had been poured in the clamp and gag were removed, they then took the blindfold off and I was carried back to my cell. I was in a state of hysterics by this time.

Marian and her sister Dolours, Gerry Kelly and Hugh Feeney were undergoing this treatment every day. The day that Marian Price describes was the fifty-eighth day. In notes at the back of my diary for 1973 I wrote out an extract from a letter from Gerry Kelly to one of his family:

> On 5 March, last Friday when I was force fed as usual I brought a lot of it up again but ... [it was] poured ... back down the tube to my stomach again.

The hunger-strikers' account of their ordeal differed from the account given by Home Office officials who said they chose the way they were fed. They said that they had never been held down or subjected to physical pressure.

Negotiations over this hunger-strike were secret and complex. I was not directly involved with that side of things, but I introduced Jock Stallard, MP, to Fr Brian Brady in the convent where they met at several intervals during negotiations. Roy Jenkins was the Home Secretary at the time and, through an intermediary, contact was established with him to start negotiations in resolving the hunger-strike.

As the hunger-strike went on, press interest picked up. The journalists got to know that the families were in a house in Brixton. When they found out the phone number, the families were inundated with calls especially at the time of negotiations. But they were secret and nobody was supposed to know anything. The families had to answer the phone because it might have been a call from one of their relatives. So if it was the media Sarah Feeney would pretend to be an answer-phone and in a tin-pan voice she would say please leave your message after the beep. If it was family she'd talk. But she forgot what she was doing one day. A man had rung from one of the prisoner's aid committees and she pretended to be the answer-phone. The man said, 'They've got a bloody answer-phone,' asked a question, left a message – and Sarah forgot and answered it. The man said, 'It's a bloody computer they have – it's answering us'.

I gave my support to the families who stayed in the Brixton house throughout the period of remand and continued to lobby MPs and members of the House of Lords. I wrote many letters. Meanwhile outside Wormwood Scrubs where Gerry Kelly was held, an Irish psychiatrist Máire O'Shea (some years later to be imprisoned herself on suspicion of conspiracy) mounted a mock force-feeding demonstration with the actress Siobhán McKenna. It made an explicit point about the pain and indignity of force-feeding – it is really a torture. I was there when they were doing it but I never know whether these demonstrations are a good thing or not.

I was not involved in the negotiations between Jock Stallard, Fr Brady and Roy Jenkins, but I was aware that the regular meetings in the convent were crucial if the hunger-strikes were to end. The meetings then transferred to the House of Commons with Fr Brady acting on the prisoners' behalf. The negotiations stopped temporarily as the six counties faced a political crisis in May 1974. The Ulster Workers' strike, fuelled by Loyalist leaders William Craig and Ian Paisley, broke out. Men with clubs, dressed in combat gear, some masked, others wearing dark glasses roamed the streets threatening violence to anyone who wanted to break the strike. Power and water were frequently cut off. The six counties came to a standstill. Car bombs went off in Dublin and Monaghan killing thirty-two people and injuring one hundred.

The strike bought down the agreement forged at Sunningdale in Kent only six months before by British Prime Minister Edward Heath and Taoiseach Liam Cosgrave in which the governments of Britain and Ireland, in consultation with Northern Ireland constitutional politicians, had agreed on power-sharing. The agreement was popular with some political parties, including the Social Democratic and Labour party (SDLP) but, ironically, it was equally unpopular amongst the rank and file Loyalists and some Nationalists. To some Nationalists it meant that their own people – the SDLP – would be colluding with the British government. To Loyalists it was a threat to the Union and their privileged life-style. On 28 May 1974 Brian Faulkner, chief minister of the Northern Ireland Executive together with the Unionist members in the Northern Ireland Administration, resigned. That ended the statutory basis for the Northern Ireland Executive and so ended the power-sharing experiment.

It was against this backdrop that the Old Bailey prisoners continued their hunger-strike, every bit as determined to get the results they wanted as the Loyalists had been in mounting their protest. During the strike the negotiations continued with every-one bound to secrecy with a threat of the end of negotiations if the media were informed. On the Wednesday of that week Fr Brady and myself were in the House of Parliament with Jock Stallard and Roy Mason awaiting a successful resolution to the hunger-strike. As we came into the lobby we met a politician who realised something worthwhile was happening and he immediately began to realise that political capital could be made if he were seen to be on the committee. Up to this point he had not been involved in anything to do with the hunger-strike. The following Friday the Home Office proposed that if they ended their hunger-strike they would eventually be able to return to serve their sentences in Irish gaols. The four hunger-strikers agreed to the terms and we were all elated. Fr Brady came to the convent to collect the chalice for the Mass we had planned to hold in the house in Brixton and he told me to have the altar ready in the house for a thanksgiving Mass. I believed that I was supposed to tell my Reverend Mother everything. Fr Brady met her at the convent and she told him that the strike was over, as she told everyone else who came there. Fr Brady was furious with me in case the end of the strike would be jeopardised and he said you don't have to tell her everything! He said Mass in a very emotional and highly charged atmosphere in celebration of the resolution to the strike in the house where the families had been staying. He read out the letter Dolours Price had written saying her goodbyes and asking that there should be no violence as a result of their deaths. The altar cloth used that evening is now the possession of the Feeney family.

On 5 June, just two days before the Old Bailey people ended their hunger-strike, an Irish prisoner from Mayo called Michael Gaughan, who had been force-fed, died in Parkhurst gaol on the Isle of Wight after sixty-five days on hunger-strike to get a transfer to a Northern Ireland gaol. Whilst it didn't deter the four others or influence their decision to end their hunger-strike, it frightened their families.

Neither myself nor Fr Brady knew the Gaughan family, nor were we involved in his protest but along with many people from the Irish community in Britain we attended his funeral Mass. I was sitting beside a Special Branch man. He was peeping into my prayer-book to see if the priests were deviating from the norm. When the funeral was over he stood up and turned right around with his back to the altar so that he could survey the crowds – he was very tall I remember.

During the following months as Marian and Dolours Price, Hugh Feeney and Gerry Kelly waited to return home, I lobbied the Labour peers Lord Brockway, and Lord Longford and Jock Stallard, MP – agitating for *all* the prisoners to be sent back. When Lord Brockway replied testily that he could not take on everything, I reminded him that he was one of the people who had guaranteed they would be sent back. Then he remembered and promised to write to Roy Jenkins.

The saddest thing of all was the mothers, their suffering. In February 1975 I went over and stayed with Hugh Feeney's family to whom over the years I have become extremely close. It was a sad occasion, the death of Mrs Price, Marian's and Dolours' mother. The sisters had not yet returned to Northern Ireland. I rang my contacts at the Commons and the Lords to try and get parole for them but to no avail.

On that first trip to the six counties Belfast looked lovely from the sky, the lights like lacework. I went on the 8.05 plane full of soldiers – well-fed, well-dressed and loud. I did not enjoy the flight. My brief-case was put into a blue plastic bag and I was searched by two women police after the baggage was examined. There were no hostesses on the plane and the stewards were more like 'strong men'. I got my first glimpse of the army with guns on the ready when I arrived at the airport. The Feeneys met me. We went over to the Price home and it was full. We met Máire and Jimmy Drumm and Harry White (condemned to death under De Valera). The remains were waked in the house as is the custom in Belfast. I stayed with the Feeneys in Belfast and they drove me to visit all the other families. They housed me and fed me. I felt very close to Hugh's mother, Kathleen, and his sister Mary. I was also close to Mrs Walsh and Mrs Holmes. Marian and Dolours Price's mother died while they were in Durham. Imagine their sadness.

Waves of joy came over me with the announcement of each one's return. First to return were Marian and Dolours Price. Five years later Marian was released, dangerously ill with anorexia nervosa, an illness that dated back to the hunger-strike. Not long afterwards Dolours was also released, she too had anorexia. On 8 April 1975, Gerry Kelly's wife Isobel went to visit him in England only to be told he had been transferred. 'I spent the day between the phone and looking up in the sky at the helicopters in case they were passing on their way back,' Hugh Feeney's sister Sarah said. I got a phone call from Lord Longford to say they were back in Ireland at 5.15 p.m.

The young men's journey had been eventful. Handcuffed to Special Branch men, they were flown to Belfast's Aldergrove Airport on a scheduled flight. Just before entering the aeroplane, Hugh Feeney stood on the top of the stairs to the plane and turned and spat saying he would never set foot on English soil again. He found when he was shown to his seat that Ian Paisley was sitting behind him. Their four co-defendants were not transferred to Ireland until many years later.

For me the experience with the four hunger-strikers was a baptism of fire, a loss of innocence, a brutal lesson in Anglo-Irish politics that was to stand me in good stead for many harsh years ahead. These years were marked by increasingly draconian British attitudes to the Irish and by a mounting death toll. I was officially barred from visiting Irish prisoners in English gaols but continued to offer whatever help I could to the many beleaguered families who were, and are, often neglected. A few months after Gerry Kelly, Hugh Feeney, Marian and Dolours Price went home, the Prevention of Terrorism Act was dragging in its wake many innocent people.

4

THE PREVENTION OF TERRORISM ACT

In Germany they first came for the Communists; I did not speak because I was not a Communist. Then they came for the Jews; I did not speak because I was not Jew. Then they came to fetch the workers, members of Trade Unions; I did not speak because I was not a Trade Unionist. Afterwards, they came for the Catholics; I did not say anything because I was a Protestant. Eventually they came for me, and there was no one left to speak ...

PASTOR MARTIN NIEMÖLLER

On 21 November 1974 two bombs went off in Birmingham pubs killing nineteen people and injuring 182. I was horrified by the bombings and deaths. I hate bombs anywhere, at any time, and I am appalled by the suffering. The anti-Irish feeling whipped itself into a rage, with petrol bombs lobbed into Irish clubs and Irish workers sent home from factories for their own safety. Things were difficult enough: families were coming over, trials were coming up and the bombings affected the outcomes.

In a frenzy to produce culprits for an enraged British population, ten innocent people were arrested for the Guildford and Birmingham bombings. All but one was Irish. The IRA has always said none of the people accused had anything to do with either their organisation or the bombings. It was enough that they were Irish or connected to Irish people. Torn from their communities and locked up, victims of official cover-up and abuse, the ten were imprisoned and sentenced to life imprisonment. Over the years I was to get to know all of them and their families, some very well. I was always suspicious of the convictions, never doubted the nine men and one woman's innocence and believed accounts of beatings and gross irregularities in methods of interrogation leading some of the suspects to make false statements. The wives and children of the Birmingham men who had lived for years in that city were forced to leave their homes

The six men accused of the Birmingham bombings were on

their way to the funeral in Belfast of an IRA man, James McDade, who had blown himself up with his own bomb in Birmingham. He was from their community, some of them had known him since school days and, in Ireland, attending the funeral of an IRA man does not imply involvement with or support for the IRA. But this was enough to justify their arrests in Britain. The only 'evidence' against them was forensic tests done on their skin and clothes revealing traces of nitroglycerine but the same results could have been gained from cigarettes, playing-cards or a range of household chemicals. The six were not released until 1991. I worked very hard for them as I did on behalf of the Guildford Four – three young Irish men and an English girl, teenagers from Kilburn squats and hostels who like a million others, had dabbled in drugs and rock and roll, and nothing more sinister than that.

I do not differentiate in my work for the wrongly accused such as the Birmingham Six, Guildford Four, Maguire Seven and Judith Ward and my work for Gerry Kelly, Hugh Feeney, Marian and Dolours Price and in later years the Balcombe Street Four – Harry Duggan, Eddie Butler, Martin O'Connell and Hugh Doherty or those convicted of the Brighton bombings, Martina Anderson, Ella O'Dwyer, Pat McGee and Gerry McDonald and many others. It is not my business to condemn this one or that. These young people ended up in gaol because of grave injustices in the six counties. People have an image of the Irish prisoner, assisted by the British and Irish media, as thugs and psychopaths. I visited these prisoners, highly intelligent young people who would never have been engaged in violence if it had not been for the oppression of their people. Later that year the British government extended its powers. These bombings were the catalyst for the Labour government to rush through the most repressive legislation of the twentieth century – the Prevention of Terrorism (Temporary Provisions) Act. Far from being a temporary provision, this act has remained on the statute book, renewed every year with a large majority in the House of Commons. Under the PTA people can be held for forty-eight hours without any charges being filed and a further seven days if deemed necessary. People can be 'excluded' under the PTA – summarily exiled from England, Scotland or Wales to Ireland for several years at a time and only allowed back after appeals which often fail. The act made membership of the IRA illegal but it did not forbid membership of any other paramilitary organisation. The law imposed a positive duty on all citizens to report any information concerning possible suspicious activities to the police, even if this meant information about family members.

Under the PTA in the first twenty years from 1974–1994, 7,397 people were held and questioned. Of these arrests 92.58% were neither charged nor excluded and of those few who were charged, most were charged with criminal and not political offences. The PTA instilled greater fear into an already fearful Irish community and for many the experience left its mark.

Over the years I worked with many such people and it was against this backdrop that my work expanded dramatically. It soon became clear that the authorities weren't really finding the guilty so much as taking in the innocent. My files and diaries are full of bits of paper with hastily written notes, details of people arrested at ports, stations and airports all over the Britain, usually ordinary Irish people on their way somewhere with no thoughts of guns or bombs. 7,397 were arrested but many thousands more were routinely stopped for short periods of time at ports of entry.

Everything about the PTA is excessive. It induced terrible paranoia and it has been used with abandon. It has allowed the tabloid newspapers to whip up anti-Irish hysteria, especially in the first six years. Thousands of innocent people have been caught in its net – including a British soldier and the daughter of Stella Rimington, now the head of MI5 although, unlike its other victims, she got compensation. The Irish government didn't care. Michael O'Kennedy, a government minister, was taken in, Joe Mulholland, head of RTE News, was also held – both were detained without any justification. Neither the government nor the media in Ireland did anything worthwhile to expose the hardships people endured under the PTA.

While people were held the press had a field day – the people were automatically culprits. The matter wasn't sub judice until they were charged so very often if it went to trial, there had been trial by media before it got to court.

My phone never stopped ringing. My name soon travelled through the networks in the Nationalist communities and became known to many Irish families. I regularly got calls asking me to find out what had happened to people on their way to England who had not turned up. I would ring round police stations, often fruitlessly as police failed to tell me if this or that person was being held. I was also involved in formal attempts to contest anti-Irish legislation but met with scant success as attitudes had hardened and there was little sympathy for the Irish.

In November 1975, a year after the PTA became law, I went to a conference called by the British Section of Amnesty International on 'Women and Torture' chaired by a Labour MP. There were workshops before the main conference and I joined one on prisoners. I introduced a resolution calling for prisoners to be allowed to serve their sentences in gaols near their homes. It was passed by the workshop to go forward to the conference but that was the last I heard of it. During a break I went out to put money in the meter where I had parked my car and found I already had a ticket. I was in a bad mood after that! I came back in and there in the foyer were some women from a group called Women United, Irish and British, calling for an end to the PTA and internment. They asked me to read out their motion, I suppose because I was a nun. When I read it out the hall was only half-full. The proposal about repatriation of prisoners was adopted by the conference – but the chairperson ruled it out of order because the British section of Amnesty International has a policy of not getting involved in domestic issues. Women United walked out in a fury. The hall then filled up and those who had just arrived wanted to hear what this resolution was so I was asked to read it again. Again a vote was taken and it was passed. Again it was vetoed. When the conference voted for our motion, the chairperson vetoed it. Then a woman stood up on the stage and proposed a motion about the Basques – it was full of bombing and violence and it was passed and not ruled out of order. Just then an old lady got up and said if the Basque woman's motion was accepted so should mine. I was asked to read it again! I thought I'd never stop reading that motion. Still it was ruled out of order. When the conference ended I made a beeline for the stage and the chairperson. A lot of blue rinse ladies were gathered on the stage as though they thought I was going to attack her. I said to her, 'you have been most undemocratic', and the blue rinse heavies crowded round her as if protecting her from me!

The *Irish Post* reported that the 'discussion of Ireland was deemed irrelevant although the majority of women were in favour of discussion of Irish political prisoners and the PTA'. I was disappointed in Amnesty International. We went to

Amnesty repeatedly. They listened and made notes but did nothing. Although Amnesty were slow to react to what was happening in Ireland they redeemed themselves in reports on ill-treatment of detainees they brought out later and their reports on the shoot to kill policy.

As well as the ever-increasing work helping those held under the PTA, I was still teaching three days a week and taking parcels up to the prisons – in itself a day's work. I was becoming exhausted and was subject to regular bouts of illness that I frequently ignored because I was so busy.

Many of those who had worked with me before – putting up families or helping in this or that way – now suffered arrests and harassment. Several Irish people in Britain packed up and went home. There were only a few left who felt able to offer hospitality to Irish families. That was a big change. Margaret O'Brien, an Irish housewife in Walthamstow, had had families to stay but then her husband was excluded under the PTA and they left. Pat McCabe and his wife Maureen, another ordinary Irish family who used to help to put up families and meet them at the airport went back to Ireland – life was too difficult here. Rose and Jim Ryan, another ordinary London Irish family, friends of mine, kept families for me. They began after the PTA when I asked them because I hadn't anybody. They didn't escape police attention but weren't harassed.

The atmosphere had changed. I remember an announcement on the radio saying that people listening to traditional Irish music should be reported. At first shocked and unbelieving, I became accustomed to stories of arrests being made in the middle of the night, or raids mounted during the day at workplaces, of van loads of policemen with guns and dogs, of doors kicked in and terrified families held in their own homes whilst walls were taken down and floors ripped up, of possessions taken away, letters, gramophone records, anything thrown into plastic bags, of children crying as parents were handcuffed and led away. The PTA caused much more terror than it prevented and remember – if you were raided – even if nothing was found and you were as innocent as the next person – you were shunned by neighbours who assumed the raid implied guilt of some sort. My files on the PTA bulge with details of people visited at work by Special Branch officers and losing their jobs as a result, of others en route to jobs in Germany held and questioned and let go too late to

catch the flight they'd paid for or the ferry crossing they'd bank-
ed on getting and hence losing their jobs. One of the very strik-
ing things about the many stories my files tell of people held
under the PTA is that, despite their treatment, few of them were
ever charged or found guilty of anything. But the toll on people's
lives was terrible. Numerous people detained for seven days suffered psychological breakdowns, many students dropped out of
college; others turned to alcohol; some began to have hallucina-
tions. Many women found their menstrual cycles thrown into
disarray. Although I found all this ominous and sinister, I could
not believe there was really anything for me to fear. However as
the lists of people disappearing into custody grew and the phone
calls multiplied, I realised the PTA was much worse than I expected. I often stayed up at night trying to locate people.

One of the saddest stories was that of a woman who for the
purposes of this narrative I have called Mary, the names of her
children have also been changed. Fr Brady rang me on 27 March
1976 and he asked me to visit Mary in Holloway gaol. Her husband suffered from depression and had disappeared. She has
three children, seventeen, sixteen and seven years old. She
reported her husband missing to the police and they came and
arrested her! I said I would try to visit her but I doubted if I
would be allowed to see her. I then rang Holloway gaol to ask if
visitors were allowed on Sunday. I was told that remand prisoners are not allowed visits on Sunday.

Mary's own account of what happened next is recorded in a
statement she gave to me. Her son also gave me an account of
what happened to him. They provide a vivid insight into the ordeals they experienced:

I came home from work at 12.30 p.m. on Wednesday 17th March
1976. The note said, 'Sorry, gone to the river'. I knew what this
meant because he talked about it so many times before. On the side-
board was the shamrock and pence from his pocket – a comb and
on the mantelpiece his diary and £1 on top of it. I picked up the
phone and rang the head master. I asked if my husband was there.
He said he had not seem him and I asked if he had left his keys
there. The head master said 'his keys are here in the office'. I told
him what the note said and I asked him to ring the police. He rang
the police and he and the priest came around to see me. The head
master stayed with me for a while and Fr Wright remained with me
and I told him about my nephew-in-law. He said that my husband

was at 9.30 Mass that morning and went out before Mass was finished. The police came around 1.30 p.m., picked up the note and took some particulars and the description of my husband. They said that they would circulate the river patrol immediately. Fr Wright left but he sent a Mrs Dunne to sit with me. John (sixteen years) was home from college at 1.45 p.m. that day. [The] police rang and asked me to go along to the police station to fill up a missing persons form. This I did under great strain and I returned home at approximately 2.30. Ciarán (fifteen years) and Fintan (seven years) came home from school. At about 4.20 p.m. the door-bell rang. When I opened it there was a man at the door who said he was from Scotland Yard. He had a pal with him. He put his hand into his pocket and pulled out a card with a photo of my nephew-in-law on it. He said, 'Do you know this chap?' I said yes he was my husband's nephew. Then all of a sudden five men and a woman rushed in. They talked for a few minutes about him, when he was there last and where my husband was. I said that he had left a note saying he had gone to the river. The first and second policemen stayed and questioned me. Two more questioned the big boys – another questioned little Fintan. The first asked to use my phone for a few minutes. He talked on the phone for a few minutes. The door-bell rang and eight more men came in with about four dogs. They started searching and sniffing – the tool-shed – everywhere. The first and second policemen stayed with me. They said I was telling lies, that I was involved in bombing. They told me that they were going to arrest John because he had a map in his room. They said they were going to arrest me. They took a lot of notes from the children. This went on for about five hours. The phone kept ringing – people ringing up about my husband. They would not allow me to answer it – they said I was busy. Only when the doctor's receptionist rang at six o'clock to see how I was and said that the doctor was expecting me at 5 p.m. and that there was a prescription for me down there – they refused to let me go for it.

At 9p.m. they said they were taking us all to the police station. I was taken in a car with a lady detective and little Fintan. The other two boys were in another car. In the police station they took my handbag, money, etc. and took me into a room – took my photograph – took my fingerprints and tested me for explosives. They took photographs, fingerprints and tests of each of my children (I did not give my permission for this – neither was I asked if they had my permission to do this.)

They then took me into a room and questioned me until about twelve midnight. I had nothing to eat or drink all day – I said the children had nothing to eat. They said, 'Don't worry we will buy you all a big steak dinner.' At about 12 midnight I asked to see the children. They took me out to where the boys were. In this room there was a big football and two of the police were kicking it to Fintan and they said that every time he scored a goal they would buy him a packet of crisps. Another policeman walked into the room and said he would like to take Fintan for a ride in his car, as Fintan had said earlier that he was out for a drive with his cousin on Sunday. The police was anxious to see where he went to. I said no to this, that I did not want Fintan to go out. He said, 'Don't worry; we will get fish and chips'. They sent out and got pies and chips for the children and fish for me. All the time they were trying to bribe Fintan about the ride. Finally they agreed that Ciarán could go as well.

They then took me into a room (it was after midnight) still being questioned by two men – questions about my husband and nephew-in-law: 'Your husband is missing because he is involved, etc.' At about 3 a.m. they said that I had better go and lie down and have a sleep. I asked to go to the toilet – they ignored me. I again asked to see the children. They said they were fast asleep. I was brought into a small room. Little Fintan was lying across a small wooden table. Ciarán was stretched on two chairs, no blankets or anything. I was not allowed to see John. I said that the children could not stay there for the night, could Fintan not come where they were going to put me. They said no that they would get a bed later on. They took me to a dirty cell with 'Male' on it (only used by men) with a bench and a dirty mattress. I just sat there. I used the toilet but there was no hand basin or tap.

At 9 a.m. the first and second policemen came and unlocked the cell and took me out. I asked to see the children. They brought me into the cell where the three of them had slept on three mattresses lying on the floor. I was allowed to talk to them for a few minutes. The first and second policemen were there. They took me up to ask me more questions. They questioned me until approximately 1.30 p.m. The same questions over again and again. I was then brought back down to the cell again. Just before they put me in the cell (at the cell door) the first policeman lost his temper with me. He said it was their intention to wipe the Irish out of Northern Ireland completely. The second policeman held a heavy metal object that held the cell keys and said that he would smash my head against the wall and if I would not have a good think, he would call the Special Branch in to me. I ignored him and sat in the cell. I was given dinner. They came back in about three-quarters of an hour and brought me up to the same room again. The first policeman said that he hoped that I was not going to tell any more lies. At this stage (approx. 2.45 p.m.) He was taking a statement of what I had already said – a statement under caution. They went on until 7.30

without a break. They then put me back in the cell. I asked on different occasions about the children. I was told my sister and brother-in-law were at the station to collect my children but that they were not ready to leave the station. (I understand they spent five hours waiting for the children.) They were told to go home and that the police would deliver the children. They did deliver the children. Sometime that night I was taken to the cell again. I asked if I could wash and the first policeman said that he would leave a message on the out to get a WPC for me. None came. I pressed the bell at 10 p.m. A policeman came to me. I asked for washing facilities and he said that there was no WPC on duty. I would have to wait until the morning.

Next day was Friday. The first and second policemen arrived about 9 a.m. They took me up to the room for more questioning. I was kept until approximately 1.30 p.m. – again the same questions over and over again. Put in cell for lunch. I was taken out again in an hour's time. During all this time I had a bad headache and I felt very ill. I asked for my own doctor – they refused – they said they would get me their own doctor. I refused. They gave me tablets for my head. I was kept in the room and questioned and threatened on a number of occasions with the metal object by the second policeman. All the time they smoked cigars and the room was heavy – they smelt of alcohol.

Saturday was the same – times, etc. approx.

Sunday was worse because they said the canteen was not open. All I had was a beaker of water. At 3 p.m. I was so weak I was hardly able to walk up the stairs to the room on the top floor. I was crying about my children and my husband. I said that I would not talk any more as I was very weak. They realised that I was in a poor state. They rang my sister and asked how my children were and the first policeman said to my sister that I was fine: 'She's just had a big dinner'. He told me that the children were all right. They kept me until 6.30 p.m. and then put me back in the cell. I again asked to wash. They said they would do their best to get someone. They rang a few police stations for a woman to come (a matron) and they got one. She took me out to the sink in the passage and I had a wash there. She said that she would go to my house and get a change of pants, a flannel, soap and a towel and brought them back to me. This was the only wash I had.

Monday: The same routine 9 a.m. – 8 p.m.

Tuesday my period came on. I asked for a WPC but there was not a WPC there.

Wednesday morning a WPC came into me. She said that she had no sanitary towels and told me to use paper towels. I was left in this condition without washing facilities and without sanitary towels until I went to another police station on Thursday at approximately 4.30 p.m. At the other police station I asked a WPC for sanitary towels and she went off to get them for me. At approximately 5 p.m. I was charged along with a young man named John. I was in a bad state at that time; I was crying and unable to stand. When John was asked had he anything to say, he said that Mary was not guilty of the charges put on her. The second policeman then turned to me and said, 'Now, Mary, that goes in your favour'.

After an hour the WPC returned and said that she had to go for sanitary towels. She gave me two and the rest were thrown outside the door for the night-time. I had to ring the bell and they would be handed in to me.

I appeared in court the next morning at 10 a.m. The police told me not to worry that I would get bail immediately. The main thing was to get a good solicitor. I got the duty solicitor.

All the time I was being interrogated, I was threatened by the second policeman– he would knock my brains out, etc.

All the time I never read a statement I made because I was in a state of collapse. I was getting a sort of visions and I just signed the bottom of the page.

Fintan's statement:

I was in the big room with a policeman. A drunk tramp came in himself with blood on his nose. The police threw him out. The two of us went into a room (Ciarán and me) and I fell asleep on the window sill. I don't know where John was. When I woke up I was in a different small room on a mattress. I had no clothes over me. Ciarán was on another mattress and John was there too. We were locked in. There was a shutter on the door and a policeman used to open it and say, 'Here is breakfast'. There was a bell in the room. The policeman said if we wanted anything, to ring. They gave us our breakfast – a horrible bun, sausage and tea. I got bubble gum. I went in a big car. They were talking about things. I forget. They wanted to know where my cousin's friends lived. I knew where one lived. We found three houses.

I went to Aunt – and stayed the night. Two policemen – the same two always – brought me there. We got a big feed and then we watched TV and went to bed.

Next morning the police came again, and took my palm prints in the house. (They took Ciarán out to get the elastics for his teeth that day.) To get my palm prints, I had to roll a paper on a bottle. There was black stuff on the paper.

When I went to visit Mary on the Monday – it was 29 March 1974 and seven days since her arrest – she didn't know that her husband's body had been found floating on the Thames. In despair and terror he had committed suicide. Already depressed, he had seen a photograph of his nephew in the paper and read of his arrest. He was terrified that his family would fall under suspicion and knew what had happened to others under the PTA. Mary had no idea of her husband's fate whereas I assumed she would have been told. When I saw her I thought the end of the world had come. There was a female prison officer beside her and I asked her where the children were and the woman said you can't have that question answered or your visit will end. Then Mary talked about her husband for ages and it dawned on me that she didn't know what had happened to him.

Mary's story made a very deep impression on me and I wrote about it at unusual length in my diary:

Went to Holloway this morning and I was just stunned all day. She was like a scared mouse. Such sorrow! Oh, Lord! I could not speak about it when I came back. I felt scared myself. I looked around at the community and wondered who was right – the ones who didn't care and enjoyed life or the likes of me – frightened after the experience. When she grasped my hands I said that we would fight for her; it was worthwhile. They did not accept a parcel for her. She said, 'Letters, letters.' Anxious that the Special Branch had taken over the house and that they would plant something; anxious over the solicitor, anxious that she would not be allowed to give her sister's phone number. Gave me the name of her curate and the priest in charge of her children at school. She said, 'You know about my husband', but later I realised that she did not know about the discovery of his body. When I was leaving, I mentioned her husband's body to the wardress, but she had not heard about it. I left that prison, and I felt like a leper, not because of the prisoners but because of the bitchiness of the wardresses. I got back home frightened and rang the priest at school. All the prison staff denied the death of Mary's husband. Mary was worried if her husband was found dead that he wanted to be buried in Ireland. The priest at school was extremely nice. He sent for one of the children and got the aunt's phone number. I rang the curate. He was nice but did not give much help. I rang the prison governor because I was afraid that the family would arrive for the visit and be turned away. She was extremely pompous and patronising, tried to make me feel like a fly. Fr Brady rang. He was pleased with the phone numbers as the family did not know where the children were. I would have told the governor where to get off only I may have to go to Holloway again.

I remember returning to the convent after this visit. The nuns were worrying over some missing spoons and I thought why were they worrying about spoons when there is such sorrow about us. Two days later Mary was told about her husband's death and they had the funeral. The Special Branch were there all dressed in black, some of them accompanying her.

On 31 March I made some more notes about Mary's situation:

> Got home after a very strenuous day. Phone rang. It was the priest from Mary's children's school. He was up in Holloway to see her. He too mentioned how distressed and stressed she was. She gave him her solicitor's address. Father could not find address in phone book. I got in the car and went to the address. The office had closed three years ago. Looked in yellow pages and found the address. I rang the solicitor and said that Mary had written to him and that she was in court tomorrow. He said that if he got the letter he would ring the court to issue a legal aid certificate ... To my satisfaction I convinced Mary to accept the services of a solicitor I knew ... Brian Rose-Smyth – a good solicitor who would commit himself to a difficult and unpopular Irish case.

Whilst Mary was in Holloway gaol I visited her sister with whom the children were staying. I was appalled by what I heard and noted in my diary on 9 April:

> Went out to meet the children. They were lovely, but they were all, even the 7 year old, told by police to tell all about their mother and then she would be released. The seven year old was kept for questioning until 1.00 a.m.

I was incensed. I believed Mary was completely innocent and this was later established. The police knew the nephew had visited her house and they took the children round London to show them places their cousin had gone.

Mary was very concerned about some of the methods used by some of the police. I myself received a call on 14 April from one of Mary's relatives who said that the Special Branch had promised the children Manchester United tickets in exchange for information about their mother.

Mary was charged with conspiracy. The solicitor said that if they could find a convent that would take her in, it would strengthen her chances of getting bail. I rang all the convents and went to the Irish Centre trying to find a convent that would take her in if she got bail. I knew they wouldn't let her come to my convent because I was persona non grata with the Home Office. I tried to get some other nuns. But nobody would take her; they all had excuses. I asked a nun down at the Irish Centre, I said families are insulted at every corner and when you brought them near the nuns they got the same. She said she couldn't ask her Reverend Mother because the convent might be blown up. Everyone shunned her. In the end Mgr Bruce Kent got a place for her in a convent; the nuns would do anything for him because he was a monsignor. Finally after several months in gaol, Mary got bail and at her trial was found not guilty.

Hundreds of cases slip out of my files and what appear here in my account of these years, are only examples, glimpses of experiences suffered by many others.

ONLY RARELY HAS MY PERSONAL LIFE interrupted my convent life or my gaol work. But on 3 May 1974 I had some sad news – my brother Michael died. I got news around 7 p.m. and flew to Dublin arriving at midnight. My cousins, Betty and John McCarthy, met me. Everything was like a dream. I had been very close to Michael and, when I took my vows, the hardest thing was to leave my mother and Michael. I came to England in 1957 and used to go back to Ireland once a year. I stayed in the convent but I was allowed to visit my home. It was hard being parted from Michael and my mother but I didn't choose a soft life. It was a year since I'd seen him. He was only fifty and left three children, my nieces. I'm very close to them and to his wife. I stay with them when I'm home. One of my nieces now lives in our old home.

My faith imbues me with a strength that carries me through the pain of bereavement. I don't know how people who believe in nothing live. I'd end life very quickly if I had no belief. If you believe in nothing then it means that when you die you say good-bye to your family. When I die I'll see my mother and father and Michael again. I know I'll see them again – in heaven. They are there. I pray to them.

IT WAS WITH EVER growing dismay that I witnessed the trauma of people held under the PTA. Their connections with anything or anyone that might conceivably be of interest to the police, even purely circumstantial, led to arrest and interrogation. They were treated as though guilty. The miscarriages of justice of the 1970s are well-known now but at the time few people either knew or cared what was happening. Another case in which I became involved thanks to the PTA was that of the Braintree Irish Society. It was a near thing for the thirteen people arrested and looking back I realise that it was thanks in no small part to the expertise of solicitor Mike Fisher and barrister Mike Mansfield that the thirteen people were eventually freed.

There are other similar societies all over Britain made up of local Irish people, small fraternities of the like-minded, very rarely, if ever, political, more involved with social events. Nonetheless, their very Irishness thrusts them into the focus of the security forces. The society in question was in Braintree, Essex, a sleepy village some thirty miles outside London. I had never heard of either the society or the town until Fr Brady telephoned me on 26 January 1979 asking me to find out why thirteen Irish people had been arrested there. I recorded in my diary:

> Phone call from Fr Brady. He is furious over the Braintree arrests. They are held under the Prevention of Terrorism Act. He asked me if I knew anything. I rang Mel McNally [a photographer with the *Irish Post* whom I knew lived nearby in Harlow] and he gave me Phil Lane (chairman of the Harlow Irish Society) who told me that the whole Irish Society had been picked up. I rang Fr Cagney (head of the Irish Centre), Tom Walshe (Federation of Irish Societies), Fr Brady. He rang and told me to ring Fr Faul in Paris and get him to get people to stir things up and told me to ring Rita Mullen [Irish Caucus worker in the USA] in Washington. Got Fr Faul about 1.00 a.m. eventually.

Phil Lane told me that the men had only the clothes they stood in and asked me to buy them some clothing. I had no idea of the sizes or clothes that men wear. I had to ask a woman shopper what a man would wear and asked her to come with me to buy the clothes. The next day I rang Charlie Haughey and left a message for him about the Braintree arrests. Sr Imelda and I went to Brixton gaol after lunch and brought a meal, fruit, biscuits, sweets and cigarettes, shirts, underpants and socks for one member of the group. We saw that he had no solicitor and we asked to visit him but we were refused. Then we asked to see the governor or his assistant. We were told there was no one there. We asked to see a chaplain of any denomination. We were told there was no one in the gaol. We said that we would remain until we saw someone. The other gaol visitors were all listening, so they asked us to go out to the office and then they decided to let us speak to the Anglican chaplain, Fr Comerford. He seemed wary but nice and took down all the information about Mike Fisher solicitor, and our names and addresses for Fr Evans [the chaplain]. When I came home I rang Rita Mullen and spoke to Fr McManus about Braintree. They asked me to send them the information in writing. I rang Fr Brady and told him all that I did.

I always found it unusual to encounter co-operation with the authorities whether secular or religious, and the Braintree case was no exception. I rang the chaplain, Fr Evans, before lunch. I was asked who I was and I gave my name. I was then put through to someone who asked me my business with the chaplain. I asked if I had to say what my business with the chaplain was. He immediately put me through. Then Fr Evans said that he would ring me back. He did so at 2.00 p.m. He wanted to know why a Catholic Sister was involved with such men – I was bringing the Catholic Church into disrepute. I should leave the work to families of the prisoners. I was frightened, and my left hand got the shakes. I felt so shaken after him that I had to go out for a walk. I went to Kenwood. It was cold with snow and ice. I fell twice and broke my glasses. I came back and phoned Fr Faul and told him about Fr Evans. He said that he could get in touch with Frank Maguire MP and that he would get the archbishop to do something. Nothing was done.

That suspects should be treated with the minimum of respect comes as no surprise but it surprised me that, in many cases, those attending court on behalf of defendants can expect to be treated as though they too are suspect. In February I attended the weekly remand session in a magistrate's court where the Braintree prisoners requested bail. We were the first to reach the magistrate's court. Then John O'Callaghan from RTE arrived. The security was mounted and a helicopter flew over the court. The doors were locked and only police (thumping loudly) were let in. We were soaked with rain. The door opened and a policeman shouted, 'Barristers, solicitors'. People made an attempt to go in and the door shut sharply after the first one, nearly taking the hands and nose off the barrister following. He had to jump back. This was repeated every time the door opened. When the barristers were in, they shouted for the press. John O'Callaghan was the only one there. Then they shouted for the sureties and they went in one by one. We waited until last and we were thoroughly searched and asked for name, address, etc. We went into court but they would not allow anyone to stand and there wasn't enough room for everyone so we thought it better to leave the families inside rather than us.

The Braintree people were arrested under the PTA because Gerry Tuite, who was wanted for bombings, had stayed with one of them and was on the run from the police at the time. When a car full of explosives was found, it emerged that the car in question had been hired from a car rental firm in Braintree. During the search for Gerry Tuite the police were looking for a suspect white Opel Kadet. One of the accused had hired the car and brought it to Ireland and sold it. A massive search resulted with sightings everywhere in Britain. One policeman in Kent reported that an Irishman driving the car had got out of the car and fired at him. The car was actually in Ireland all the time. The accused was very lucky it was because he would have been given a long sentence if he had been found guilty of conspiracy and shooting at a policeman. All thirteen were charged and eventually the case went to the Old Bailey where they were all found not guilty of conspiracy to bomb.

Many of the people arrested under the PTA, despite never facing charges or trials, have been profoundly disturbed by the experience. Peter, a man I knew and helped, was arrested under the PTA three times in the month of May in 1979. I rang Peter on Monday 28 May 1979. He said he was arrested at 6.00 a.m. and he and his wife taken to the police station. The children were sent to his mother-in-law. The interrogation went on from 7.00 a.m. to 11.00 a.m. – same old questions over and over again, a history of his life since 1976. He is twenty years here. The first and second time he was arrested Peter was lying in his bed and they came in, told him to get up. They pushed him. Peter fell against the wall, and they kicked him in the chest. The second time Peter was arrested he was slapped in the face two or three times. This does not seem much but it is frightening. There was a bit of pushing during Peter's third arrest. He had no sleep at any time.

After Peter was released Dave Clarke, a reporter, was in his sitting-room. The phone rang and Peter's wife answered it. A voice said CI3 (interrogation section of MI5) wanted to speak to him. Dave Clarke took the extension in the kitchen. The voice said that the police wanted to offer Peter protection and added, 'Your life is in danger'. Peter refused protection, as he said that no way was his life 'in danger'. Presumably the police wanted to tempt Peter into working for them or frighten him.

One night very late I got a call from a man saying he was being harassed by the police. I asked him how he got my number and he said the name of someone I vaguely knew. Then he said he was being driven crazy and didn't know what to do. I advised him to ring a solicitor and gave him Mike Fisher's number. A few nights later he rang back saying Mike Fisher was very left-wing. I said I wasn't interested in his politics, that he was a very good solicitor. A few nights later he rang again and I suggested that if things were as bad as he said he should maybe go back to Ireland. He rang one more time saying he wanted to say goodbye to me. I never knew who he was – perhaps he was a policeman trying to unnerve me by his strange behaviour. I always suspected my phone was tapped because it was never out of order!

In 1980, there was a swoop and some of the people netted suffered badly. I remember getting a call from Fr Faul saying a family had been raided in Southampton. One had been taken straight from the interrogation to the psychiatric ward. I went to their house in the snow with Theresa Hynes and a member of Civil Liberties and all the cupboards and fittings were pulled out – it was a complete mess and the wife was in tears. We went to the psychiatric hospital – the husband was very frightened and wouldn't talk at first but a religious habit has a very calming effect on people who are disturbed. He asked me who I was and where I was from. He had two big round bruises on his chest and kept running into the corner with his head down. He thought everyone was a policeman. The thing about the PTA is that it's indiscriminate: no matter what your state of mind or your age, you can be held.

At 2 a.m. one morning another couple, in their sixties, were woken by policemen demanding entry to their house. The problem for them was, that like Mary, they had a distant relative involved in bombing. Once in the police station, they were separated and Annie was stripped, item by item, starting with her glasses and her teeth, and then each article of clothing. Everything was singly wrapped in sealed plastic bags. Annie was left naked in a police cell with nothing but a filthy blanket covered in vomit and a concrete bed. She told me she had never in her life felt so depersonalised, so denigrated as at that moment. She said she was a poor woman who had brought up a large family and had suffered a lot, but had never suffered as much as in that police station sitting naked in the cell. She was then given peculiar ill-fitting clothes and was finger-printed, photographed and interrogated for hours. She has never quite recovered from the experience. After several days of this degrading treatment the couple was released without charge. They were severely traumatised and Annie died soon after from cancer.

During the summer of 1980, I had an American visitor, Bishop Thomas Drury, then of Corpus Christi, Texas, USA. On 9 August I drove Bishop Drury to visit Annie who told the bishop all that had happened to her and her husband. Bishop Drury was horrified at their treatment. Here was a bishop coming to see me who readily agreed to visit prisoners' families, people who felt shunned and scorned by everyone and deserted by the Church. I brought him to the prisoners' families all over the country and he always gave them a bit of money. He was very welcome to these people who had suffered so much. They felt crushed, bruised, despised and it gave me great pleasure to be able to bring them a bishop.

The arrests continued. Another typical example was in June 1990. I had a call to tell me that four young people had been arrested and taken to different police stations. After sixteen years I was familiar with the tactics. The police seemed to recognise the effectiveness of the intervention of a solicitor familiar with the workings of the PTA immediately after a suspect's arrest.

Jim Canning of Coalisland rang to say a young man named Terence had been taken in under the Prevention of Terrorism Act. I rang Mike Fisher [Christian Fisher & Co.], but the police would not let him in. The next day Mike Fisher did finally get to see Terence but he was not allowed to visit Eileen, another of those arrested. Meanwhile, the parents of these four young people were ringing me frequently. On 6 June I got a call from one mother who was distracted over her daughter's situation. At 7.30 p.m. that same day I got a call from Eileen's mother telling me that her daughter Marie had been released and asking if I could I pick her up at the police station and take her to the airport. She would have the tickets for the British Midland 9.30 flight. I rang Theresa Smalley (Paul Hill's aunt who sometimes helped me) and she came with me. Marie was frighteningly white and very upset. The police were courteous enough but unfriendly – especially the women. Two hours twice daily she was told she would be charged with conspiracy – a twenty-year sentence – or charged with withholding information. She cried all the way to the airport – degraded, abused, filthy dirty. We got her magazines and cakes and coffee and said goodbye at the barrier.

When I went to the young girl's flat to collect her few belongings, the locks had been changed and the landlord refused to help. Marie never got her things back.

Spread over the years as these cases are and featuring people of all ages, they have one thing in common, they happened to people who were vulnerable, unworldly and innocent. They were not people who knew how to resist the pressures or who knew how to make a fuss. I have noticed that when detainees are either well-connected or articulate and educated, interrogations are courteous by comparison. People are rung up and asked if they'd like to visit the station for a chat rather than finding themselves on the other side of a beaten down front door.

Amongst those who have spoken out against the PTA is Dr Amphlett Micklewright who published an article in the *Irish Democrat*, the magazine of the Connolly Association, in December 1977.

> This Act must be repealed because it is a threat to the liberty of the citizen, destroys the harmony between Irish and non-Irish communities in Great Britain and makes for injustice as well as bad law.

Solicitors Mike Fisher and Brian Rose-Smyth have worked successfully for Irish prisoners since 1973, with Gareth Peirce and Neil O'May becoming involved in the early 1980s. They have seen the PTA in action countless times. Gareth Peirce says it has added a whole excessive category of powers to annihilate the individual. Detaining people for up to seven days is an extraordinary phenomenon. No individual can sustain this kind of interrogation and not be affected. She describes the psychological effects of the PTA as the frightening sound which the law makes in the ears of ordinary people. I witnessed the psychological effect on people when I picked them up after a period in police custody. There were young men like broken reeds. Even strong women one would think nothing could break would come out of those police stations in a state of collapse. I saw that time and again. I brought them to the convent and the first thing they would ask for was to wash. Sr Gemma and Mother Marian Bernard always showed great kindness to these people, giving them a meal, and they appreciated the sense of security offered by the convent in their frightened state.

I met opposition where I might have expected co-operation amongst middle-class Irish people in Britain and apathy from the Irish government. There were even suspicions about my work among a few members of my religious community. I noticed that when I tried to tell both the community and others what was happening to people under the PTA, the topic of conversation was suddenly changed. They did not want to know. Here I was, one of the few religious helping prisoners and families and I could not understand why there was nobody backing me except Fr Faul, Fr Murray and Fr Brady. Even when Bishop Drury visited he too came under the spotlight. I began to question myself: was I doing something wrong? Should I be doing these things or not? Then I would read the Gospel: 'I was in prison and you visited me, I was hungry and thirsty and you gave me to drink'. The Gospel was in my thoughts all the time. I also read Bishop Camara's book on justice. How truly he speaks of those who are afraid of being branded 'subversive'! – 'Fear of speaking, fear of listening, fear of thinking'. Sometimes I think I must be subversive.

There were times when I felt, and feel, lonely and isolated – times when my heart cries out to say something but if I do it backfires. I go and make the Stations of the Cross; Christ's sufferings were worse. Sometimes in bleak moments I take some comfort from Psalm 3:

> I am a reproach, an object of scorn to my neighbours and of fear to my friends. Those who see me in the street run far away from me; I am like a dead man, forgotten in men's hearts.

I remember one morning going to early Mass at 6.30 at St Joseph's near the convent and feeling the whole world was on top of me, I felt so alienated. It was a time when things were going particularly badly with the prisoners. I said, 'God, I'll give up everything now and just run away'. I was in a really bad state; I couldn't stand it any longer. The priest came out and before he began Mass he said, 'Today the reading is about Daniel in the lions' den. We are all in the lions' den at some time with people around us making life hard and things seeming intolerable. But we must be like Daniel and trust in God'. I knew the story and I often felt like Daniel. The priest said, 'God got Daniel through and the lions came and licked him instead of eating him up.' It was a direct answer to my prayer. I felt better. I decided to stay in the lion's den.

Nevertheless my work was devastating and difficult. The kind of response I got from Church and State was that they'd ignore me, they would ostracise me, they would attempt to silence me but that was one thing they never achieved. Several prison chaplains – who had never even met me – told prisoners to have nothing to do with me. I wasn't important enough to be a thorn in their side – I was a nuisance on the edge of their vision and not under their control.

5

EXCLUSION ORDERS

Get up, take the child and his mother with you and escape into Egypt.
MATTHEW 2:13

One of the PTA's most devastating powers is the exclusion order under which a 'suspect' can be virtually deported from England, Scotland or Wales, and sent to Ireland where he or she must stay. It's shadowy and sinister – like sending people to Siberia – and often the people involved are completely innocent. Police or immigration authorities can arrest people of whom they are suspicious and hold them under the PTA while they apply to the Home Secretary for an exclusion order. Whilst this is being processed, a suspect is held in custody for forty-eight hours or the extended seven days. The authorities seek to exclude, expel or refuse entry to 'suspected terrorists' and 'anyone suspected of harbouring them'. There is no trial, no judge, no jury, just an order by which the 'suspect' can be denied entry into Britain or be arrested and sent from England to Ireland. Between 1975 when the act became law and 1992 (the last year for which figures are available) there have been 463 applications to the Home Office for exclusions, 403 of which have been successful.

I remember endless documents falling on to my desk on which the final word was 'excluded'. I saw the effect of this exile on families who often broke under the strain. There was no reason given for the exclusion order, so individuals and families were destroyed without ever knowing why a member of that family had been excluded. Since no evidence against the excluded person is required, and the documentation compiled by police, immigration and other security personnel is secret, and often gathered by paid informants the security forces seek to protect, it is almost impossible for solicitors to provide an adequate defence.

Those served with exclusion orders are invariably denied even the most basic of rights. They are not given a chance to go home and see their families, to collect their possessions or to explain to employers what has happened. Since most of those excluded are

70

men, it is the women who are left alone and traumatised, often with children, and have to cope with the fallout and survive as best they can. Until the change in the law in 1984 people could not be excluded if they had lived in Britain for more than twenty years. This was subsequently changed to three years – a slight improvement but ten years too late for those already excluded.

In June 1982, Patrick, a twenty-two-year-old man, who had already served four years in Magilligan gaol for political offences, wanted to leave Ireland and get away from the political situation so he decided to go and stay with relatives in England. His family and friends told him that things might be difficult for him in England – but he thought, having put violence behind him, he would be given a chance to lead a normal life. He planned to go to Birmingham with his grandmother where they would stay with relatives. Any hopes of a chance for a 'normal' life were shattered when police boarded the coach out of Stranraer, called out his name and said he was arrested under the PTA. His grandmother was left to travel on alone. Patrick was taken to a police station, shoelaces and belt were removed and he was left alone in a cell. He was so scared he wept. A little later he reported: 'A cop came in and deepened my anxiety. He made it clear to me in no uncertain terms that I could be "fitted up" with ease. No one, he implied would bat an eye lid because I had a record – and after all I'm Irish. I knew only too well that his words were true. They had done it in the past and they could do it again. My isolation was compounded by the fact that they wouldn't allow me to contact anyone ... Things got worse once the interviews started. The two interrogators were very menacing. They told me that they could help me to get into England if I agreed to co-operate with them. They wanted to know what information I could give them. I told them I had none and was only interested in a quiet life away from the Troubles.' Patrick was held for two days without being allowed to wash or exercise and then held for a further five days during which every night they took away his clothes, leaving him naked in his cell. After these seven days he was given an exclusion order. I remember this young man's case very well. He was taken in in Stranraer and I had to find him a solicitor there. I just got the solicitor for him when they moved him to Dumfries so I had to get him another solicitor.

After Leon Brittan, the Home Secretary, announced that the period for appealing exclusion was to be cut from five to three years, Patrick thought he could visit England without a problem as his three years were spent and he tried again in March 1987. What he didn't know was that his exclusion order had been renewed for a further three years. Again he was arrested, and held for three days. Once more he was excluded but he fought for an appeal and an explanation. Two years later he was granted an interview and a few weeks after that the exclusion order was revoked – but no reasons were given why it was being revoked nor was any justification given for his exclusion.

In 1987 Lord Colville, a former Conservative Home Office minister, reviewed the PTA and recommended that exclusion orders be abolished because they were a severe infringement of human rights. His was not the only dissenting voice from the Establishment: Sir Cyril Phillips, a former chairman of the Police Complaints Board, also recommended the abolition of exclusion orders. Interestingly, these orders relate only to people involved in the Irish conflict and cannot be used against other nationalities suspected of terrorist involvement.

The people excluded under the PTA are still vivid in my memory. I remember the phone call from one of their wives to say these men had been excluded. I wasn't sure what it even meant and when I understood I was horrified. I don't think people in England realise the devastating effects laws applied to Irish people have on them and their families. [For the purposes of this narrative I have changed the names.] The first three people to receive exclusion orders were three Irishmen, Joe, Seamas and Tom. They were in Sinn Féin and Tom and Seamas had spent short periods of time in prison for political offences. All three were excluded. They lived in England and, like five of the six men charged with the Birmingham bombings, went to Belfast for James McDade's funeral in November 1974. I had met Tom at civil rights meetings but until I heard from their wives about the exclusions I had no knowledge of Joe or Seamas.

Joe's wife phoned me saying she'd been given my number and told I would help her. There were the partners, and all their children, stranded in England. Their husbands had been told exclusion orders would be served. They decided it was better to stay in Ireland as, if they tried to return to homes, families, and jobs in England, the order would be served and then become part of their personal records. Joe was in the merchant navy. The exclusion order meant that while it was in force he could never enter British territorial waters. He could never visit Patricia, his wife, and their two small children in London. I suppose some people might wonder why wives don't necessarily join their husbands but I can understand it. They would have to uproot themselves completely which is particularly hard if you have children who are settled into a routine. So some wives decide to stay for the sake of their children.

In my diaries I often refer to Patricia and the children whom I did my best to help after Joe's exclusion. I had many conversations and visits with Patricia whose distress continued for several years. I was saddened but not surprised when their marriage ran into terrible difficulties. On 20 May 1978 I had a phone call from Joe before 9.00 a.m. He stayed on the phone for two hours talking about Patricia. In early June that year she took the children to Ireland where they were all reunited with Joe – but the reunion did not go well. On 11 June, I began my yearly visit to Ireland and visited the family on 16 June, a visit which I recorded in my diary:

> I went to visit Patricia, Joe and her father and mother and the children. It was a very sad visit – tension. Joe is a very fine man and he is deeply hurt.

Having returned to London, Joe phoned me on 9 and 10 July. On both occasions he was asking for my help. The marriage ended with Patricia's suit for divorce and the usual divisions for the children. Now, so many years later, Joe is in the USA. He has never returned to England but maintains his relationship with his children and returns to Ireland.

Tom, the second of those first three to be excluded was a senior official of Sinn Féin at the time and was running a successful business in England when he travelled to Belfast for the McDade funeral. Once in Belfast he, like Joe, was informed that were he to return he would be issued with an exclusion order. His teenage children tried to maintain their father's business but eventually it collapsed.

Four years later, one February morning, I had a phone call from Clara Reilly of the ALJ in Belfast to tell me about a twenty-two-year-old Belfast man who had by then been in Brixton gaol for a week. [For the purposes of this narrative I have changed the names.] He was married to Jane, an English woman and they had two little daughters aged one and two. Brian had lived in England for five years. I immediately phoned the number Clara Reilly gave me and spoke to Jane, arranging to visit her at her father's house where she had gone with her children. Three days later I took a statement from Jane:

> At 5.00 a.m. on 23 January 1978, there was a knock on the door. Brian got up thinking it was someone from work and I came downstairs. I saw a plainclothes man with a gun. Another man put handcuffs on Brian and took him away. They then searched the house. We had to sit and wait about twenty minutes while they obtained a dog from a neighbouring town. I said not to bring the dog upstairs without a lead because one of the children was terrified of dogs. They went upstairs to search the house and let the dog off the lead. The frightened child screamed and went stiff. They asked me how long we were married, why Brian came to England, with whom he drank, how long we had been over here, if any of his friends came from Ireland, and if he had any Irish friends here.

I remember Jane telling me that one of the Special Branch men asked her for tea. She refused to make it. He said he'd make it himself and she said no because there was only a little milk and it was for the children. Brian was taken from his home to the police station. Four members of the RUC came over the following day to question him about his alleged involvement in the murder of a British soldier. Jane's statement says, 'They (RUC) punched him in the stomach and accused him of murdering a soldier. They held Brian in the police station until Saturday.'

On 24 January the RUC officers who had questioned Brian said that he was no longer a suspect in the soldier's murder. Nevertheless Jane records:

> On Friday night I found out that they were going to deport him. He said he would appeal. On Saturday afternoon, 28 January, they sent him down to prison. On Tuesday, 31 January, they brought him to Brixton for his appeal.

Jane told me that Brian's solicitor said that he had been arrested on information the police had received. This 'information', it later transpired, was in an unsigned statement flashed in front of him during his interrogation. It was allegedly made by a man awaiting trial in connection with the murder of a soldier – he had allegedly named Brian as the hit man. During the interrogation, one of the men questioning Brian said, 'Come along and say you did this crime. Go over and do a year or two and come back and we'll have a drink.' Brian said that he would not sign for anything he had not done.

I told Jane that I would meet her the next day (6 February 1978) at Charing Cross and we would visit Brixton gaol and our MPs. She asked to go in alone. (I would not be let in anyway). She brought a little parcel to Brian. She was supposed to see the MP, Sidney Irwin. After the visit she said that Brian said not to go to parliament but to leave it all to the solicitors. We left Brixton at 4.00 p.m. On 8 February I collected Jane at 1.55 p.m. at Charing Cross. We went to the gaol. She was very quick. It was very cold, and there were not many there at first. Brian was very sad. He cried when she was leaving. The next day I again took Jane to Brixton gaol. She got a long visit because there were very few there due to the snow. As I recorded in my dairy:

> If Brian gets an exclusion order, he will ask to see the children. He told Jane today that he thought the food was drugged and he was very dizzy. He fainted once already.

We did not arrange to meet again, but Jane promised to ring the minute she heard anything. Subsequently Brian told Fr Faul that he felt he hadn't been drugged, but had fainted having been shown photographs of a dead soldier during his interrogation He told the *Sunday Times,* 'They kept showing me photographs of the soldier's body. There were pictures of him naked and of him in his uniform hanging from the ceiling with a hook through the back of his uniform.'

On Friday, 10 February, Jane rang to say that Brian was to be deported. I rang Fr Faul. I rang the Association for Legal Justice. I rang the solicitor. He was not given any details. Jane rang and asked me to ring the prison about visiting Brian before he left. The police rang her and said that she could visit him. I told her that I would take her to the prison. I rang *The Irish Post* and *The Irish Times.* The next day – the day of exclusion – I met Jane, the two children and Jane's mother at Charing Cross – a forlorn little group. It was 11.30 a.m. before I got to Charing Cross. I took them all to the convent and gave them a good lunch. We then went to Brixton gaol. There were police in the waiting-room. The family saw Brian who was pleased to be getting out. As they were coming out, the police asked Jane if she was staying in England. She did not answer them. They asked if they had money to give Brian.

Neither of them had any. Brian was given a choice of going on Saturday or Monday. He was expecting to be held by the RUC for a few days, so he chose Saturday so he would be with his parents on Monday. I left them at Charing Cross. Jane promised to keep me informed.

At 7.00 p.m. I rang her, but she still had not heard anything. Fr Faul phoned to say he would try to see Brian. I rang Clara Reilly who gave me his sister's number and when I rang her I learned that Brian had arrived home, thank God. I asked her to ring Fr Faul and tell him where Brian was. Jane phoned and said she was talking with Brian on the phone and gave me the number to ring. I rang Brian and he was pleased it was all over after three weeks in prison. He was not held by RUC at the airport but was deported without a penny in his pocket.

Through his solicitor, Brian appealed against exclusion but, despite having been ruled out of the RUC's enquiries, his appeal was turned down. In my various efforts to publicise this case I contacted the National Council for Civil Liberties and many other people. I was dashing round everywhere to find somebody who would speak out. None of the calls helped Brian and Jane. The NCCL had all the information, and they could perhaps have taken the case to the European Court of Human Rights. Nothing, however, was done internationally to expose the injustice this young couple suffered.

On 14 February Jane and the children went to Belfast where they stayed with Brian's parents. For Jane, an English woman, living in a Nationalist area of Belfast made the situation very hard. To add to their difficulties, Brian, like so many young men in the six counties, was unemployed. I was not surprised to hear that Jane and the children had returned to England. Later that day I spoke to Jane who asked me to ring Brian in Belfast and ask him to phone her. She was afraid he wouldn't speak to her as they had quarrelled and she was sorry she had left Belfast after the quarrel. I rang Brian and he said he would ring Jane but he didn't. Brian and Jane's marriage was over and they were left to pick up the pieces of their shattered lives. The word exclusion cannot express the sorrow of families, the heartbreak.

Danny, a Derryman, came to England to find work, but he was rewarded with an exclusion order. He was thirty-five, and had not been in trouble at all since his early twenties when he spent two years in jail. In an affidavit made in 1989 Danny declared:

Following my release I have been constantly harassed and have been arrested upon a number of occasions. During my periods of arrest I would have been subject to assaults and the arrests would all have been politically motivated. When there was any activity at all, the police would have subjected me to harassment and I would have been arrested on a number of occasions. There would have been no firm grounding for any of these arrests. I would always have been held for the maximum amount of days allowed and during the time held, I would have been pressed to make statements, etc. However, I would always have been let go at the end of the detention period.

Fed up with this constant difficulty, in 1987 Danny took up an invitation from friends in New York who asked him to visit and said they could get him work. But he was refused a US visa. Sufficiently desperate to improve his position, he entered the US via Canada but was picked up by Immigration. 'They held me for twelve days ... constantly insinuating that I was there to get arms for the Republican Movement which was totally incorrect. I went to America to seek a new life and get away from the situation.' Danny had planned to settle, find work and then his wife and three children aged from four to eight at the time would join him. His friends in New York had actually found him a job which he could have started more or less immediately:

> I simply wished to seek a new beginning and get work and earn some money to improve the quality of lifestyle for myself and my family ... In view of the fact that our initial emigration plan had failed, I now wish to go to London where I have a number of friends who can arrange for me to get work and indeed have work lined up for me at present. I am therefore most anxious that this plan to go to London for work can proceed and I can escape from the harassment in my home town. I am most anxious that I will not be subject to any harassment in moving to London on this occasion.

Danny arrived in England and worked as a labourer on building sites while his family remained in Ireland. He managed to send money home to ease the tremendous financial burdens they faced. In October 1989 he was arrested. When I heard of his case I recognised the potential for another miscarriage of justice as there were immediate echoes of Annie Maguire's story: Danny was charged with having traces of explosives on his hands. He wrote to me from Brixton gaol:

The police have made a terrible mistake, but with the help of God everything will rightify itself sooner if not later. I'm sure I can rely upon some of your prayers to help my family and myself to come through this ordeal. As you probably know the work situation where I come from in Ireland is very bad. I would estimate that the unemployment rate in Derry is upward of 60 per cent. A few years ago my wife was able to get a job in a local cafe, I could not get any work at all. The extra few pounds that she earned was a great help. Then our youngest son George got sick more frequently, he had always been sickly from birth. He has been in hospital sixteen or seventeen times up to date and is now five years old. The doctors diagnosed chronic asthma and TB. He had to be on a nebulising machine for four hours every day. My wife left her part-time work so she could spend more time with him. By the beginning of April this year our financial situation had been getting very tight and something had to be done. It was then I decided to come to London with a friend to seek work ... we came on 2 May and after about six days searching we found a good job by Tower Hill. I worked for about eight weeks approximately, I sent money home weekly and was able to save a lot as well. The job I was on was coming to an end, so I planned to come home. But my wife wanted to come over to see me so we decided that she come over and I go home with her. She came on a Friday at the end of June and we went back home the following Tuesday together. We had a great weekend together. We then had a holiday with the children in Blackpool in August. I came back to London on 17 September to work to get some money for Christmas. This visit turned into a nightmare, although I had started work and things started to look up, not in my wildest dreams did I think anything like this would have happened. Hopefully in the near future, justice will prevail and it will come to a happy ending.

I advised the family to get Gareth Peirce on to the case but the acting solicitor was reluctant to hand over the case which was not uncommon. Ultimately Gareth Peirce took over and subsequently the charges were dropped from lack of evidence. But there the process of justice stopped and in spite of the fact that the charges were dropped Danny was excluded from Britain and sent back to the prospect of unemployment in Derry.

Although the majority of exclusion orders were handed out between 1974–1980, they still go on. I calculate that I had some involvement with half of these cases. As recently as 1993, a young man called John was excluded. He had been in England for about ten months and planned to return to Belfast to live. He was working as a porter in a hospital and staying with an aunt in North

London. He was on his way back to Belfast when he was arrested at Heathrow airport and questioned about the recent Bishopsgate bombing. During his detention Gareth Peirce acted for him. His alibi for the day of the Bishopsgate bombing eliminated him from that line of enquiry. He was then accused of hijacking a taxi on the day in question and telling the driver to go to Downing Street. He was remanded, bail was refused and the Crown Prosecution Service (CPS) announced that they had evidence against him. Two and a half months later the charges were suddenly dropped. The CPS had no evidence at all.

His story might have ended there but as he left the court a free man, he was immediately re-arrested and an exclusion order was produced by the next morning signed by Home Secretary Michael Howard. It was explained to him by a Home Office official that the Home Secretary had reviewed his file and was satisfied that he had been involved in terrorist offences. Like any other person issued with an exclusion order, he was told that if he tried to come back he would be arrested and could face custody once more. The maximum penalty for being in breach of an exclusion order is five years imprisonment. His family was not told he was being sent back and he was subjected to the humiliating and unnecessary indignity of being handcuffed throughout the flight. John was furious – he was never a member of the IRA, something the IRA have publicly announced. During the seven days of his interrogation, having nothing to hide, he was open with his interrogators and told *The Guardian* newspaper in London, 'I would have signed anything they put in front of me just to get out of that cell. I was actually glad to be taken to prison, just to be able to have a shower and some sleep, and to talk to people.'

He found an ally in the unlikeliest of places, the Conservative Party. Peter Bottomley, MP, said, 'John is as innocent of IRA offences as I am'. Michael Howard stuck to his decision and said that crucial evidence leading to the exclusion order could not be made public in court. John was granted an appeal but the appeals procedure for someone with an exclusion order is farcical and heavily weighted against the appellant. Until 1984 when Lord Jellicoe reported on the working of the PTA, anyone wishing to appeal had to remain in custody whilst awaiting the appeal. After 1984 appeals could be made retrospectively, as John's was. The people who hear the representation are known as 'advisers' and are not required to have any legal qualification, nor any specialist knowledge of the situation in the six counties. The adviser sends a report to the Home Secretary who is not obliged to act on it.

When John went to the British embassy in Dublin for his 'representation' – the appeal procedure – he felt the 'adviser' had made up his mind already as nothing of any significance was discussed. Results of appeals are not accompanied by any reasons or explanations. The use of exclusion orders and the methods of appeal could be said to be in breach of the European Convention of Human Rights of which Britain is a signatory. The British government argues that in matters of public security it can derogate from its responsibilities to the convention. When John Hume raised John's case at the European Commission, the British government criticised him saying matters of internal security should not be investigated by the European Commission.

At the time of John's ordeal I was more or less blind but I still did everything I could. Despite his innocence, John's employment prospects looked very bleak as the odour of exclusion hung around him. He couldn't return to do post-graduate work at Queen's University in Belfast because he would have been an obvious Loyalist target. The irony for John is that he was born in England. 'How can I be expelled from a country I was born in?' he said in an interview with *The Guardian*. 'I thought this was only supposed to happen in the old USSR. Does this mean people living in Northern Ireland are worth less than people living in England?' In July 1996 I received a copy of the document John received from the Home Office revoking his exclusion order.

Saddened but no longer shocked I am not surprised by the account of John's experiences. It conjures up a world of broken homes and broken hearts, of anger and despair, of injustice and racism.

At present, the most recent Irish prisoners to be released from jail have, at the whim of the Home Secretary, been forced to remain in Britain for an indefinite time. All have served more than twenty years in jail.

6

THE FAMILIES

The struggle to deliver history from its dead past and oppressive present in the name of all non-persons has a prophetic meaning. It keeps hope alive – that hope without which human persons would no longer see any reason to be.
LEONARDO BOFF

I was lined up with the other gaol visitors in Brixton gaol's dingy visiting area waiting to hand in my parcels. In the middle of this grim room a woman stood on her own weeping uncontrollably. She looked around wildly and saw me and as she looked at me it was as if she'd seen a beacon, something she could recognise and identify in these terrible surroundings. She came over to me and, holding me by the arm, begged me to tell her son she was there. She must have thought I was a chaplain. I was trying to tell her I was only another visitor like herself. But I said I could bring him a parcel every week – I explained that I wasn't allowed to visit the prisoners since the time of Marian and Dolours Price. This was this poor woman's first experience of a gaol – let alone a high security one – and she looked so vulnerable and so forlorn. Any doubts I'd ever had about the work I was doing were dispelled. I knew as I looked at her I was right to devote my energies to helping these people.

It was mid-1976 and until this time my energies were divided; I was stretched to breaking point between prisoners and their families and teaching. With the weeping mother very much in my mind, I went to see Mother Provincial, Mother Christopher, with a request. I told her about the woman and other families. I asked to be released from my teaching obligations. She was very good to me and generous: she supported me in all I did. She was sympathetic and before she left at the end of the 1970s she let me buy a new car for my work.

Kathleen, the woman I met weeping in Brixton gaol, and her family are still visiting their relative in a British jail. For twenty years the family have been trekking to England, scrimping and saving to get the fares, bolstering themselves for every heart-stopping greeting and heart-breaking farewell. Kathleen has never come to terms with her son being in gaol. Like most of the Irish prisoners whose families I got to know, they would never have been inside a gaol had it not been for the political situation – this was certainly Kathleen's thinking.

The Irish prisoners are always put in remote 'dispersal' gaols on moors – far from anywhere in inaccessible places and that means the families have to stay in bed and breakfast places. I remember a mother telling me that she'd have her visit and then she had to walk the streets because the Bed and Breakfasts would not let her back in before 6 p.m. Other Bed and Breakfasts have a captive clientele – because they are nearer to the gaols than any others so they charge well over the rate. When I saw what the families had to go through I decided that I would concentrate my efforts on them because in some ways they suffer even more than the prisoners as many a prisoner has told me. One woman, Geraldine, gave me a statement about what happened to her:

On arrival to the prison [in the morning] with my luggage and 4 year-old daughter, I asked a prison officer to put all my luggage into a locker until my afternoon visit was over ... he searched the bags, locked them in a locker and held the key of the locker at all times ... on my way out of the jail I noticed my bags sitting at a doorway, I enquired as to why my bags were there as the same officer was still on duty ... He replied, 'I'm not allowed to keep them ...'

So I started on a 3 mile walk into the nearest village, Stanfordbridge (as there is no public telephone at the prison to phone a taxi), with my 4 year-old daughter and two grip bags.

On return to the prison for the afternoon visit ... a different prison officer was on duty. He took the bags from me ... The afternoon visit was over at 4.30p.m. ... and we searched for accommodation in Stanfordbridge but there were no vacancies. I knew of a Bed and Breakfast around 1.5 miles outside Stanfordbridge, at this stage it was pitch black, with heavy rain on a January's night. Because there was no taxi service at the time I had to walk the distance along the dark country roads with my 4 year-old daughter and two grip bags.

When we arrived at the Bed and Breakfast they no longer did this service, so we had to walk back to the village. Half way back ... Danielle started crying, stating, 'it's all right for my daddy he has a roof over his head, we've got to sleep in the fields'. I had to reassure and comfort my child that we would get somewhere to stay.

When we got back to the village I phoned for a taxi ... to come from York and collect me at the village to bring me back to York trying different Bed and Breakfasts as we passed them. After the fourth we got a room.

As my work load grew and my commitment to the families increased, I got more and more phone calls from Fr Brady, Fr Faul and Clara Reilly in Belfast. Clara Reilly lives in West Belfast and she was, as I have said, a founder member of the Association for Legal Justice (ALJ). Clara Reilly is not a solicitor; she is what the newspapers call an 'ordinary housewife'. Over the years she has worked tirelessly to support those caught in the web of the law, learning the legal intricacies that enabled her to help people. A woman of considerable warmth and integrity, she has made it her business to understand the complex legislation that so directly affects many Irish people.

Clara Reilly and Fr Brady and Fr Faul would alert me to people who had travelled to England and had disappeared – often into police custody. Others they told me about were families visiting relatives in English gaols or people living in England who had disappeared. I would arrange somewhere for them to stay, sometimes with friends Rose and Jim Ryan or Annie Duffy, and sometimes I booked them into the Irish Centre in Camden Town and paid for rooms for them. I would always have to remind the hosts that they were automatically in danger of being searched and even arrested.

I often rang the newspapers, trying to get journalists to cover stories of arrests, imprisonment, unfair treatment by prison officers or police or the difficulties the families faced on their journeys to visit prisoners. I doubt if this endeared me to the Home Office. The newspapers I rang were *The Irish Times* and the *Irish Press*, a paper that was usually good. Two of the journalists I admired were David McKittrick and and John O'Callaghan, RTE – I'd ring them before I'd ring anyone; they were very objective. It's not that others were incompetent; it's just that they didn't want to know. Breandán Mac Lua who edited the *Irish Post* was always very helpful. He kept the memories of prisoners alive down the years, the Maguires, the Birmingham Six, the Guildford Four. It was very hard to get anything into either the Irish or the English papers in the 1970s and 1980s. It was the same with television. I would talk to journalists for hours and then nothing would happen.

When I went to the gaols to leave parcels for the prisoners, I always stood in the queue with the relatives. The queues were often long and in some gaols in the open air without shelter. It was all right for me but imagine if you'd just travelled from Ireland and you were tired and had your children with you! First you've to queue to hand in your visiting order, then another queue to hand over your parcel and then get in the next queue to get in for your visit. For me the queue was an education: I learned a lot about the lives of prisoners' families, their grievances and hardships, the injustices they suffered. At first people thought because of my habit I must be part of the system. They would come to me with their problems but I had to tell them I was as powerless as they were. It was better that I didn't go in through the chaplain's office because it meant I could be independent; I could speak out. The gaols couldn't control what I did or said and I could denounce ill-treatment and write to or ring up the press. Had I been part of the chaplaincy I wouldn't have been allowed to do that. I was in a small way a help to those queuing – people I'd never met before, strangers.

I would not otherwise have known, either, of the treatment of prisoners' visitors by the prison officers, something I not only witnessed but experienced first hand. Rules were arbitrarily changed – one day a parcel would go in with no comment, another day it would be refused. The Irish prisoners' visitors were treated as lepers – segregated from other visitors – a prison officer would often call out 'IRA' indicating that the Irish visitors should move away from the others. Any anonymity was at once ruined– I was also treated this way. All the others would regard them with hostility – the normal practice is to shout out people's names. It happened to me in Wormwood Scrubs gaol. There was one prison officer there who would never let anything in. I remember him saying that the 'Dubliners' sheet music was political and refusing to let it in. Taking in the parcels was a real penance, having to face the hostility of most of the prison officers. They were always making derogatory comments and throwing things back at you – it was terrible. They must, I felt, have been trying to force me to give up bringing the parcels because they disliked the prisoners. There was one, in particular, who was extremely anti-Irish and when he was there I knew I was in trouble.

They seemed to enjoy taunting me. When they made me sit outside with my parcels I wouldn't contest their orders or argue. I would read from my spiritual readings and pray for patience to endure whatever taunting came my way. The prisoners had a right to their parcels and I'd told the families I'd bring them. *Two Mules for Sister Sarah*, they'd often say to me just to wind me up. I saw that film and she wasn't even a nun. They were trying to insinuate that I wasn't really a nun at all. In Wormwood Scrubs they would not let me in with the other visitors at all to deliver my parcels. The other visitors could go in but I had to wait outside until a prison officer accompanied me just to bring my parcel to reception. There were times when I was being searched with the electronic scanner and the prison officers would shout 'IRA, IRA'. I had all the usual searches and then would be taken to a special room and a prison officer with a big knife would cut into the parcels, opening everything, slice it all open, cut up the tomatoes, stick their noses in the milk; it was pure harassment.

The prisoners and their families were always on my mind and, occasionally, some of the other sisters at the La Sainte Union convent would help me. When they witnessed the kind of pressures I was up against in my work they were amazed. One day when I was ill, my friend, Sr Imelda, accompanied a family to court. She was harassed at the door to the court by a policeman who said, 'Oh, from the North London Convent? You are notorious'. Sr Imelda complained to a senior police officer about him.

IN 1973 FR FELL, BORN in England and public-school educated at Cheltenham Boys College, was arrested. He was a Protestant but converted to Catholicism in his last year at school and had a parish in Coventry where he was very popular. He used to help with collections for the families of Irish prisoners as so many of his parishioners were Irish. I remember a rumour going round that a clergyman was to be arrested and Fr Fell thought it would be a Birmingham priest who was very outspoken in favour of a United Ireland – he never suspected it would be himself. I myself didn't know Fr Fell, although after his arrest I corresponded with him.

Fr Fell was charged with conspiracy along with six others, amongst them Frank Stagg who later died on hunger-strike. Three were acquitted; the others received ten-year sentences apart from Fr Fell who got twelve years. Fr Fell was found guilty of conspiring to commit arson somewhere. His family always maintained that he was innocent of the charges.

I got to know Fr Fell's parents and began to correspond regularly with them. Through my contacts and the Relatives and

Friends of Prisoners Committee (set up and run by myself and a small group of dedicated friends and associates) I worked tirelessly on Fr Fell's behalf.

A consultant psychiatrist described the medical condition of Fr Fell's elderly parents a few months after the verdict passed on their son. 'Mr Fell has had four coronary infarctions, and suffers from anxiety and depression. Mrs Fell is in congestive cardiac failure which is secondary to hypertension. This condition has reached an advanced stage. She also has Parkinsons disease, arthritis and severe depression'. Undaunted, Harry Fell never gave up the fight for his son – and I helped in any way I could. Frs Faul and Murray drew up a plea in 1980 to win parole for their colleague, based on Harry Fell's account of what his son was up against. (In the event parole was denied six times.) This document was sent to international human rights groups that had taken up his case. Harry Fell's account is succinct and shocking.

After his arrest his son was interrogated for thirty-four hours and denied access to a prominent lawyer who had come to his aid. During that time he was given nothing to eat or drink, nor was he allowed to sleep. At his trial a detective-inspector said he had not asked for a lawyer. The trial, lasting twenty-eight days, was held amidst massive security, giving the impression to the jury and the public that these were extremely dangerous men. The tabloids had a field day after conviction with headlines such as the *Sun*'s which read, 'Rebel Priest gives orders to IRA through Confessional'. After the trial Fr Fell was held for several years in Wakefield gaol of which Harry Fell wrote, 'The treatment meted out to my son was brutal and degrading. They wanted to reduce him to something like a wreck such was the harsh régime'. There followed several years in Hull, a gentler régime where he was allowed to study. He was in Bristol for seven weeks where he was held in solitary confinement because the gaol lacked the security required for Category A prisoners. He had done nothing to exact this punishment. It was during this period that his mother died (3 June 1976). He was denied parole to go to her funeral. Over 730 Mass cards and letters sent to him in sympathy were returned to the senders – amongst them mine. My letter and the curt note returning it are still in the box file. I had written:

Words mean very little in a time of great sorrow but somehow at such a time words mean everything. Your mother is gone to God and as

God is everywhere she is with you in your prison cell. I too lost my nearest and dearest recently and it was from the suffering of you and your colleagues that I took my strength. God bless you and I wish we had a few more who cared about justice.

The letter with a Dear Sir/Madam letter signed simply Security. It evokes something of the heartlessness of the gaol régime:

No: 501557 Fell, I refer to the letter received here and addressed to Fr Patrick Fell named above. As you are not one of his approved correspondents I regret that I must return the letter.

Fr Fell was then moved to Albany gaol in the Isle of Wight. This was the most inaccessible of all gaols for his ailing father who lived in Donegal. For the first two years his son was in Albany, Harry Fell was physically unable to make the journey. Had it not been for pressure exerted by Fr Faul, myself and others, the old man would not have been able to see his son. Fr Faul urged the prison authorities to arrange for a visit for the father and son in a gaol in London. He was aided in this by Frank Maguire, Independent MP for Fermanagh. I remember picking Mr Fell up at Heathrow – the tips of his fingers were blue and he was very weak and deaf.

In my diary for 5 September 1976 I wrote:

Went to airport to meet Harry. Saw two gentlemen – Harry is tall and thin in dark grey pin-striped suit. Beautifully and immaculately dressed – Mr Maguire likewise. Mr Maguire waved across to me, and I knew they were the people I was meeting. We went up to the cafeteria to have a chat. Found out that Mr Maguire was born in Galway, grew up and educated in Athlone. He knew all my friends. We said goodbye to Frank Maguire who returned on the next flight and we headed for the convent. Nuns very kind to Harry. Rang Fr Cagney who said Harry could stay with him. Went to Mass at St Joseph's at 5.00 p.m. (A priest from Westminster preached about youngsters falling away from the Church – it made me cross, as he blamed all the wrong reasons.) Left Harry at the Irish Centre. He was tired as he was up at 4.00 a.m. plus the journey. There was to be a phone call from the home office for me early Monday morning.

The next day Harry went to visit his son:

Collected Harry and brought him to convent. I then rang Mr Jeremy Page of the Home Office. I told him who I was and that Harry would like two visits each day. He said he would have to arrange that with the governor of Wormwood Scrubs. We rang [Wormwood Scrubs] and were told it was most irregular. We mentioned Mr Page and Frank Maguire and got through to the governor; handed over phone to Harry. He was asked name, address, date of birth, etc. Got permission for two visits per day, for a watch to be handed in, etc. First visit at 1.30p.m. Harry and I left convent at 12.50. He was worried about how he would find his son (at the same time the son was worrying about how he would find his father) two and a half years since their last visit. I waited outside, and at 3.30 I went up to about 100 yards from the prison gate. Security man made me move off on the order of a hard cruel-looking gentleman who passed the car. Harry was emotionally upset when he came out, although he was treated very correctly. He tried to keep smiling, but the tears rolled down his cheeks.

He had found conditions there very harsh. He was searched and taken to a room twelve feet by six where there was a table between them and they were locked in. Imagine having to shout across long table to a deaf father!

On 7 September I collected Harry for his second visit:

Called for Harry at 8.50 a.m. He had not slept. Went to prison. Wrote six letters and said my prayers and did my spiritual reading and meditation. Visit lasted only from 10.00–11.20 a.m. but Harry could not find where I was. I got worried at 12.05 and drove past the gate to find him standing there. Lunch was a rush. Back for 2.00 p.m. visit. I went for a small walk up the road to East Acton. Found a beautiful church with a Graham Sutherland Crucifixion. Made Stations of the Cross and said my prayers.

On 12 September I drove Harry to Heathrow airport and he returned to Donegal.

Fr Fell was escorted to Albany gaol and got back at about the same time as a new Irish prisoner, Brendan Dowd arrived. Brendan was put into solitary confinement whereupon five Irish prisoners, Eddie Byrne, Seán Campbell, John McCluskey, Con McFadden and Liam MacLarnon went to see the governor to protest. He received them and as one prisoner's wife said in the statement she was later to make, 'He treated them all right'. But Brendan remained in solitary confinement so they returned to see him a second time having on this occasion asked Fr Fell to be their spokesman. They were met by an assistant governor who refused to listen to them. Their reaction was to sit in the corridor in a peaceful protest. They were confronted suddenly by twenty warders in riot gear who set upon the prisoners backed up by another thirty prison officers.

Harry Fell's letter to Fr Murray picks up the rest of the story:

> Patrick had to have several stitches in his head, his nose was fractured and his right wrist fractured. In this sorry condition Patrick was brought before the prison visiting committee and charged with mutiny. This committee found him guilty and he lost 690 days of remission. Along with the loss of remission he was given ninety-one days in solitary confinement on 24 December 1976. He still suffers from what he himself thinks are migraines but I have spoken with a specialist who said that he is suffering from post concussional syndrome.

Harry Fell ends his letter to Fr Murray more in sadness than in anger:

> I am 75 years of age. I am living alone and have a heart condition. Sometimes I grow despondent and wonder will I be alive to see his release and welcome him home. I am most grateful for all the many endeavours made for my son's release. At Knock I met his Holiness John Paul and he gave me a medal. On this I pin my hopes.

So disgusted was Harry Fell with the injustices endured by his son that he relinquished his British citizenship and applied for Irish nationality.

Fr Fell's loss of remission cost him not only his parole – to which he had a right – but home leave during the last six to nine months of his sentence. I in my capacity as secretary of the Relatives and Friends of the Prisoners Committee wrote:

> Father was due for release in March this year (1981). He challenged the loss of remission in the courts and lost. He is now appealing to the House of Lords. He has nine months more to serve because of loss of remission.

In the year leading up to Fr Fell's original release date, another Republican prisoner also convicted on a conspiracy charge was given a week's leave before his release. My note ends: 'Fr Fell writes, "I feel totally surrounded by discrimination after eight years ...". Fr Fell's father is in hospital recovering from a serious operation in which he had a leg amputated.'

Having served eight years Fr Fell was released in July 1981 –

his father died at 4 p.m. on 7 August 1982.

I WAS VISITED BY Mrs Campbell. She stayed at the convent. Her husband Seán was the prisoner most badly wounded during the attack at Albany gaol. He had a broken leg, a broken jaw, two broken fingers and badly damaged ribs and was taken to the gaol hospital where he had to be fed intravenously.

Mrs Campbell was the first relative, along with her father-in-law, to see any of the wounded men. The Albany attacks were taken up by Amnesty International, the National Council for Civil Liberties and the Howard League for Penal Reform who compiled a detailed dossier of statements and made enquiries to the Home Office. In her statement for the dossier Mrs Campbell reported what her husband told her:

> They thought Seán was unconscious, they jumped on his legs, they held him down until they broke his leg. Then they said, 'I think he has a punctured lung, let's take him to hospital.'

He was left in a cell for two days having returned from twelve days in the gaol hospital but could not walk to the canteen for his food and so did not get any food or water for those two days. On the third day he was moved to the punishment blocks where his bed was a three-inch thick piece of foam that was removed between 8 a.m and 8 p.m. His leg was still in plaster at the time and his other injuries had not healed – fractured ribs, a broken jaw, two broken fingers and a broken arm. He had a hard chair and a pot in his cell and nothing else and was locked in 23 hours a day. His wife wrote: 'His worst injuries are his chest injuries and his back – he keeps spitting up blood. He cannot move his left hand.' When Mrs Campbell asked for an independent doctor to visit her husband the request was turned down.

Seán Campbell's wife wanted to call the media's attention to what had happened to her husband and the other men. To this end she and the prisoners asked me to help them organise a press conference. It was at this point that I ran into my own problems. At breakfast one morning the Reverend Mother approached me. She said she had a phone call from a man in Luton who said I was not to talk to the press, that he would not allow me to make statements. I replied that the man in question was a member of Sinn Féin and that Fr Faul had said I was not to take orders from anyone – he had told me I should call the conference and talk to the press. She beamed at me in relief! I was walking a constant tight-rope up against Sinn Féin, the Church, my own superiors but I knew I had to walk that tightrope to help the families. The greatest thing you can do for the prisoners is to help their families.

In 1985 Fr Fell and Seán Campbell won a case they had taken to the European Court of Human Rights. The case concerned rights of correspondence and legal representation for prisoners. The court found that there had been a breach of their rights in that they were obstructed from access to legal advice in relation to a personal injuries claim against the warders and set a precedent whereby all prisoners in British gaols were granted increased legal protection.

Prisoners have different ways of registering their protest against their own treatment or that of their fellow prisoners and their visitors. Fr Fell's co-defendant Frank Stagg, a Coventry bus driver, was also convicted of conspiracy. He too was in Albany in the early part of his sentence where his wife visited him and was only allowed to see him behind glass in a closed visit surrounded by prison officers. (Frank Stagg's sister Veronica Phillips gave me a long statement after Frank's death.)

Frank Stagg refused to have further visits in these conditions and refused to do gaol work. He was held with Paul Holmes and Michael Gaughan for the first three months of 1974 in a cell eight foot square in which they had both to eat and use a bucket for a toilet that was not removed regularly. It was when rats appeared that the men went on hunger-strike. On the twenty-second day of their hunger-strike – they were in the gaol hospital at Parkhurst by then – Michael Gaughan had been, as usual, force-fed in a crude and agonising manner. He was refusing to drink any water as the only tap was also used to wash out the slop buckets. His family were sent for and on 3 June he died.

After Michael Gaughan died Frank Stagg ended his hunger-strike when promises were made that he would not be made to work and would be transferred to Long Lartin gaol in the Midlands – nearer to his family. This happened but when his wife and sister visited him there on 26 July they were taken individually into a side room and forced to strip and subjected to a body search both before and after their visit which upset them profoundly. At one point his sister refused to removed her bra and the warder physically ripped it off her. Frank resumed the hunger-strike – this time for thirty-one days – when he was told he had to have a strip-search before being allowed on a visit with his wife. He refused and was put in the punishment block.

I recall going to the Connolly Association Bookshop where I would buy books for the prisoners to be sent in to them. Not knowing that Frank was again on hunger-strike I sent him in a copy of *The Great Hunger*. I was relieved, for once, that the book never reached him. During this hunger-strike Frank Stagg's father was dying of cancer but he was refused permission to write to him. After the intervention of Frank Maguire, Frank was told there would be no more stripsearches and that he would be allowed to write to his father every week.

On 17 February 1977 I visited Brixton gaol and again found two women in tears. In the waiting area Mrs Hackett and Nuala were in tears; they were refused a visit. Patrick, with only one leg, refused to stand and give his name and number to the prison officer before the visit. This was never required before. Patrick's mother and sister had come from Ireland to visit him. On 26 August I went to Brixton gaol to deliver parcels and saw Mrs Hackett and her son-in-law in the reception area for Category A prisoners. Both were clearly upset. Her son-in-law had not been allowed in because he had no identification on him although he had been in the day before without any problem. Mrs Hackett was in tears. She said that she had seen Patrick on his crutches for the first time that day and she got a shock.

I remember how Patrick received the injuries that led to his handicap. He was carrying a bomb in the Chelsea area in March 1976. I heard that bomb going off while I was at a party with the students in the art college. Nobody was killed but he had to have an arm and a leg amputated. As he lay in hospital so badly hurt they interrogated him to find out who he was. He told his sister that a policeman had poked him in the amputated stump of his leg.

As the mother and sister wept that day in the gaol, I suggested the family left the gaol with me at once. We rang *The Irish Press*, *The Irish Times*, *The Cork Examiner*, and the Irish embassy. Because of his amputation, Patrick Hackett was held on remand in the gaol infirmary. I remember his sister weeping as she recounted what she had found when she, a nurse, visited her brother. Because of his injuries he couldn't slop out. But if the stench of urine was anything to go by, nobody else was doing this for him. His cell was full of bottles of old urine.

In May 1977 Patrick Hackett's trial began, so his family stayed in London for some time. I helped the family to put pressure on the authorities so that Patrick would be able to see an independent doctor. I was pleased when the Irish embassy said they'd try and help – they often disappointed me. Patrick was so badly treated that he sent out all his things to his mother while he was at Wormwood Scrubs. He was transferred to Wakefield gaol where he refused to wear the gaol uniform and they wouldn't let him wear anything else so he was on the blanket for a long time, I think it was about two years that he spent in the punishment block. His sister did everything she could for him – she went to see anybody she could. Amnesty International wrote a report on his condition. She arranged for people from the Irish embassy to go and see him but before they went he was transferred to Parkhurst gaol on the Isle of Wight. He was put in hospital there where he was with people with psychiatric problems. He served most of his sentence there and was allowed to wear shorts and T shirt. He was given permission to use the gym and this was a great help to him.

Harassment continued at every level. Allies with influence were rare and were inclined to be unreliable. When Giuseppe Conlon's daughter Ann was to be married in the spring of 1978, I lobbied Richard O'Brien, an Irish embassy official, to help to secure permission for Giuseppe to attend the wedding. He said there was nothing he could do. I turned to Lord Longford, the Labour peer famous for championing the causes of a variety of prisoners, amongst them Myra Hindley. Lord Longford had just been into Wormwood Scrubs where he had seen Giuseppe Conlon, Gerry Conlon and Billy Power – now he was not quite so sure they are guilty. But no amount of pressure would soften the administration and the wedding went ahead without Giuseppe. I appealed to Lord Longford for help on several occasions. I went to see him about the Maguire family – what was left of it. It was immediately after Annie Maguire had been convicted and her sister Mary McCaffery had come over to mind the children. Annie's son John, about fourteen at the time I think, was being harassed by the police so I went with Mary McCaffery to lobby the MP Arthur Latham. We were waiting to see him and Lord Longford walked past so I grabbed him. I said something terrible had happened, that an innocent family had been locked up and introduced him to Mary McCaffery. He turned to me and said, 'They tried to kill my son-in-law', [Hugh Fraser, a Tory MP had a bomb left under his car by the IRA] and he kissed me on the cheek and walked on. Years later, at the end of the appeal that finally cleared the Maguire family who spent many years in gaol, Lord Longford approached me – I reminded him of what he had said and he shook his head, 'It was a terrible thing to say, it was shameful of me to say that'.

IT SEEMED AT THIS TIME that the British were gripped with an anti-Irish hysteria that gave them licence to wreck the lives of innocent people. I always remember Chrissie whose husband Brian was in gaol in England. She used to come over to visit him regularly. Sometimes I met her and took her back to the airport but other times she arrived very late at night and would go straight to her friend Val's house. There was one time in 1979 when she was late and went straight there. It was midnight when she arrived and the two women sat talking until 2 or 3 a.m. Suddenly the door was smashed down and the police burst in arresting both women. Chrissie couldn't think why they were being arrested and both she and her friend wondered what the other had been up to. They were taken to a police station and stripped naked and ordered to wear these ridiculous police-issue clothes and then paraded in front of all the policemen to have their finger prints and pictures taken. They let Val go fairly soon but Chrissie was charged first with withholding information and then with conspiracy to help her husband escape. She was held for six months on remand without bail while her six children were cared for by relatives. She was eventually allowed bail, but had to report to a police station twice a day. I collected Chrissie but did not recognise her as her gaol ordeal had taken its toll. At least, after bail, she could see her children who came over to visit. At her trial she was found not guilty but she had spent eighteen months on remand.

THERE HAVE BEEN SEVERAL PRISONERS whom I have known whose parents have died whilst their sons and daughters were imprisoned. Paul Holmes' mother was near death in 1980 and when I visited her that year I remember the dying woman begging me to take her to England to see her son one last time. On 19 August 1980, I wrote in my diary:

Phone call from Clara Reilly. She and Fr Faul went to see Mrs Holmes; she is very very low, could barely speak. When they mentioned Paul she said, 'I love him; I love him'.

I remember many prisoners' mothers, amongst them Noel Gibson's. Noel Gibson was recently released from gaol having served over twenty years. In August 1982 his mother came to England to see him. I had visited her a few months before during my holiday in Ireland and had found her very unwell. When she arrived she had really made a big effort and she looked lovely. She didn't tell me then that she had terminal cancer. It was over four years since she had seen her son who had refused to send out visiting orders as his visits had to be taken behind glass. However, his mother was determined to see him before she died. I picked her up and took her to the Scrubs. Of course they wouldn't let her in and her son wouldn't take a visit behind glass. We contacted the Irish embassy and eventually they agreed to let her have a twenty-five minute visit the following day and thirty minutes the day afterwards. The visits had to be conducted behind glass. She didn't tell her son that she was so ill. Two months later she died.

There were others who died, Ray McLoughlin's father, Hugh Doherty's mother, the Gillespies' father, the Prices' mother, Brendan Dowd's mother, Joe O'Connell's mother and father, Roy Walsh's mother, Paul Holmes' mother, Brian Keenan's mother, Giuseppe Conlon and many more. Irish prisoners did not get compassionate visits to see a dying parent nor were they allowed to go to their funerals. I only remember one being allowed out for a funeral and he had influential political strings pulled for him. As far as I remember Gerry Conlon was the only one allowed to see a dying parent, and he was only allowed once even though Giuseppe was dying in the same gaol. Sometimes the chaplains who gave prisoners news of deaths were very hard.

On 26 July 1981 I met Mrs Doherty [mother of hunger-striker Kieran] and spoke to Mr Doherty when I was in Long Kesh. She went there during the day and Mr Doherty stayed at night. He had given up hope. Kieran was lucid but very, very ill. Mr Doherty is very proud of his son. I had looked after Mrs Doherty during a trip to London. Poor woman, I was very sorry for her, her heart was breaking and the Reverend Mother said she thought she should go home and try and make her son come off the hunger-strike. I was in sympathy with the hunger-strikers' demands – as far as I was concerned they were political prisoners and many would never have been in gaol if it hadn't been for the grave absence of human rights in their society. I had very little to do with the strike except for my contact with Mrs Doherty (and seeing Michael Devine's family in Derry). I don't like hunger-striking because it causes so much sorrow to the families already deep with grief.

It was during the late stages of Kieran Doherty's hunger-strike that the royal wedding of Prince Charles and Lady Diana Spencer took place. At the time I was fed up with the endless coverage of it on the news and the interest taken in it, particularly since at the same time Kieran Doherty was sixty-eight days into his hunger-strike and Kevin Lynch sixty-seven. Both men were going blind and close to death. Ken Livingstone was joining a forty-eight hour hunger protest on the steps of County Hall and all day long it was wedding wedding wedding. Mrs Reagan was there with five hat-boxes and a hairdresser. I felt I should go down and stand with the protesters at County Hall. The prince and princess passed the hunger-strike demonstration and the commentator said that they looked at the demonstrators – let's hope it reminded them that all was not well in a so-called part of the United Kingdom.

On 2 August Kieran Doherty died after seventy-three days on hunger-strike. I was shocked when I spoke to his grief-stricken mother who told me a priest had said that Mrs Quinn, the mother of a young man who had come off the hunger-strike, would go straight to heaven – implying, as she understood it, that she would not, implying even more distressingly, that her deceased son wouldn't.

A few weeks later in August 1981 I visited Ireland. I spent several days in the six counties seeing prisoners' families and seeing for myself at first hand what was happening on the streets. Here are extracts from three days – three typical days in the life of the embattled Nationalist areas of Belfast:

17 August: Mary [Feeney] and I went to Mrs Storey's. Mr Storey was there but Mrs Storey was out. Bobby [a former H-block prisoner] does not live there because of harassment but he calls sometimes. We then went to Mrs Doherty. She was out so we called on Mrs Hill. She had gone to England. We called back to Mrs Doherty. She was delighted to see us; she is still heartbroken but very proud of Kieran. She found that a priest putting pressure on her was the hardest thing but she had to endure. She gave us copies of Kieran's letters to her. She has lovely sons, well spoken, polite. Life is so cruel to these poor people. The Iranian embassy sent representatives to her. They gave

Mrs Sarah Conlon with a photograph of her husband, Giuseppe [Pacemaker]

a　　　　　　　　　*b*　　　　　　　　　*c*

[a] Mrs Kinsella, Mother of Seán; [b] The late Mrs Dowd, mother of Brendan, travelled to remote corners of Britian for 20 years until she died: [c] Mrs Kathleen Feeney, mother of Hugh

a

b

[a] Mrs Annie Walsh, mother of Roy, travelled for 18 years to remote corners of Britian until she died; [b] Mrs Hackett mother of Patrick and Mrs O'Dwyer, mother of Ella; [c] The late Mrs C. McComb, mother of John and Damian. They were held in different gaols and this made it difficult for their mother to visit.

c

Mr & Mrs Bill Butler have travelled for 22 years to remote corners of Britian

[a] Mrs Lily Armstrong, mother of Billy; [b] Mrs Briget Duggan, mother of Harry;
[c] Mrs Lily Hill, mother of Paul; [d] Mrs Sheila Gillespie, mother of Ann and
Eileen; [e] Mrs O'Neill, mother of Eddie; [f] Mrs Hayes, mother of John

Mr and the late Mrs McLoughlin, mother and father of Patrick

Bishop Drury, Catherine Madigan and Mrs Madigan, mother of Tony

The late Mrs Madge Doherty, mother of Hugh, outside Parkhurst gaol in the 1970s, with [l] Sr Sarah, Anne Doherty and [r] Judy Kupersmith, an American friend of Sr Sarah

her a picture of the Ayatollah Khomeini framed in minute shell mosaic. We then went to Mrs Lennon. Her husband is suffering terribly from arthritis. She has all her sons in prison now so the army leave her alone – they took [shot] her dog last year. Going home we passed silent protests standing in single file in the centre of the road. We are asked to blow the horn in solidarity with H-Blocks.

18 August: Went to 9 a.m. Mass. After breakfast we went to Long Kesh, Mrs Feeney, Mary and myself. Hugh was in good form. We had an hour's visit. Hugh told us that Martin Hurson's [hunger-striker] body was handed over to the family wrapped in a Union Jack flag ... On the way back we were stopped outside Long Kesh and each one was asked for identification. We were joined by French visitors from a Catholic French organisation. Mr Avril [from the French delegation] was shocked over what Mrs Conlon [Giuseppe's wife] told us. Gerry's brother-in-law was refused permission to see him but film actors and actresses are allowed freely into the Yorkshire Ripper – Peter Sutcliffe. Gerry saw his file with the mark suicidal on it. He told his sisters next day. A prison officer called the sisters and showed them the file – there was no suicidal mark on it – they called after Gerry who came and looked at the file and then pulled at it – the prison officer had stuck paper over the suicidal mark – only a medical doctor could put such a mark. Gerry was never at the doctor since he went into prison. We went then to see Mrs Sands; Mr and Mrs Sands were there. They are a lovely family. She gave me signed copies of Bobby's writing and two signed copies of his diary. They had the smuggled letters from Bobby framed – some on toilet paper and some on cigarette paper.

19 August: Up early. After Mass I heard that Michael Devine died on hunger-strike this morning. The whistles and dustbin lids were banged. After breakfast there was a lot of shooting and it sounded quite close. Mary said she would take her car and take me out. Mr Avril came with us. We went up to Twinbrook. There were cars burning. The army was everywhere with road blocks. We visited Mrs Smyth, she was heartbroken [her husband Seán Smyth is Annie Maguire's brother and one of the Maguire Seven, and her eldest son, who had been seriously ill, had died]. We went to Turf Lodge to Clara Reilly. While we were there Suzanne Bunting, Ronnie Bunting's wife came in. She had a Greek lawyer with her and two other Greeks. She showed us her big scars after the assassination attempt. She had her two children with her also. [In October 1980 Suzanne's husband Ronnie and a friend Noel Lyttle were murdered by assassins in front of their young children. Suzanne was left for dead.] We called to see Mr and Mrs Sheehan, the parents of the latest hunger-striker. They realise the awful cross ahead and asked us to pray for strength for them to bear it ... Bobbie Storey was arrested with two others in a car

in Kennedy Way. I rang Mrs Storey, she is brave – he is in Castlereagh now.

On 21 August I went to Derry. Having visited various people we went to Creggan to where Michael Devine was laid out. [The tenth hunger-striker to die – 30 August.] We went to Mrs Walker's [wife of Johnny, one of the Birmingham Six] and to see Mrs O'Hara [mother of Patsy, a hunger-striker]. Patsy had daily Communion. He asked for the last rites while he could participate in them. He told his mother to help him continue the fight when he was unconscious and she understands.

On 22 August I drove all over Donegal visiting families in fog and rain and at one point had a collision – partly my own fault, partly due to aggressive male chauvinist. My car was the only one damaged and I hastily left the scene without taking names or addresses, I was shaken and upset. When I got out of the mountains the mist and rain ceased. I went to Mr Fell. He was sitting in the kitchen with his dog beside him. He had become very thin but he was alert, aware, and his memory remarkable. Fr Fell phones him on Fridays at 10.40 and speaks to him for twenty minutes.

The next day I went home to Eyrecourt for a few days' before spending my last three days visiting families.

There were occasionally families who couldn't accept what their children had done and could not accept that they were in gaol. Most would say, 'He's my son or she's my daughter and I love him or her'. I remember one man whose wife died whilst their son was in gaol. He could not accept that his son had ever been implicated in anything to do with the IRA. On the request of the prisoner, whenever I was in Ireland I would go and see the father, who, although always polite, could not forgive his son. When the prisoner's mother died it was I who went to see him. After several years the father finally accepted his son again and, when the prisoner was released, father and son renewed their relationship.

It is the families of prisoners who are always uppermost in my mind. The Stagg family had to endure many torments during Frank Stagg's repeated hunger-strikes and Harry Fell's ordeal was made worse by his advanced age and physical frailty. Other less dramatic torments, the petty irritations, have worn families down over the years. Some notes in my box-files highlight the difficulties prisoners' families are subjected to, as if the mere fact of having people they love locked up is not enough of a punishment. Harry

Fell's visits in 1977 cost him £133 – a small fortune by the standards of the time. He had to endure the pettiness of the authorities as I documented:

> Visiting hours 10.30–11.30 a.m. and 2 p.m.–4 p.m. on Thursday, Friday and Saturday. On Thursday he lost twelve minutes of the morning visit and fifteen minutes of the afternoon visit. The visitor was on time but the officer in charge did not bother to call him in time. The visits ended every day five minutes before time. On Saturday he lost fifteen minutes at the beginning of the visit; Friday he lost approximately twelve minutes in the morning and fifteen minutes in the afternoon. The man was deprived of sixty-nine minutes out of the nine hours that were his allotted visiting time. This man last saw his son in August 1976. The only family visit the prisoner has had. This father had to travel for twenty-eight hours. He saw his son for forty-five minutes. It cost him roughly 30p a minute.

In mid 1980 my Reverend Mother suddenly told me that I could not have any more visitors. Shocked, I asked for clarification and as I mentioned various names -- Mrs Tuite, Mrs Bennett, Bishop Drury – Reverend Mother went through all my faults and failings and I got the impression if God had made me differently I could have had all the visits I liked. I made up my mind to get 'takeaway' meals in the future and just use the parlour. She told me also that the writing was on the wall for me, but if I am doing God's work the writing will only be on the wall when he wants it. Looking back now I remember this was a hard time. But I can't help smiling when I think back to the man in the local Kentucky Fried Chicken takeaway – he must have thought I was very hungry. It was several months before I could bring visitors to the convent again.

I always made a point of meeting families at stations and airports, but there were two occasions in the last twenty years when it was impossible for me to be there either to meet people or see them off. The first of these occasions concerned Geraldine, a prisoner's wife from Belfast. I couldn't be there to meet her because I was in hospital. For some time I had been subject to bouts of weakness and illness. Sometimes the illness confined me to my bed, other times I would continue working in spite of having a temperature. It was at the time Geraldine came to London that I discovered I had gallstones.

On Monday, 9 April 1984 I noted in my diary:

Phone call from Geraldine. She is coming Wed–Sat. I booked her in at the hostel but I won't be able to meet her as I am at the hospital. I had a chat with Sr Anthony (at the hostel), and all is well there.

On Friday 13 April, just out of hospital and still weak I had my first and only actual contact with Geraldine during that visit. I went to Victoria:

Picked up Geraldine, and we went to Brixton. She got a fairly longish visit and they told her to come early tomorrow and they would see what they could do about extra time. On the way back she asked to call in to Mike Fisher (the solicitor). He was not there. I left her back at the hostel and told her to tell Sr Anthony that I would send on the money for her bed and breakfast.

On the Saturday Geraldine was due to go home and I regretfully told her I wouldn't be able to take her to the airport because I had a previous commitment.

Late that evening I got a phone call from Belfast asking where Geraldine was. Mike Fisher rang Scotland Yard and was told they had not got her. I rang the Irish Centre. Sr Anthony said she was trying to get me all afternoon. She had bad news. Geraldine was arrested at 11.30 a.m. The Special Branch came to the hostel and searched her room and took what was in the wastepaper box. I rang Belfast and the solicitor, asking him to ring the police station. I rang Fr Faul who rang the police and accused them of bullying women. The police put the phone down on him. I rang and suggested that he ring Bishop Cathal Daly who had been in to see her husband the week before. He did and Bishop Daly rang the police. The Church is very powerful and can do a lot of good to relieve anguish and suffering, but I think they don't always realise they have this power.

Two days later Geraldine surfaced – she had returned home. According to her statement:

I was walking along with my suitcase and a man came up behind me and he said my name and I turned round and he tapped me on the shoulder aand he said, 'I arrest you under the special powers act'. He showed me a card ... there was another lady with him ... he radioed for a car ... the car came along and another woman jumped out and they put me into the car and they put my suitcase into the back of the car ...

We finally arrived at [police station] ... I got out of the car and the man who arrested me started searching the car ... then they brought me into the station and they booked me in ... they then brought me down to a room, there was desks and chairs ... so I sat down. Then they opened the suitcase and started looking at things ... the men left ... one of the women said 'we're going to strip-search you and we want you to take all your clothes off'. So I started talking my clothes off and they started searching all my clothes. I said to them that I had took my periods that morning and I had a piece of toilet roll and I took the toilet roll out and handed the girl it and I said 'are you actually going to search the toilet roll?' It was stained. She took out the toilet roll and had a good poke around it. I had nothing on or around me. After they went through my clothes ... they then said to me 'you're going to have to come down now and see the doctor'... he examined my ears, my nose, my throat ... he says 'you need your pants off you I'm going to examine your back passage ... I was stark naked ... he put his finger in my back passage and he pressed up really hard and I told him it was sore. He took his fingers down and took the glove off and threw it away and took the woman to the side and said something to her ... he says 'put back on your clothes' ... they brought me back to the room I was in ... one of the women came back again with the Tee shirt and a skirt out of my suitcase and says 'you're going to have to strip again' ... so I stripped again ... I had to change into the skirt and top and they took my clothes away then.

They started asking me questions and then said they were going to take my finger prints ... I needed to go to the toilet, so they brought me into this room ... like a shower thing ... I started to go to the toilet. There's no doors ... as I was going, police officers walked by and I jumped wiith embarrassment. After I went to the toilet, the police-woman was with me all the time in the toilet, she says to me 'don't be flushing the toilet'. She then took me in so I was able to wash my hands afterwards. She then took me back in and they brought the stuff in to do my hands and under my finger nails ... she says 'it's for explosives, to see if I was handling any explosives or stuff like that' ... they put me in a cell and they ... kept checking me every half hour through a wee thing in the door

I got up the next morning ... they came again and took another set of prints ... they started interviewing me all that day ... at the last interview they says to me 'if we release you where are you going to go?' and I says 'home' ... They left me at the door ... they drew me a map of the Underground and said there was an Underground place just near to it. So I took the Underground and went straight to the airport.

Geraldine was finally released after a weekend that was tantamount to rape by the Establishment and she was told by the police not to talk about what happened to her.

The only other time I wasn't able to take a family on their visit, was the occasion when there were arrests under the PTA culminating in the exclusion of the sister of a prisoner in England. Martina had been imprisoned in September 1987 with two other young people arrested under the PTA and charged with conspiracy to murder. Martina's family, especially her sister Deirdre, did all they could for her. Deirdre visited Martina almost every week, as they were very close.

On 27 February 1988 Deirdre and her brother Paddy arrived in London for the committal hearings preceding the trial of their sister and her companions. I met them from the coach and drove them to Brixton gaol to visit Martina. After the visit I drove them to my friend Steve who sometimes put Irish visitors up for me. The court proceedings began on 29 February and continued until 3 March. Each day I collected Deirdre and Paddy and accompanied them to court. They were scheduled to return to Ireland on Friday 4 March, but plans were changed because the psychologist who was monitoring Martina's condition needed two hours with the family at a hospital in Denmark Hill. Deirdre and Paddy had to cancel their 11.00 a.m. train and were worried about a friend called Lisa whom they had planned to meet at Euston Station. I volunteered to go to Euston to collect Lisa. I searched and searched and finally found her sitting outside in Merton Road. We got through heavy traffic back to Denmark Hill and picked up Deirdre and Paddy. It was one o'clock and we started back to London. On the way, as they had missed the train, we decided to go to Slatterys (a coach station) in Paddington and dumped the cases. It was after 3.00 p.m. and the traffic was awful. We stayed for a while. Then I took them to nearby shops to get something to eat and to while away the time until 8.30 p.m. I brought them to Marble Arch, then said goodbye. I was back after 3.30 in the convent.

Five minutes after I left them at a nearby Kentucky Fried Chicken restaurant, just as they were carrying their trays to a table, Deirdre, Paddy and Lisa were suddenly approached by three Special Branch men with guns and arrested under the Prevention of Terrorism Act. A startled Paddy, misunderstanding the situation exclaimed, 'But I'm going to pay!' The Special Branch men were not amused. They quickly whisked the three off to three separate police stations, strip-searched and interrogated them and, several days later, presented Deirdre with an exclusion order, ensuring that, while it was in effect, she could never visit Martina again in a British gaol.

About 9.00 p.m. that day I learned of the arrests from a Dublin journalist. He knew before the parents did – he must have had a tip off from the gardaí who must have been told by the Special Branch. I rang Fr Faul, asking him to ask Irish bishops to phone Scotland Yard in protest. I also rang the anxious relatives in Ireland who had no idea why the three were missing. On Sunday 6 March I rang Gareth Peirce again. They had applied for an extension of two days. Gareth was going in at 3.00 p.m., but she sent in books and sweets. *The Morning Star* rang and took a statement from me. Then Clive Soley, MP, rang to ask what had happened. When I learned the time of the arrests, I could only conclude that the Special Branch had followed me all day, since my passengers were arrested only moments after I left them.

On 8 March Gareth Peirce rang me to tell me Paddy and Lisa had been released and Deirdre sent back under an exclusion order. I went down, got Paddy and took him to the Irish embassy. Lisa was there already. Paddy had lost weight and they were talking, talking, talking. One of the things Paddy talked about then was the strip-search to which he had been subjected. He told me that he was used to being naked in a sport's changing-room and wasn't embarrassed about taking his clothes off. But this was something totally different – he felt defiled, disgusted and humiliated by the probing eyes and hands of the police.

The embassy wanted them to take the tube to Heathrow. I said that, darkness or not, [my sight was by then not as good as it should have been to drive at night] I would drive them there. We arrived after a slow journey.

A week or two later I rang Deirdre. She was still feeling shattered. She went on television and described exactly what happened when she was strip-searched.

IN MARCH 1988, a month in which there were many horrific deaths, I went to Belfast for the funeral of Roy Walsh's mother. The funeral was on 23 March and I arrived the day before. The Feeneys were at the airport to meet me – what would I do without the Feeneys? In the evening we went to visit the Farrells, the family of Mairéad Farrell gunned down by the SAS on 6 March in Gibraltar with her two friends Danny McCann and Seán Savage in an extra-judicial killing orchestrated at the highest levels of the British government.

I knew the Farrells well. I had visited Mairéad in Armagh gaol where she had served a lengthy sentence.

The next day I went to Mrs Walsh's funeral with Mary Feeney. When we got to the church Gerry Adams was behind us on the way in. He is very tall and thin. I shook hands with him. The Mass was beautiful. After the Mass at which I met several relatives of prisoners in England, I went with Mr Farrell up to Milltown Cemetery in West Belfast, the graveyard where his daughter Mairéad was buried in the Republican plot several days earlier. During the funeral of the three killed in Gibraltar, a lone Loyalist gunman, Michael Stone, shot at random into the crowd and hurled grenades killing three and injuring fifty. He claimed it was in revenge for the Enniskillen bombing in which 11 were killed and 63 injured in November 1987. Mrs Walsh was buried near where the mayhem was – the whole plot was a mountain of flowers for all those killed.

On my holiday to Ireland in 1989 I went to see Joe O'Connell's father who was in hospital (and shortly to die). I took him flowers saying they were given on Joe's behalf – he said, 'From Joe', and the tears rolled down his face. Life is so hard for some.

IN THESE TWENTY-FIVE YEARS SINCE I began my work with prisoners, children who were babes in arms, carried to English gaols to visit fathers, are now themselves grown up and bringing their children on the visits. It makes me reflect on the shattered lives of these families and the vow of chastity with which I have lived happily for fifty years. The wives of prisoners had not taken such a vow, yet those who are faithful to their husbands are condemned to lives of celibacy for twenty or thirty years. These women have never had a visit with their husbands except in the presence of two prison officers, nor have they exchanged words, greetings or letters unread or unheard by others from the day of arrest. It's a marvellous marriage that can survive such a sentence.

Some marriages didn't survive the strain. I remember a prisoner's wife who wanted to split up with her husband telling me how she felt. Some wanted to break with their husbands. It wasn't for me to say anything but I would ask them to keep writing and visiting and I'd make sure they had enough funds to do that for the children's sakes. I think that if you're married, you're married forever whether a man is in gaol or not, whether his is a life sentence or not. It's the same for a man if his wife is in gaol but I don't think the men would be as faithful as the women. The women were wonderful; they kept visiting despite all the harassment. I do think the gaols ought to allow conjugal visits. Why should these wives be condemned to celibacy – it's quite different if like me, you chose it – they didn't.

I marvel at the families that have stayed together and the marriages that have lasted in spite of the terrible ordeals faced by the wives travelling to see their husbands in English gaols. I am amazed at the loyalty and love of mothers, fathers, sisters and brothers, facing all the dangers and humiliations awaiting them as they make their way from Ireland to England, some for twenty years or more.

7

THE RELATIVES AND FRIENDS OF THE PRISONERS COMMITTEE (RFPC)

... a religion which is about 'saving the soul' while allowing the body to be brutalised is a complete distortion of the Gospel...
JOSEPH MCVEIGH *A WOUNDED CHURCH: RELIGION, POLITICS AND JUSTICE IN IRELAND*

As time wore on the needs of people arrested or imprisoned and their struggling families increased steadily. Support from the community, however, dwindled. By the mid-1970s support for Irish prisoners' families was ebbing away as the anti-Irish atmosphere grew in England. This atmosphere was caused by legislation designed to dampen resistance to the British presence in Ireland and sympathy for Irish Nationalism in England. Many returned to Ireland driven away by the harassment and hostility they met. Of those who remained many were subject to surveillance and intimidation and it was difficult for them to help the families. One by one people fell away. You wondered who would be gone next but God never closed one door without opening another – somebody always came to help.

I understand how people felt because I was scared. Some people thought the Special Branch were around every corner and I used to laugh at them. The laughter faded when I heard from two friends that the Special Branch had suggested they try to get me implicated in something. It wasn't being followed that worried me – they could be sitting beside me for all I cared because I had nothing to hide. It was the idea that I might be incriminated. I was worried because I didn't want anything to prevent my work for prisoners' families.

Sometimes other people made me nervous with their perceptions of possible dangers. A sixty-six-year-old retired Irish psychiatrist, Máire O'Shea, was arrested and charged with conspiracy to bomb a SAS man's home in 1985. During her remand she was strip-searched continually despite her age and frail health. Máire O'Shea had worked in Birmingham for many years so I rang the Birmingham MP Clare Short to see if she could get some help for Máire. Clare Short's reply made me anxious. She said I should watch out, I'd be next – it made me extremely nervous. Máire was subsequently released.

I turned to people in Ireland for help, going straight to the top by making contact with prominent TDs: Michael O'Kennedy, Brian Lenihan and Máire Geoghegan-Quinn – ministers in the Irish government of the time. I told them about the dire conditions of Irish prisoners in English gaols, the treatment of families visiting them and of the costs and the hardships of journeys to England. I told them that prisoners were often held in solitary confinement and were not allowed letters or visits except from relatives. Frequently families were not even able to visit because they could not afford it, or were old or ill. I informed them I was shocked and saddened by the Irish failure to do more for its citizens in English gaols.

Their response was sympathetic, if limited. I met Brian Lenihan at Leinster House and he received me well. He listened to me but I could feel I was knocking on a stone wall. I met Michael O'Kennedy at his home and it was he who advised me to start a group. The Irish government, the TDs, would always receive me very nicely but one minister took me out to the courtyard in case he would be heard speaking about Irish prisoners in English gaols.

Fr Faul and I discussed Michael O'Kennedy's suggestion that I start a committee to support improvements for prisoners and their families. Remembering my experiences with NICRA and ICRA and the inherent dangers of in-fighting and infiltration in any such group, I was wary. The way to avoid such dangers was to be careful about who joined. Having decided to call the group Relatives and Friends of Prisoners Committee (RFPC) we invited a few dedicated people to join. The committee consisted of Theresa Hynes, Oonagh Milner, John O'Brien and myself. We worked closely with Clara Reilly of the Belfast group ALJ and Sr Miriam Corcoran, Colonel John McGuire and George Korb in America. The founding objectives and philosophy of the RFPC were conceived in response to the needs of Irish families with

107

prisoners in British gaols. Aware of the particular stresses and worries which the imprisonment of a relative brings to families, the committee provides help, guidance and a sense of security for the families. When an arrest is made, the committee locates the prisoner when contacted. A twenty-four hour telephone service is maintained for this purpose. A file of solicitors is kept, both for London and for points of entry to Britain, and legal assistance is provided for those unfortunate enough to be detained. The families are kept informed during this stressful time by telephone.

If a prisoner is charged, the committee ensures that the prisoner has the best legal representatives for that particular charge. While he/she is on remand in or near London he/she is provided with a weekly parcel or with cigarettes and daily papers, on behalf of the family at home. This is a time of acute anxiety for the family and close links are maintained with them by telephone. Accommodation is found for the family when they come to visit the gaol. They are met at the airport/station and accompanied to the gaol. They are introduced to the complexities of gaol visiting – a formidable experience initially – by a member of the committee, who is familiar with the procedures. They are also accompanied to the trial. When the family cannot be present, the committee will send someone to the court on their behalf.

After conviction accommodation is found, where possible, for families to stay on visits to the prisoner, near the gaol where he/she is serving the sentence. An essential important link is kept with the prisoner and his/her family during the years by letter and by visits. The RFPC acts on behalf of the family in trying to safeguard the rights of the prisoner and the family by informing the Irish embassy, Amnesty International, the Howard League and the National Council for Civil Liberties of irregularities. Where publicity is desirable, the press and the media are informed.

We were all already doing the work; it's just that at this time we decided to give ourselves a name taking the minister's advice – it gave us a group identity. I couldn't say how many people the RFPC has been involved with since then, probably thousands. On 8 October 1977, for example, several committee members attended the meeting of the Roman Catholic Justice and Peace Committee of England and Wales to honour the tenth anniversary of the encyclical *Populorum Progressio*. Fr Faul and Fr Murray had just published their book, *The Birmingham Framework*, supporting the innocence of the Birmingham Six, so the RFPC thought that a celebration of *The Progress of Peoples* would be the ideal place to circulate information on wrongly convicted prisoners. We were in for a surprise. Although the bishop in charge had welcomed me warmly at first, congratulating me on my good work, he shrank in horror when I offered him a copy of Fr Faul's and Fr Murray's book. I was walking down the stairs – it was in a church behind Oxford Street – when I saw the bishop approaching me. 'You do good work Sister Sarah', he said, after I had introduced myself as a La Sainte Union nun. I was carrying copies of the book and wondering who to give them to, so since he had congratulated me on my work I gave him a copy. I assumed he was talking about my work, not that of La Sainte Union in general. Stupid of me, I was naive. He looked at it and was almost afraid to touch it. I pressed the book on him and asked him just to read it. He said, 'Well I will read about these six men but there is all this work to be done for the Third World and I cannot neglect it just for six men'. In a letter to Fr Faul about the incident I wrote, 'I prayed all evening that he would realise that, as a shepherd of the flock, when the sheep stray into the bushes, he is bound to leave the ninety-nine and go after the stray.'

Where I might most have expected some sympathy for the six wrongly convicted Irishmen, I repeatedly found hostility. Something similar occurred with a columnist for a paper. When he was offered a copy of the book, he rejected it, saying, 'Yes, I believe the Birmingham Six were beaten, but they deserved to be because they're guilty'. And yet in the gospel Jesus said we should, 'seek and save what was lost.' These men had lost their liberty unjustly. In later years thanks to the work done behind the scenes and despite the intransigence of the judiciary and the unsympathetic attitude of the general public, the six men became something of a cause célèbre and were eventually released. In the face of such opposition, the RFPC campaigned for years on behalf of people unable to fight their corner without support.

In 1977 the Committee challenged the authorities in Ireland about the treatment of prisoners in Portlaoise gaol. On 16 April I wrote a respectful but forthright letter to Liam Cosgrave, then Taoiseach, decrying the humiliating practice of strip-searching prisoners, sometimes several times a day. I reminded Mr Cosgrave that a Catholic who receives Holy Communion must have the greatest reverence for the Body of Christ and should, in turn, respect the bodies of all whom Christ came to save.

On 4 December 1977, three Belfast women, mothers of Irish prisoners, sponsored by the RFPC, demonstrated on the steps of Westminster Cathedral to draw attention to conditions in Long Kesh. It was Prisoners Sunday, a date in the Catholic calendar. I and other members of the committee were there in support of the three mothers and again found ourselves up against official hostility. I noted in my diary:

> The priest there said he wished we had not come because they were concentrating on prisoners of conscience (we embarrassed the cathedral, in other words). Russian TV came and German, French, Belgium, and Italian photographers, but no Catholics or English people were interested. While the Belfast women sat outside the church, a special display inside dramatised Russian injustice. Near the main altar, Pax Christi had erected a ring of barbed wire surrounding a woman dressed as a Siberian prisoner of war. When the bishop celebrating Mass came out and spoke to the Belfast group, they asked why Irish political prisoners had been omitted from his prayers. Incredibly, the bishop told these women, 'Do not worry, for God will take care of it all in the end'.

Undaunted, the RFPC returned the following year to protest again at Westminster Cathedral on Prisoners Sunday. I was preparing the leaflets and I got a phone call from Fr Faul. He said the administrator of the cathedral was very truculent and did not want us in the cathedral. When he said that we would have to get permission from the Westminster Council to give out leaflets on the patio, Fr Faul said we would give them out on the street. He said the administrator said we could be arrested for obstructing traffic. Fr Faul suggested we go down and see what would happen. I rang Sr Bernadette Naughton and she said she would come with me. I went to Mother Provincial and told her what we were doing.

The next day I collected Sr Bernadette and got to the cathedral at 9.40 a.m. Theresa Hynes, Pat McCabe and Maureen, all RFPC members, arrived. We sorted out the leaflets and took up our position. It was pouring with rain. I went to the cathedral steps to see what would happen. I was there about a half-hour when a priest with a beard came out and told me to get off the steps. I told the priest that Fr Faul had been in touch with the administrator. He said that they did not get enough notice about our coming. I then got off the steps and stood at the bottom of them giving out copies of the leaflet, saying it was written by gaol chaplains.

STRIP-SEARCHING WAS A CONTINUAL PROBLEM. In April 1978 a modest Catholic woman was forced to remove her sanitary towel. Another pregnant woman was made to pull up her skirt and pull her tights up around her because they thought there was something in the folds. Through the RFPC, I raised the issue of strip-searching and tried to think of anyone influential who might be actively sympathetic.

As the RFPC's objectives say, one of our main concerns was to safeguard the rights of prisoners and their families. Clearly, these rights apply to spiritual as well as material needs. I had already had problems with chaplains in English gaols and their ministry to Irish prisoners. Many prisoners' families, not only Irish ones, were complaining to me about the chaplains. They would approach me in the visitors queues outside the gaols. This happened every time I stood in the queue and in the end I felt compelled by my conscience to do something. So in the winter of 1978 we, the RFPC, wrote to Cardinal Hume, to the bishop in charge of gaols and the head chaplain of the English gaols. The letter called their attention to the prisoners' rights to every consolation the Church offers any other member irrespective of crime, politics or anything else. The cardinal formally acknowledged our letter as did the bishop who added that he was sending it on to Fr Richard Atherton, the head of the Catholic English Chaplains – a Home Office employee.

Fr Atherton rang me at the convent saying he would like to visit me there to discuss the letter, but the meeting was not a success. He was not impressed by my work and the meeting ended acrimoniously. The mother of a prisoner Ronan Bennett was with me at the convent that day. She had come over to England from Belfast to visit her son, held on remand in Brixton gaol. He was attempting to get bail at the time. He had been held on remand for eight months as one of six young people charged with conspiracy and subsequently tried in a famous case known as the 'Persons Unknown Trial'. The other defendants were granted bail but Ronan was denied it. His mother, despite living in what is called part of the United Kingdom, found that the law was different in Britain when it came to bail. If she was to stand surety –

unlike residents in Britain – she would have to produce £4,000 in cash in court to provide bail for her son. Despite rulings that previous convictions should not be heard during bail hearings, when Ronan's case was being heard, the recorder mentioned a previous conviction and a spell in Long Kesh. This was very unfair as he had been freed by the appeal courts and the conviction overturned.

Mrs Bennett was in a state of great anxiety about her son and I was doing my best to help to console her. Fr Atherton was upset when Mrs Bennett came in. I felt he was cross with me because I said I felt it unfair that if all the others got bail Ronan should have got it too. He disagreed with me. Fr Atherton continued quibbling about something I said. I got cross. I stood up and said that it was a waste of time talking to him. I took the tea tray and opened the door. He quickly put on his anorak and turned to go still trying to talk down to us. He took his bag and said, 'Happy Christmas' and I let him out the front door at 8 p.m. I was in a state of collapse with it all.

After this visit, I received a letter from Fr Atherton dated 19 December and sent from the Home Office. In this letter he said he was delighted with my concern for the welfare of prisoners but went on to say, 'I feared that your very enthusiasm might have led to a distorted view of things. Yesterday [the day of the visit] I discovered that my worst fears had been realised'.

I repeatedly met hostility from gaol chaplains, something that still shocks me. I remember Richard Glenholmes being told in Long Lartin by the chaplain not to have anything to do with me when he had failed to get me added to the list of people he wanted to correspond with. I had never even met the chaplain. Another time I wrote to a prisoner who had been transferred to Lewes from another gaol and I got a letter from the chaplain there asking how I knew he'd been moved. At the time of the gaoling of the Braintree people I was told on the telephone by a chaplain that I was bringing the Church into disrepute by acting on behalf of men on a very political subject. I replied that politics had nothing to do with my work. He continued by saying that only prisoners' wives should be taking in parcels. I pointed out that Irish prisoners' wives were hundreds of miles away and could hand in parcels only when they came for rare visits.

The RFPC, realising the power of the media, pursued publicity. The *Irish Post* was one paper we could rely on for accurate coverage. On 14 February 1981, for example, this paper told readers that:

> The London based Relatives and Friends of Prisoners Committee has written to the Home Office regarding the recent transfer to prisons in Britain of two British army sergeants who were convicted of murder in Northern Ireland.

The article then cites the committee's reminder to the Home Office of its seven-year-old promise to return the remaining prisoners involved in the Old Bailey bombing to Northern Ireland when they had served a significant time in Britain. Finally, the RFPC called the Home Office's attention to the unfairness of sending British prisoners to England while continuing to refuse a transfer for Irish prisoners. The headline read, 'Whitelaw reminded of promise to transfer prisoners.' Publicity kept the issues and concerns of prisoners and their families alive. We had to get publicity since the prisoners themselves were practically entombed in British gaols.

In November 1981 Pope John Paul II issued the encyclical *Familiaris Consortio*. On 12 December I bought copies for myself and Fr Faul. The busy pre-Christmas tasks of sending postal orders and cards to prisoners prevented me from reading the encyclical until February 1982. I received a great boost from it as it was very pertinent to what I was doing for prisoners. It was heartening, after all the opposition. I rang Theresa Hynes to tell her that families of prisoners were mentioned.

The encyclical was an inspiration to me and others on the committee. It gave credibility to our work. In Section IV, 'Pastoral Care of the Family in Difficult Cases,' the document reads:

> An even more generous, intelligent, and prudent pastoral commitment ... is called for in the case of families which ... find themselves faced by situations which are objectively difficult. In this regard it is necessary to call special attention to particular groups which are more in need of assistance but also of more incisive action ... in order that the causes of their need may be eliminated. Such, for example, are the families of migrant workers, of those obliged to be away for long periods, such as members of the armed forces ... the families of those in prison, of refugees and exiles.

This was in sharp contrast to the statement made by a chaplain to me when I complained about the treatment of prisoners' families. He said they could punish the prisoners by punishing the families.

By 1982 I had been working with prisoners and their families for approximately eleven years. After I read the encyclical I wrote a letter praising a support group I was familiar with for their work with British prisoners overseas and said that the Holy Father had now brought out an encyclical on the family. I said that I hoped the Irish Church would do something for Irish prisoners abroad. A week later the letter in question, approved and co-signed by Theresa Hynes, was completed. After Mass and breakfast I wrote to Bishop Dermot O'Mahoney, Cardinal Tomás Ó Fiaich, Archbishop Dermot Ryan of Dublin, the editors of *The Irish Times, Irish Press, Sunday Press*, Neil Blaney, MEP and Brian Lenihan. Each got a covering letter and a copy of the letter to the press. I was expecting to be excommunicated:

> Eleven years of contact with families coming from Ireland to visit their relatives in British jails, 11 years queueing with and witnessing the hardships, the harassments, the escalating expenses, the fears and frustrations of these families have highlighted two aspects of the situation: the heroism, faith and self sacrifice of these wives and mothers and the stunning silence and seemingly total lack of concern of the Irish State and people for their plight.
>
> There are about 800 prisoners in English jails who were born in the Republic of Ireland. At the moment no statistics are available to show how many of these prisoners are serving long-term sentences. Allowing a rough estimate of 200, 60% or more would be domiciled with their immediate family in England. Our concern is for the families domiciled in Ireland whose sons and husbands are in prison in England.
>
> The British people, as a whole, show great concern for their own citizens in trouble abroad. The British passport holder is not allowed to languish long in a foreign jail. No harassment is allowed to be quietly meted out to relatives of prisoners, even to the perpetrators of the most heinous crimes – and rightly so. Questions are asked in Parliament, constant pressure is put on Prime Ministers and foreign Governments. A release, not transfer, is invariably the result.
>
> Irish women, on the other hand, are dragging their children across Ireland and the Irish Sea to the remotest corners of England, at regular intervals, staying a few days in bed and breakfast to get a half hour or an hour's daily visit under extremely harsh conditions, to keep the 'irreplaceable importance of the father' alive in the family unit. Some women/families/marriages have endured this sacri-

fice for over eight years and may have to do so for 20 or 30 years more. Other women/families/marriages have understandably broken under the strain. The long journeys and constant switching of prisons and the varying harshness of visiting conditions are part of the policy of punishing the prisoner further by punishing his innocent family and relatives.

We therefore read with great interest Part Four of the recent Encyclical on the family – *Familiaris Consortio* – where the Holy Father refers frequently to families in difficult circumstances and he calls on the Church as a matter of urgency to show pastoral concern to such families. I quote: 'the families of prisoners ... the families discriminated against for political or other reasons ... In this regard it is necessary to call special attention to certain particular groups which are more in need not only of assistance but also of incisive action upon public opinion and especially upon cultural, economic and juridical structures, in order that the profound causes of their needs may be eliminated as fas as possible.'

Innocent or guilty, political or non-political, we are bound to these prisoners by race, religion and Christian commitment. Dare we hope that this Encyclical will be a guide-line to the TDs and others with power and influence to make a continual and concerted effort through the Dáil and the European Parliament, the United Nations and even the Vatican to ensure that prisoners serving long term sentences in foreign countries, regardless of the crime, get the right to serve their sentences in their own country, after a stated period, to facilitate the innocent family? It should be a feature of penal policy to enable relatives to visit prisoners without excessive expense and travelling, especially in the case of prisoners serving long sentences.

We would, therefore, urge the Irish Government representatives to press for the introduction of the policies indicated above and for the Church to lend its support.

On Monday, 1 March Fr Faul rang to tell me that my letter was in that morning's *Irish Times*. There were positive results. The next day journalist John McEntee phoned me about the letter and asked if he could interview some families when visiting gaols in England. On Wednesday, 3 March I got a letter from Neil Blaney, MEP, saying, 'God's blessing on Sister Sarah and her great work'. Several days later a Dubliner who read the letter in an Irish paper sent me a cheque. As letters and phone calls continued to come in I was pleased that most approved of the letter. (Unfortunately, Theresa Hynes, whose address had not been published, received hate mail delivered to her home.) One of the most welcome responses arrived on 11 March from Cardinal Ó Fiaich. He said he intended to ask Irish Justice and Peace to contact English Justice and Peace about Irish prisoners. I wondered should I write and put him in the picture about what was happening here.

The effects of the letter continued for many months. There were many responses to it and one that was particularly significant and welcome for me came from Rev. P. J. Byrne of Dublin, Secretary of the Irish Episcopal Commission for Emigrants, at the request of Bishop Casey, head of the Committee for Emigrants – whose job it was to look after prisoners in England. Fr Byrne wrote showing the concern of that Church group. His letter was a reminder that the Commission for Emigrants operates in England through the Irish Chaplaincy Scheme there under the direction of Fr Bobby Gilmore. Fr Byrne offered to discuss my ideas with me as soon as an opportunity arose. On 19 April I met both priests in the Commission offices, Dublin. We met for an hour and a half and agreed that the chaplaincy's scheme would back me.

This chaplaincy scheme is quite separate from the English scheme – it is a group of priests whose duty it is to look after the needs of Irish emigrants. On 21 May I met Fr Byrne again and this time Fr Faul joined us. Fr Byrne certainly backed us, and he showed me his report to the bishops – Fr Faul was very pleased.

I returned to London in late May. On 14 June Fr Gilmore invited me to lunch with the priests at the Irish Chaplaincy Scheme. Fr Gilmore said he would give me every help, but I wondered if I was selling my families out in the meantime. I wondered whether I was doing the right thing and if the families would approve because of its [the Irish Chaplaincy Scheme] former hostility to Irish prisoners and Bishop Casey's attitude. I was not sure why there was this seeming change of heart – could it really have been my letter that made them suddenly take an interest in the prisoners?

During the summer Fr Byrne invited me to be the keynote speaker at the Annual General Meeting of Irish Emigrant Chaplains in Dublin the following December. With mixed feelings I accepted the invitation but dreaded it. I received a large packet from Paddy Hill of the Birmingham Six – he sent out a long letter which gave an excellent account of the plight of the Birmingham Six from his point of view and other letters. I made six copies of Paddy's information for the Irish bishops. I began to write the statement that I hoped would persuade Fr Gilmore to establish a National Council for the Welfare of Prisoners Overseas. My great hope was that the Irish Chaplaincy Scheme would support a voluntary ministry in Ireland, similar to mine in England, staffed by a nun serving prisoners' families by offering moral support – a twenty-four hour service – financial help and practical information.

In July I visited two English women at the National Council for the Welfare of Prisoners Abroad (NCWPA) and was pleased to learn that their work closely resembled my own. They gave me a copy of their constitution and I promptly sent Fr Gilmore six copies of this document as he had requested. On 23 August I called on a friend, Gerry Corr, at the Irish embassy and told him he must be sure to back this Council for Prisoners' Welfare in Ireland.

When I visited Ireland I called on a prisoner in Limerick gaol and promptly complained, in the name of the RFPC, of the terrible conditions in the waiting-room. It is not a welcoming place. I stood at the barrier for a while before realising that I had to go under it. I went to a hut with guards in it; they told me to wait in the nearby hut. It was a very dirty place with torn bits of linoleum on the floor. When I got in, we were in a big room with a prison officer at the top. Two officers sat behind the prisoner and two behind me, standing at the door. The prisoner was uneasy and said he wanted the extra prison officers removed. Having gone in and gone out, like something in a Gilbert and Sullivan operetta, as the senior prison officer ordered them, the prisoner ended the visit. I said that I would complain to the Minister of Justice. I remember vividly the prisoners were behind two sheets of glass and two rows of wire.

When I returned from the visit I wrote to Charles Haughey about the conditions in the waiting-rooms in Limerick gaol. It seemed the RFPC was making a few waves; it was effective. We got a reply to the complaint about the waiting-room at Limerick gaol. I received a letter from Charles Haughey, the Taoiseach, on 9 September 1982, assuring me that action was being taken to clean and refurbish the waiting-room. This response was very encouraging, the work seemed to be hitting the mark. My confidence in the Irish government was growing and my hopes for the chaplaincy were higher. It seemed that the kind of work I was doing in England would now be done in Ireland.

I rang Fr Gilmore on 4 October and learned the bishops had given a green light for the formation of a group for prisoners. The intuitive suspicions and misgivings I had in June returned shortly afterwards. I went over to Fr Gilmore on business. I mentioned that I was going to telephone Mr Haughey about a gaol problem that needed urgent attention. I was told that I could not do that because I was now a member of the Irish Chaplaincy and I would have to go through the Dublin committee. I rang Fr Faul when I came back because I was so unhappy and he suggested I should think about resigning.

The delivery of the lecture in Dublin was a major event for me. I was unaccustomed to public speaking and had never seen myself as someone occupying the centre of any stage however small. I had prepared my speech for months and when I spoke to the meeting of Ireland's Emigrant Chaplains on 1 December I was scared. I was all right, however, when I got going. They listened intently. It was a pleasure to have an opportunity to share the stories of the families and to cite their just claims on the Church's ministry. However, some priests accused me of IRA propaganda when I mentioned the Maguires and the Birmingham Six. I was so stunned I was unable to reply but the archbishop stepped in and backed me up.

On 13 January 1983 Fr Murray and I visited Fr Gilmore and emphasised the need for a nun to help prisoners' families in Ireland. We also stressed that we were trying to get a good priest for the prisoners. I prayed for this thinking that then I could retire in peace.

Instead of planning retirement, the next move was an effort to secure a grant from the Greater London Council (GLC) to help finance my work. I asked Fr Gilmore for permission to apply for a GLC grant – using the charity number of the Irish Chaplaincy. He agreed. I applied and took it to the GLC where I was told it would be dealt with straightaway.

I am dependent on my religious community's personal allowance and on the gifts of friends. My finances until this time had all been from voluntary donations for clothes, travel and stamps for the prisoners and their families. I hadn't the money to buy anything – in the early years not even newspapers. Nuns never had money – you had to ask for everything – even a stamp. Then in the early 1970s we got a bit of pocket money and that increased a little as time went on. I didn't need much for myself;

for clothes I'd take the old habits the other nuns discarded when the La Sainte Union started wearing ordinary clothes. They were leaving off collars and veils. I didn't have to buy anything because I always wanted to wear the habit. I did it partly to save money but also because my identity as a nun is important.

Right from the early days there were people who would help me financially in my work for the prisoners and their families. Fr Faul, Fr Brady and Fr Murray would give me cheques now and again which would go a long way and Mother Provincial paid for the car. As word spread about the work I was doing, people would give me small sums that helped with the parcels and the needs of the families but it was always a struggle.

Meanwhile, my old concerns were resurfacing. On 11 March 1983 I had a meeting with Fr Byrne in London that alarmed me. His attitude had changed. He said he was talking to other priests and told me that, in his view, the chaplains in English gaols were better than I said they were. I had told him of the complaints I used to get. I decided to drop my affiliation with the Irish Chaplaincy. On 18 March I rang Fr Murray and told him of my disillusionment with the chaplaincy. I learned the GLC grant was approved but the paperwork had not been completed. Later I learned a new application was resubmitted on behalf of the chaplaincy but it was turned down because the chaplaincy had no gaol work to its credit. I felt then that all my efforts to get this grant and my months of involvement with the chaplaincy had come to nothing. Instead of setting up a service in London that closely resembled the NCWPA's for British prisoners abroad, a totally different body – the Irish Commission for Prisoners Overseas (ICPO) – emerged. It did good work but not the work, I felt, that was indicated in the Holy Father's encyclical.

On 22 April I got a letter from the Episcopal Committee in Ireland to discuss commissions and groups, but by then I was so disillusioned that I had lost faith in anything good coming out of it.

Whatever the final disappointment of my attempts to improve the conditions of prisoners and their families through official committees whether religious or secular, my experience shows how the meek can rattle the cages of the mighty. What was most important to me in the end after the meetings, the correspondence, the phone calls and the disappointment was that to some extent the prisoners and their families benefited. If the family of only of one prisoner received more Christlike recognition as a result of all these efforts, they were worth the many storms through which we sailed. The endeavour was best summed up by Eamonn Andrews in *The Catholic Herald* of 9 July 1982:

> Two ladies – one a nun, the other a housewife – have been pursuing that most unpopular cause of all – convicted prisoners. Worse than that, Irish convicted prisoners in British jails. Their solicitude is for the unfortunate relatives and friends who suffer so much hardship and heartbreak making long, difficult and expensive journeys to see prisoners. They hope that perhaps John Paul's encyclical on the family will stir someone somewhere to pity. I hope so, too.

8

GIUSEPPE CONLON

Sons, I'm sorry I have to apologise. I always told you that British justice was the finest in the world and that you should trust and respect it. I was wrong.
PADDY MAGUIRE'S COMMENTS TO HIS TWO SONS VINCENT THEN 17 AND PATRICK THEN 14

In the autumn of 1974 four young people were arrested and accused of planting bombs that went off in pubs in Guildford, Surrey on 5 October. The four: Gerry Conlon – Giuseppe Conlon's son – Paul Hill, Paddy Armstrong and his English girlfriend Carol Richardson were innocent and uninvolved. Gerry Conlon was arrested on 30 November from his family home in Belfast and taken to Springfield Road Barracks. Gerry's parents, Giuseppe and Sarah, called repeatedly to the barracks but were not given permission to see their son. On 1 December Gerry was taken to England for further questioning about the Guildford pub bombings. The next day, Giuseppe went to England to try and help his son. He was only 52 years old, hardly an old man, but he was very ill with emphysema in his lungs and dependent on special medication. When he arrived in London he went to his in-laws, Hugh and Kate Maguire, but as they were not in, he went instead to the house of his brother-in-law Paddy Maguire in Kilburn.

Unknown to those who were at the Maguires' that evening (among them Seán Smyth, Annie Maguire's brother and Pat O'Neill a friend who had dropped in) Hugh and Kate Maguire had been arrested. Paddy Maguire was worried about his brother – he had been gone two days and it was unusual for him to disappear like that. At about 6 p.m. on the Sunday evening, not wishing to cause anxiety to the others, he slipped out unnoticed to the local police station to ask for their advice about his brother's unusual absence. He was told that Hugh's lodger had also made enquiries. Paddy said perhaps they should go round and break the door down and the policewoman told him that there would be no need for that. Shortly after this, a friend arrived at the Maguire home and told them that Hugh and Kate had been arrested the day before, Saturday, and taken to Guildford for questioning. They

121

were all deeply shocked as they had no idea why this should have happened.

On 3 December, bewildered and shocked, Giuseppe, Annie, Paddy and two of their children Vincent (16) and Patrick (13) Pat O'Neill and Seán Smyth were arrested,

Two years later they were found guilty of the possession of nitroglycerine, the implication being that they were bomb-makers. Annie and her husband were sentenced to fourteen years. Giuseppe, Annie's brother Seán Smyth, and Pat O'Neill, the friend who had dropped in on the day of the arrests, got twelve years, whilst seventeen-year-old Vincent was sentenced to five years and fourteen-year-old Patrick went into youth custody for four years. The convictions of the Maguire Seven had completed the crown's victory over all the Irish suspects arrested in November–December 1974. The Birmingham Six lost their case on 15 August 1975 and the Guildford Four lost theirs on 23 October.

From the beginning I worked behind the scenes for all of these wrongfully convicted people. I can't remember exactly who told me about an elderly man who had been arrested under the PTA, held for seven days, charged, and remanded to Brixton gaol. The old man's name was Giuseppe Conlon, a name that meant little to me then but was to haunt me for the rest of my life.

I travelled to Brixton immediately to see him. I went into the visiting-room and sat at one side of a table in a small room reserved for the Category A prisoners, those deemed the most dangerous; it had extra surveillance. I had been asked to visit this man but nothing could have prepared me for the sight of him as he came in – an emaciated old man gasping for air. 'I am an innocent man', he said to me. I knew of the injustice to him and to the others because Fr Brady had told me. He moved very slowly, he was panting for breath. I was very worried. I had never seen a prisoner so ill. He was almost crushed and broken. With every breath he said, 'I'm an innocent man', and then he would say he had faith in British justice as I myself did at the time. I asked him if he had been in touch with anyone. He said yes, shortly after his arrest he had contacted his MP, Gerry Fitt. Gerry Fitt told him that everyone knew he was innocent – so there was no cause to worry.

That first visit I had with him was short and it seemed no time before he was shuffling out again still saying, 'I am an innocent man, tell everyone'. I felt powerless. It was terrible. I left the gaol devastated and as the door closed behind him I resolved to tell everyone about this innocent man. I became like a cracked record – constantly repeating Giuseppe's story.

In March 1976 the Maguire Seven were tried, and to my regret I could not attend the trial as I was still teaching. I came home and after supper the telephone rang – it was Dr Amphlett Micklewright. He told me the news of the conviction of Giuseppe and the Maguires. He was very worried because he felt there was something very wrong with these convictions. I had just driven home in the rush hour traffic after a day's teaching and then this awful news. I was stunned. No sooner had I put the phone down than it rang again. This time it was Mary McCaffery, Annie Maguire's sister, ringing from Annie's house. She had been over during the trial and was staying there. She was heartbroken and weeping.

I knew little about the Maguires as I concentrated my efforts on Giuseppe who was far from home whilst the Maguires by contrast were surrounded by friends and family. They had lived in England since 1957. I felt so powerless as I drove to the house. Teresa Kearney, Annie's aunt, was there with Mary McCaffery and Anne-Marie, Annie's little girl and John her son who was in his early teens. They were all distressed and crying and told me about what had happened. I noticed Giuseppe's suitcase in the hall – he hadn't even opened it. I was struck by this household – certainly not a Republican home – there was a bust of Churchill on the mantelpiece. They told me that at first Annie had been charged with the Guildford bombings because she couldn't remember where she was on 5 October 1974, the day they happened. At first Annie had thought she was at Chipperfield's Circus that day, but then she remembered that it was two days before her little girl's birthday and that day had been the birthday of an English neighbour's daughter. The neighbours came forward saying she had been with them. They dropped the bombing charges against her. I didn't know much about the evidence but I remember thinking I must keep notes of where I am in case anything like this ever happens to me. So they charged her with possessing explosives because they didn't want to let her off the hook and there was no evidence of bomb-making. That visit to Annie's house, the house inaccurately and damagingly referred to as 'Aunt Annie's Bomb Factory' by the tabloid press, made a deep and lasting impression on me because it was a very comfortable house. The famous kitchen was very small for a 'bomb factory'. The children and aunt were very shattered as were all the English neighbours and children who were used to running in and out.

Despite the bombing charges being dropped, Annie Maguire was convicted of possession of explosives on the flimsiest and most dubious of evidence. Having been sentenced Annie Maguire was sent to Durham gaol to the maximum security wing. She was a long way from home – from John and Anne-Marie, the only two of her four children not locked up – and from relatives and friends. Her imprisonment also coincided with a rail strike so members of her family who had planned to visit were unable to.

FR FAUL AND I WERE disturbed by the case against the Maguire Seven from the outset because we felt it was stage-managed from the very top, the government. It came out years later that there was a conspiracy to obstruct the course of justice by those very people whose job it is to promote and protect justice. Even though it came out in court eventually that this cover-up and conspiracy had been going on, nobody was ever charged. The aspects of the case that we found most disturbing were that there was no evidence against any of the Maguire Seven apart from swabs taken which the prosecution said showed traces of nitroglycerine. These could have come from hundreds of ordinary household things. At the May Enquiry it was disclosed that the officer who took the swabs had been handling the debris at the bomb blast and the boxes of swabs were left open in the police station.

Moreover if they were really clearing the house of nitroglycerine, why had Paddy Maguire gone to the police the evening they were arrested and expressed alarm about his brother Hugh who appeared to have gone missing? The timing was crucial. There was half an hour during which the Maguires and their family and friends – in a house where there were several young children to look after and only one exit [the front door] – were said to have been clearing out the bomb-making equipment. The house was under observation by the police at this time and nothing suspicious was seen to have been taken out of it. Throughout gruelling interrogations none of the accused said anything to incriminate themselves or others but restated their positions.

On 14 March 1976, I drove Mary McCaffery, John and Anne-Marie to and from Durham gaol. We went to Mass and then went to the priest to find out where gaol was. He was most uncivil. After a good hot meal in a cafe we went to the gaol. It was bitterly cold. The children and Mary were much happier after the visit. Their mother looked lovely – she had a new hair do. We made a little pilgrimage to St Cuthbert's grave and we promised to come back and make a second pilgrimage when their mother got out. [We never did.] I remember that drive home because they were greatly relieved to see Annie looking well despite her appalling ordeal. Perhaps they weren't aware that on a visit prisoners put on their best clothes and make themselves as presentable as possible. They often try to minimise their hardships to spare the family.

I decided to see if Annie Maguire's MP, Arthur Latham, could be of use. I visited him with Mary McCaffery on 18 March 1976 at the House of Commons. We went up to Committee Room 5. Arthur Latham was well-informed about the Maguire case. He was worried about a number of things – the children being left without a home, the family being scattered, etc., about the police harassment. Although he was courteous to us there seemed to be little he could do.

After this we went to the Irish embassy because we wanted to say there was a terrible injustice done and that they were all innocent. I knew Richard O'Brien the first secretary. He listened to us and gave us coffee. He had sympathy for Mary McCaffery – she was in a state – but I'm not sure they were convinced of Annie Maguire's innocence.

After his conviction and sentencing Giuseppe Conlon became a Category A prisoner and I was unable to visit him for a while until he was de-categorised, although we corresponded regularly. During this time he was at first in Wormwood Scrubs where he was relatively well-treated but in April 1977 he was transferred to Wakefield gaol where the vital medical and dietary help he needed was withdrawn. Within three months he was coughing blood and had lost two and a half stone. In January 1978 he returned to Wormwood Scrubs but his health was permanently and fatally damaged. As a result of his illness he was de-categorised and again I could visit him. Despite his alarmingly bad health, Giuseppe continued to fight not only for his own case, but for his son's and all the others wrongfully convicted in the Guildford and Maguire cases.

Giuseppe also told me about another prisoner, Frank Johnson, whom he had befriended and who was innocent. I started then to help Frank and it was a very bizarre case – Frank Johnson worked for an Irish newsagent called John Sheridan in the East End of London. There were many attacks on newsagents in those days because a lot of them were run by Irish people. Frank Johnson got on well with Mr Sheridan and had no reason to hurt him. The shop was fire-bombed and Mr Sheridan was set on fire. Frank doused the flames. He wasn't initially a suspect. He visited poor Mr Sheridan in hospital for weeks until he died of his burns. The evidence in the case was not strong and some people feel he should never have been convicted. I still write to Frank and he writes to me – he is still in gaol.

Right from the start I was working away quietly behind the scenes doing what I could to help Giuseppe prove that he and all the others were innocent. I never thought of myself as subversive although perhaps the gaol authorities and the police did. In 1977 I read Bishop Camara's book on justice. How true it is that those who are afraid of being branded subversive have a fear of speaking and a fear of listening.

Time and again Giuseppe asked me to go to Cardinal Hume because he said Cardinal Hume knew he was innocent. It is almost impossible for somebody like me to see the cardinal but with Fr Faul to back me up I managed to see him. Fr Faul arranged the visit through Cardinal Ó Fiaich. After our visit Cardinal Hume went into the Scrubs. In his biography of Cardinal Hume Peter Stanford wrote, 'Their [Fr Faul, Fr Murray and myself] interest ... brought Cardinal Hume along to meet the men and as a result he began in the late 1970s to ask for their convictions to be looked at again.'

Cardinal Hume visited Gerry and Giuseppe Conlon. Gerry recalled his impression the first time he met the cardinal in his book *Proved Innocent*:

> All of a sudden I saw this tall, thin grey-haired figure waiting for me, wearing a black cape and a red skull-cap, and my first impression was, here was Batman come to see me. Then I heard this screw saying to him, 'Your eminence, this is Conlon'.

Having met Giuseppe, Gerry remembers the cardinal turning to a prison officer and alerting him to treat him and the others well saying, 'There may have been a miscarriage of justice'. Poor Giuseppe, he was even weaker by then – more emaciated, almost a corpse. I continued to visit him and it took him a very long time to get to the visiting-room. It was so strange, there was this ill old man brought in by two prison officers with a guard dog. What a waste of tax payers' money apart from anything else!

Despite the efforts being made to clear the names of Giuseppe and all the others, the process was slow and met with continual rebuffs. The weight of evidence pointing to miscarriages of justice in all the convictions piled up right from the start. Even before the trial of the Maguire Seven began, Eddie Butler and Joe O'Connell were arrested after the Balcombe Street siege and signalled their responsibility for the Guildford pub bombing. In 1977 Joe O'Connell said during his trial that the Guildford Four were innocent and if the Guildford Four were found to have been the victims of miscarriages of justice, it would immediately cast doubt on the convictions of the Maguire Seven.

Meanwhile Giuseppe was getting weaker and weaker. In September 1979, already desperately ill, Giuseppe wrote to his wife Sarah:

> I have lost 11 lbs in weight in the last 6 days and my weight is down to 7 st 5 lb. I have not eaten any solid food for over a week now and all I am taking is 3 cups of Complan and two cups of tea a day, so please get in touch with somebody and try and get me home out of this place for if you don't you will hardly see me again for I am getting worse every day. I don't know what kind of people these are that are keeping 'INNOCENT' people locked up for something they are not guilty of. Sarah I am locked up 23 and a half hours a day and I only get out for a breath of air half hour every day and being locked up in these cells you can't get a breath of air at all and I wake up suffocating. If you saw me now you would not know me at all. I feel very depressed and all my nerves are gone, so please get in touch with someone to try and get me home before it's too late. Sarah tell all at home I was asking for them also tell them that I love them very much. Sarah I love you and all the family.

In the summer of 1979 prisoners in Wormwood Scrubs held a peaceful protest and the riot squad were used against the protesters. The riot had nothing to do with the Irish prisoners. Giuseppe remained in his cell during the riot. As a result of the riot no contact with the outside world was allowed and chaplains, gaol visitors, etc., were not allowed access to the gaol. During the followup searches prison officers removed the small element Giuseppe used to heat his Complan, the only food he could eat. As a result there was nothing to eat – an enforced hunger-strike. Giuseppe was then moved to the hospital wing of the gaol. When Gerry eventually saw him his face was blue and he was gasping for air.

Gerry ran to the dispensary and when the warders failed to respond quickly he wrecked the place. This started alarm bells ringing and Giuseppe, under full escort, was moved to Hammersmith Hospital – next door to the gaol.

In January 1980 I visited Giuseppe in Hammersmith Hospital. I had no trouble finding him – I followed the line of security guards along the path that led to his bedside. When I got to the ward I asked a nurse if I could speak to Mr Conlon. I asked the prison warder who spoke to another warder who phoned the gaol. The answer was yes. I went in. He was in the main ward with a curtain around his bed and was guarded by three prison officers. He looked dreadful – like a corpse. He was very, very ill. I was very sad because I was very fond of the old man. He was good; he was saintly. He was on a drip and he had an oxygen mask on him. He told me to keep on doing what I was doing for him. He said he asked to see Cardinal Hume and he did not want his freedom on humanitarian grounds but he wanted the cardinal to speak out about his innocence. Kate Maguire came in and then Fr Ennis who gave him the sacrament of the sick. It was a privilege to be present. Then a nurse came and said Gerry Fitt was there so we left. Despite being so ill, Giuseppe Conlon was holding on to the hope that Gerry Fitt would be able to help him prove his innocence.

I went back the next day and he was moved into a private room. Two police officers were sitting outside the door. I went in. He looked worse than any corpse I have ever seen and he was obsessed by his innocence – always claiming, 'I am an innocent man'. He was so thin. He told me all his family were innocent and he never doubted his son. He knew Gerry had done nothing; he just knew. He always thought he'd get out and so had I.

On 7 January, I called to Giuseppe again. He looked worse. He said that he was not going to get better and to get Fr Faul to do something about Gerry – and the other innocents in gaol and – not to bother about him. Gerry, handcuffed, was brought to see him with police and twelve warders at 10.30 a.m. Giuseppe was trying to read the papers. I felt so helpless.

Theresa Hynes and I were trying to help Giuseppe every day. Theresa rang *The Universe* who told her to ring the Catholic Prisoners' Welfare Association which she did and spoke to a man who when he heard it was political said he would have nothing to do with it. Clean hands like Pilate. The day after Gerry's visit to his father, 8 January, I went to Brixton accompanying a prisoner's wife and delivering parcels. On my way home I went to see Giuseppe at Hammersmith Hospital. Sarah Conlon and her sister were there. Giuseppe was a little better but still very ill. Sarah got in to see Gerry for half an hour. When Gerry went back, having seen his father on Monday, he cried. A prison officer said to him, 'I hope your f— father dies'.

Gerry Fitt was trying to secure parole for Giuseppe. Previous requests had been turned down. On 11 January Gerry Fitt obtained an appointment with the Home Secretary, William Whitelaw, for 15 January. That day I took Giuseppe's wife Sarah to the hospital. I left her at the door to Giuseppe's room and returned to collect her later. There were two prison officers guarding his door and two in his cubicle by then as well.

When we got back to the convent I had a phone call from the chaplain telling me not to visit Giuseppe again. I asked why but he could give me no answer. There was a big security alert because in the middle of the night a nurse heard the sound of someone running and thought it was the IRA coming for Giuseppe. The next day when Sarah Conlon arrived at the hospital she saw all the police and saw Giuseppe being wheeled out and into a car surrounded by motorcycle outriders and he had all the drips pulled out of him. There were sirens going – he was pushed into some kind of van in a wheelchair, brought to the gaol next door and put in the hospital wing. Sarah was extremely worried because he wouldn't eat the food there. She felt that if only he had had some decent food it would have prolonged his life. She had to go home – she had no choice. She had to go back to her job, to keep a roof over her head. She told me she knew he would die and that she would never see him again. She was heartbroken. Sarah Conlon never cries. She becomes silent. As I drove her to the airport she was silent.

A few days later I had a call from Hugh Maguire. He said that Giuseppe was nearing death and had been taken back to hospital. He wanted to see me. I said they mightn't let me in but Hugh said they would. I rang security at Wormwood Scrubs and they said I could visit him – adding that it would do him good. That was the one and only time anyone in the prison service has admitted that anything I did was good. I went there with Hugh Maguire – we didn't need to ask the way. Giuseppe was on the first floor and there was a policeman at the bottom of the stairs, one on the landing and about five or six uniformed police and prison officers outside his door. Hugh was searched thoroughly and had to take everything out of his pockets; then they wrote down his name and address. I saw the Nursing Sister and asked if I could see Giuseppe. A policeman asked for my name and address and then they let me in. The tiny room was full of prison officers and policemen, they were even standing right against Giuseppe's bed. There must have been four or five of them. Giuseppe pulled the oxygen mask off his face and said to them, 'You shouldn't be here. You have no power over me. I'm an innocent man'. I went to Giuseppe and he grabbed my hand. He tried to sit up again and he said to the men again, 'You have no right to be here!' I said, 'Giuseppe don't! They're only doing what they're told.' I had to say something. I was kind of sorry for the policemen. I'd have been embarrassed to be them.

Giuseppe clasped my hand and said, 'Sister, I'm dying, will you clear my name and my family's? We are innocent. We are all innocent.'

'We know,' I said, 'we know and we will clear your names.'

The nurse came and he was in terrible distress. I said this is dreadful – a man dying in this little room full of people – she said there was nothing she could do.

Then I said goodbye. I told him I would pray for him. I could see his big eyes, his face shrunken like a skeleton.

As I left he said again, 'Clear my name. I'm an innocent man'.

I came out of that room heartbroken and sick.

Giuseppe died on 23 January 1980. The next day Sarah Conlon received a letter from the Home Office saying that because of all the representations made to the Home Secretary on his behalf, William Whitelaw had arranged for his release. The letter was signed by an official.

EVEN IN DEATH GIUSEPPE CONLON was appallingly and badly treated. For three days after he died Giuseppe's body went missing. A very distressed Sarah Conlon was told to ring a Hereford number. She was told there had been a post-mortem and the coffin was at an RAF base in Oxfordshire. Finally the coffin was brought back to Sarah Conlon but she had to pay £1,000 before it was released. After I heard of Giuseppe's death I thought again about the security operation mounted around the dying man. I thought of this man on his deathbed and the British Empire so frightened by a poor dying man that they had him guarded even then. But perhaps they were right because when he got to heaven he turned the whole thing round. When he was dead people who hadn't wanted to know started to ring up.

British Airways refused to carry the coffin with his body in it. Since they were the only airline flying directly to Belfast the coffin would have to go on Aer Lingus to Dublin and on to Belfast by road. I and many of my friends have never flown on British Airways since then.

In a moving letter, the first I ever received from him, Gerry Conlon wrote to me about his father's death:

Dear Sister Sarah,
I am sure you'll be surprised to receive this letter from me as I never wrote in the past.

I would like to thank you for all the effort you have made on my behalf over all these years. And the efforts you made for my father who I miss very much. My father always spoke highly of you and thought you were a lovely person. I remember when you used to come and see him in the Scrubs, how he would look forward to seeing you. I honestly believe that he thought that you were one of the few good things to happen to him in his last few years. I suspect that he depended on you greatly as he knew that you had tried to get people interested in our case and how unselfishly you worked to prove our innocence. I feel at times so lost without him because I know he was a good and decent man. I still find it hard to believe he's gone. At times I expect to look over my shoulder and see him standing there.

It's so hard for me at times to understand how innocent people can spend so long in prison for crimes they didn't do, especially when the establishment know they're innocent. I know that people outside are becoming aware of the serious miscarriages of justices that are happening in this country and the likes of Panorama, World in Action, etc., etc., are doing their best to expose and highlight these cases. But somehow I feel our case and the case of the six innocent men convicted of the Birmingham pub bombing are different from the rest. Different because we are Irish but if we were English I honestly believe we would have been freed years ago. I think I'm not so much a prisoner as a hostage. I feel as if I'm being held up as an example to Irish people in this country of what can happen to them.

I understand at present there is an awful lot of interest being shown in our case by the media; any interest is always welcome. But help and honesty is what's really needed. I believe over the years we have been neglected by the people who mean most to us, the first being the Church (yourself, Fr Faul and Fr Murray being the excep-

131

tions), second, and most importantly the Irish governments from 1974 onwards – I feel totally betrayed by them. I wrote to them and received no reply; my family petitioned them with no success. They have stood by while their country men and women have been rail-roaded to prison; they have turned a blind eye to the framing by British police of their citizens and then object to the methods of the South African police. I often wonder how they sleep at night.

Anyway Sister Sarah I hope you have a happy and peaceful Easter. I will be thinking of you.

Love and Best Wishes
Gerry Conlon

The campaign to free the Guildford Four and the Maguire Six as they were after Giuseppe died, intensified as a result of Giuseppe's death. I have a special place in my heart for Giuseppe Conlon. I was delighted when one day during the appeal for the Maguires in May 1991, Giuseppe, I felt sure, had returned. I arrived at court with Sarah Conlon only to discover that nobody was to be allowed in. We wondered why. It turned out that two pigeons had flown in and the judges, barristers, appellant – everybody was at their mercy. Four court ushers tried to get the birds out using long poles but they were stubborn and wouldn't leave. In the end the court sat with the birds roosting in the public gallery. But they swooped and flew at will almost invariably towards the judges. The judges were at the mercy of the birds.

As Giuseppe's case came up one of the pigeons did a particularly spectacular swoop and I said, 'There's Giuseppe', to Sarah Conlon. Noting the other pigeon she said, 'He must have got a new wife'.

9

CAMPAIGNS AND VINDICATION

If you want peace, work for justice.

POPE PAUL VI

Giuseppe Conlon's death galvanised me as deeply as it shocked and distressed me. I was devastated by his death but I said now we have someone in Heaven who'll clear the names for us. I thought, as I often do, of the Gospel, of the seed that falls into the ground and dies as a seed but lives in the fruit it yields. At the time of his death, the others with whom he was convicted were still locked up as were the Guildford Four, the Birmingham Six and Judith Ward. We already knew they were innocent – Fr Brady and Fr Faul were working as chaplains in Long Kesh in the 1970s and spoke to a top IRA man imprisoned there, who assured them the Guildford Four, Maguire Seven, Birmingham Six and Judith Ward had nothing to do with any of the indictments against them. In 1976, after the convictions, Fr Murray, Fr Brady, Fr Faul and myself interviewed family and counsel, collected documentation and information in London, Guildford, Birmingham and Ireland which was sent to Germany, France, the USA and Australia.

When I met Giuseppe I just knew he was innocent. Somehow you know; it's a sense – an intuition you have of someone. At the same time there is always the chance that you're wrong so one has to be very careful. When we started to do the interviews and make contact with the lawyers, it was even clearer to us that all these prisoners were victims of anti-Irish racism, public and press hysteria, police brutality, frame-ups and biased courts.

It was clear to everyone working in the campaigns that the evidence, such as it was, was seriously flawed from the outset. For years we had been saying, and it had been proved, that the government scientists on whose forensic evidence the cases depended, had been wrong all along and in Judith Ward's case they had actually lied. The lies told in Judith Ward's case, the first of these, were largely responsible for the subsequent convictions. The cases against the Guildford Four and the Maguire Seven were intimately linked; if one fell, so would the others because they depended on the false forensic 'evidence' and the 'confessions' of Paul Hill and Gerry Conlon.

During their interrogations by police, under immense psychological and physical pressure, Paul Hill had named the Maguires, and when Gerry Conlon was told of this, he was coerced into panicking and backed up Hill. Both young men thought in their terror that the mere act of giving some names – names picked at random, names of people so utterly blameless that nothing could ever be proved against them – would give them respite from the relentlessness of the interrogations. Because they knew those people named were entirely blameless, like themselves, they assumed that once the nightmare of their wrongful arrests ended, everything would be all right. Since Paul Hill and Gerry Conlon originally involved the Maguire Seven, it was clear that if the Guildford Four could be vindicated, the case against the Maguire Seven would collapse.

The Maguire Seven's case was also linked to that of the Birmingham Six because the prosecution again relied heavily on the seriously flawed forensic evidence. Like the Maguires, two of the Birmingham defendants were accused of having handled nitroglycerine, an ingredient used in bomb-making. The tests used to prove this were in question as early as 1974 during the case against Judith Ward and again in 1976 at the trial of the Maguire Seven. At the Maguire trial Dr Howard Yallop, the former principal scientific officer in charge of explosives at Woolwich Arsenal who originally developed one of the testing systems used in finding traces of nitroglycerine, said that many common household things could produce results that looked the same as nitroglycerine – for example, carpet shampoo, silver polish, shoe polish, even cigarette smoke – things people come into contact with every day of their lives.

A number of the Birmingham men signed 'confessions' as a result of the beatings they were given – these 'confessions' and the inherently unreliable and subsequently discredited swab tests were the basis on which they were convicted. The Birmingham Six were forced into making these so-called statements in which some of them, terrified and panic stricken like Gerry Conlon and Paul Hill, had agreed with their interrogators that they had carried the bombs but the information they were inventing during their 'confessions' didn't even tally! For example, they described the bags they were supposed to have carried the bombs in wrongly – the police knew what the real bags had been like.

Fr Faul, Fr Brady and Fr Murray and myself visited Birmingham several times to see the families of the six men before their trial. We'd meet in the station because at first nobody would lend us a place to meet in, then reluctantly, eventually, the Catholic Church lent us a hall. I remember meeting Kate, Richard McIlkenny's wife, Sandra, Gerry Hunter's wife and Eileen, Hugh Callaghan's wife. They were very frightened and they had met with great hostility. Sandra Hunter had to leave her house as did Theresa, Johnny Walker's wife. Their houses had been stoned. They all had small children and were very, very scared. Later we went to their houses and saw what they had been through. At one of their houses all the windows had been broken. After Sandra Hunter moved she didn't tell her neighbours who she really was. Billy Power's wife Nora came to London. I saw her quite often in her house in Walthamstow. She was so heartbroken, herself and her little children had nothing. She had heartbreaking letters from Billy. I remember the agony on her face and the little children huddled around her. She was so poverty-stricken; there was nothing in the house. One day I was there when she just got this powerful letter from Billy – I felt humbled and powerless:

6 February 1976

Dear Nora Love,
This is just a few lines to let you know I'm OK, and am thinking of you and hoping you are well.

I hope, Love, you received my last letter OK. If not let me know and I'll find out if there has been some mix-up here. It probably was held up in the post like you said.

By the way, Nora Love, I've been counting up the VOs I've had since coming in and believe I have an extra one to come, so I'm applying for one tomorrow morning and the other on Monday morning and will send them to you straight away. So you can come up as soon as you get one of them. It was a hell of a lot better the visit on Wednesday, wasn't it, Love. You know, Love, I felt worse after the visit than the other ones, because it was open. Just the touch while holding your hands, your embrace and goodbye kiss, then watching you leaving, tore my heart out. But I was soon over it and looking forward to next week, thinking what it will be like with the children, just to touch them, the enjoyment, always my disappointment afterwards.

There are only a few things for me that are real, your visits and letters. Between these is not real, like limbo, except God and the Church. Everything else is superficial, Judges, Juries, Barristers, Prisons. What is it that we are going through anyway, but the will of God, and look, Love, what joy he granted me in you and the children. He has granted me a little suffering, but with a clean conscience, just think what we have now, when seeing you brings so much happiness alone that it blots out all the injustice done to us, Love.

I can hardly wait to see you again next week. I can just see the children's reaction to the news that our visits are not closed anymore. It was a pity you had to have the news about the legal aid not being granted to cover the solicitor on Wednesday, but tell him to come and see me about the other proceeding. When you write, tell Mary and Richard I was asking for them, Love. I was expecting a line from my Mum, but haven't heard from her. Could you find out, Love, if she got my letter. I haven't received a word from Betsey or Patsy, you said they were writing to me. I'd love to have a line from one of them. Nora, Love, don't forget to tell Neddie, thanks for everything. Give the children a kiss for me. I think that's all for the moment. I wish this was next week to tell you how much I love you and miss you, but in the meantime, God Bless and take care.

Love you more, Billy,

P.S. Don't forget to let me know what day you will be coming up again. Write soon, Love Billy.

It tore the heart out of me to see the suffering these women endured. They were too frightened to say who they were because the public were baying for the men's blood. Even when it was accepted that the men had been beaten, one particular Catholic journalist said they were guilty so you can't blame the police or prison warders for beating them up.

In the beginning the wives were too shocked and frightened to do anything but in time their courage returned. I distinctly remember two or three of the times as we drove along on the way to Birmingham we were followed bumper to bumper and the women recognised the men who were following us – they were Special Branch. The atmosphere in Birmingham was understandably very tense, twenty-one people had died and 182 were injured in a horrific bomb attack and the Birmingham people felt the men were guilty. They believed the police had got the right people. The anti-Irish feeling there at the time was appalling. I kept driving as fast as I could and I didn't look at the men in the car. They were right behind us – then we lost them.

From the start Sandra Hunter was wonderful and as time went on the other wives got braver and organised their own campaign; they printed leaflets, wrote letters and worked hard. I couldn't get these women out of my mind – what they were going through, especially in the early years when nobody wanted to know them and I mean nobody. They had all lost their husbands and four of them lost their homes. And when eventually the men did get out sixteen years later, the time they had spent inside made adaptation to family life nearly impossible. Most are now living apart.

In those early bleak days in the 1970s I was often downhearted, because as I continually brought up the subject of all these innocent people I found very little sympathy for them. One or two innocent people maybe, people would say – but eighteen – they couldn't believe that. I returned often to the Gospel: 'The truth sets people free' and this thought sustained me.

Within my own order, I found doubt. I handed them the information I had about the innocence of all these people. I remember one day in particular a group of American La Sainte Union sisters were returning from Rome. They were our justice and peace representatives. I handed them the Birmingham Six book and asked them to help but I could see other sisters signalling to them to ignore me as I was unreliable. Of course, they did not heed me. I heard the nuns talking about people in gaol in other countries and I'd say we have them here. I'd talk about Giuseppe and the others and they'd say it couldn't happen here and change the subject. Nuns were very slow to sign papers about prison reform. One begins to understand how Hitler got away with murder in Christian Germany. However a religious community reflects the larger population, and most people believe – and still do – in a sense of British justice. I did myself. The Catholic Church remained, on the whole, detached from a problem on its doorstep as though more comfortable with issues in Africa, Asia, and South America.

On 24 July 1979 I went to see an MP, with Bishop Drury. The bishop said how awful it was that Giuseppe Conlon was dying in gaol and the MP said, 'How much worse that Monica Craig is dying in Armagh'. He brought Monica Craig into the conversation because I had gone to him to his surgery to tell him about her months before and had told him that she was dying of anorexia in Armagh gaol. I told him that Monica Craig was released over six months ago. He obviously had not looked into the case at all. We went into the Chamber and Bishop Drury was fascinated and amused at the scene before us. There was a Tory lady stretched out asleep on one bench.

Early in the campaign Fr Murray concentrated on examining the highly doubtful forensic evidence. He and the other campaigners knew that none of the defendants had handled explosives – so the tests on which their convictions rested must have been faulty. Fr Murray and Kieran Morgan, a solicitor with a background in science, did a study of the forensic evidence in the Birmingham Six case and together they produced a pamphlet detailing their results. They printed 10,000 copies and distributed them as widely as possible. Fr Murray took copies of this pamphlet and legal papers that he had managed to get from solicitors working on the men's cases in the early stages to Washington. He handed the documentation to Congressman Hamilton Fish, a Republican. Mr Fish, a member of the Ad Hoc Committee on Irish Affairs, had already expressed an interest. Fr Murray went to the USA twice to lobby congressmen on behalf of the Birmingham Six. Mr Fish indicated that he was prepared to pursue the additional forensic testing Fr Murray and Kieran Morgan planned to work on. Fr Murray and Kieran Morgan had been perusing scientific journals searching for a department in an American university that would be interested in following up an experiment they wanted to carry out. In this experiment ten men would be asked to handle a variety of substances which would then be put to rigorous tests, the results of which would, Fr Murray and Kieran Morgan felt sure, confirm conclusively that mistakes had been made in the case of the Birmingham Six.

In the end Hamilton Fish didn't help to set up the experiment but along the way Fr Murray had an interesting experience in media misrepresentation and political manoeuvring. At about this time, Tony McClelland, a young man whose family Fr Murray had known for years, was killed in a car accident. This young man, as far as Fr Murray knew, had never been involved in any political activity and had no brushes with the law, but after his death it emerged that he had been a member of the Irish National Liberation Army (INLA). Fr Murray gave a homily for the young man at his funeral in which he spoke warmly of him and his family, but made no mention of the deceased's political involvement which to him was irrelevant. Nevertheless, the homily was used by the gutter press and distorted in headlines such as, 'Priest

Praises Terrorist.'

As a result of these press reports, an *Irish Times* journalist wrote a short piece in which he asked a prominent Nationalist and a member of the Loyalist Orange Order for their comments which were critical of the priest. Meanwhile Seán Donlon, the Irish ambassador in Washington at the time, wrote to Hamilton Fish about the representations Fr Murray had made to him. Seán Donlon had evidently seen the piece in *The Irish Times* quoting the Nationalist and Unionist and indicating their disapproval of Fr Murray. Seán Donlon's letter, Fr Murray thinks, was an attempt to undermine him in the eyes of Hamilton Fish. In the letter he mentioned that Fr Murray was not accepted by either side implying that he should not be listened to since both the Loyalists and the Nationalists disapproved of him. Mr Donlon was not personally hostile. Fr Murray was, as he puts it himself, the 'fall guy' in the political manoeuvres of the Irish government. The Irish National Caucus, with which Fr Murray had close contacts, pursued a strictly non-political, non-partisan line lobbying for human rights in Ireland. It was hugely popular with the Irish American community as was NORAID which was backed by Sinn Féin. But the Irish government wanted to control the Irish American lobby and sent in SDLP representatives to diffuse the other organisations' popularity. Fr Faul phoned me on 21 November 1979. He said that Seán Donlon wrote to Hamilton Fish about *The Irish Times* article and he enclosed the cutting of the attack on Fr Murray. I went to the Irish embassy where I was listened to but you rarely find out if anything happens as a result of your visit – they are very polite but very noncommittal. They took a copy of the letter but I heard no more about it.

My role was to try and set up the experiment Fr Murray and Kieran Morgan had tried to get Hamilton Fish interested in. Fr Murray and Mr Morgan got in touch with Dr Yallop, the forensic scientist who had acted in Annie Maguire's case for the defence. He had said other substances could produce the same results. Dr Yallop agreed to do a further test. There were to be ten men leading similar lives to the Birmingham Six, coming home at the same time of day in the month of November, and tests would be run to establish what other things would have the same effect as nitroglycerine. I went to see a priest in one of the Irish centres in Birmingham to see if he could help us to find the ten men. He was very abrasive and told me I was being used – he didn't say by whom. I came out feeling very deflated. At another Irish centre I rang the man in charge, and Theresa Hynes and I went to Birmingham and asked him to help to find the ten men. He was very arrogant and unco-operative and said he would have to speak to his committee. He contacted us a few days later saying his committee refused to co-operate. He said whoever heard of a scientist just working with ten men. We never got the ten men.

The experiment was doomed. When Fr Murray and Kieran Morgan initially contacted Dr Yallop he seemed interested in helping but later he changed his mind and I don't know why. Such setbacks upset me and the priests and hampered their work but did not deter them.

An article in *The Guardian* of 19 February 1980 by David Leigh argued convincingly against the accuracy of the forensic evidence on which the Birmingham convictions greatly depended. Fr Murray appreciated this analysis that supported the theory he had advanced earlier. Fr Murray immediately republished David Leigh's article together with a full synopsis of the forensic evidence written by Kieran Morgan in a new pamphlet on the Birmingham pub bombing case. The campaigns ground on for many years but there were turning points and the issue of the doubts surrounding the forensic testing never went away.

After Giuseppe Conlon died in 1980, suddenly, almost miraculously it seemed to me, journalists from all branches of the media were interested in the Maguire Seven where only a very few had previously shown any inclination to doubt the convictions. In the traditionally Unionist *Belfast Telegraph*, 15 February 1980, reporters Derick Henderson and Michael Bromley discussed the doubts surrounding the convictions. On 12 February *The Sunday Times* Insight Team rang me for information on Giuseppe Conlon. I got the papers from Mrs Kearney [Annie Maguire's aunt] and I told them Fr Murray was in England. Two days later BBC Belfast rang me about Giuseppe Conlon. I told Gavin Esler [BBC] all I knew and gave him all the addresses I had. He wrote a powerful article under the headline 'Aunt Annie's Bomb Factory' for the *New Statesman* in March, giving the reasons why the Guildford and Maguire cases should be reopened. Giuseppe Conlon was obviously working hard in heaven at this time.

There was a scattering of individuals chipping away at the edifice of injustice but the overwhelming mood was one of anti-Irish hostility. I encountered it everywhere; we were branded, shunned as though working for prisoners and their families meant that one had guns under the bed. The hostility cropped up continually. At the HMSO (Government publications) bookshop in London when I asked for a copy of Lord Jellicoe's *A Report into the Operation of the PTA 1976–83* the salesmen at first said they didn't have a copy. After I insisted he agreed that they did, only to add, 'Are you going to blow something up then?' Another time I was buying rosary books for prisoners in a Catholic repository and was very taken aback when having explained that they were for prisoners, the sales assistant nearly had a fit – he said I was offensive.

My work for these prisoners and their families was unpopular and not the kind of work most nuns would have been allowed to do at that time. I don't think I would have been allowed to do it without the support of the priests – it was still a man's world. They were powerful priests and I felt very alone when they weren't there but revitalised as a Christian when they were. They were the closest we had to liberation theologians and it was through them I learned of liberation theology and human rights. I got books for them in London and stayed up all night reading them before sending them off. I always feel that we as nuns are made to feel the lowest form of womanhood but these three always treated me as an equal. In the Church in general had I been on my own I wouldn't have had half the hearing I got without Fr Faul, Fr Brady and Fr Murray. I wouldn't have been so well received and listened to. The attitude was – 'You are just a silly little nun'. Having every door shut on you makes you feel powerless, worthless. I always had to keep going to the Gospel and to liberation theology where I found what I was doing was the right way. Armed with the support of the three priests and reassuring myself by prayer and reading the gospels, I kept going. After all, I told myself, Jesus said, 'Woman, great is your faith' – that faith was continually put to the test over the years!

Each opportunity grasped was one more seed scattered but the level of ignorance, hostility and confusion surrounding these cases took its toll, especially among those convicted prisoners who were innocent. That point came for Paddy Hill at the beginning of 1982. He went on a hunger-strike. I remember this vividly. The campaigners also got depressed and downhearted; we would be subject to feelings of futility and it would sometimes take a shock like Paddy going on hunger-strike to shake us out of our despair. I wrote to him and told him that if he came off the hunger-strike we would intensify our efforts for him. He came off the hunger-strike and his spirits rallied. He got together a bundle of papers which he sent me and I contacted people throughout the world for him. As well as the letter, Paddy Hill had compiled a dossier of press cuttings highlighting the discrepancies in their case.

When Paddy Hill's bundle arrived I was delighted. Here was something from one of the prisoners showing that he was not beaten by the system that had so wrongfully locked him up. With it came a letter saying Fr Faul had sent a copy of his book, *The Birmingham Framework* and other useful material, and had sent him £40. Paddy wrote to me 'With his money, your money and the few £s I have of my own, I purchased 40 sets of photocopies and large envelopes and I wrote the enclosed eight page letter and sent a set to the following people ...' There followed a list of some twenty-five individuals and organisations, amongst them the NCCL, the Howard League, Cardinal Ó Fiaich, Charles Haughey, Lords Gifford and Longford and the editors of all the major Irish newspapers. He went on to say that he would like to send many more but it would cost him £1,000. He asked me to reprint and send out as many as I could because, 'You are one of the few people who have fought to prove our innocence from the start'. Paddy's letter, covering several pages of gaol notepaper in his meticulously clear longhand, was painstakingly written and covered the background with extreme precision and vividness.

It was clear that the due process of law was not going to go the men's way. Lord Denning said the case should not be allowed to proceed as the issues raised in the civil case being brought by the Birmingham Six against the police for assaulting them had already been decided at their criminal trial:

> Just consider the course of events if this action is allowed to proceed to trial. If the six men fail, it will mean much time and money will have been expended by many people for no good purpose. If the six men win, it will mean that the police were guilty of perjury, that they were guilty of violence and threats, that the confessions were involuntary and were improperly admitted in evidence and that the convictions were erroneous. That would mean that the Home Secretary would either have to recommend that they be pardoned or he would have to remit the case to the Court of Appeal. This is such an appalling vista that every sensible person in the land would say: It cannot be right these actions should go any further. This case shows what a civilised country we are. Here are six men who have been proved

guilty of the most wicked murder of twenty-one innocent people. They have no money. Yet the state continued to lavish large sums on them in actions against the police. It is high time it stopped. It is really an attempt to set aside the convictions on a sidewind. It is a scandal that should not be allowed to continue.

Paddy Hill told me that he got very few replies to his bundle despite all his work. Amongst those few the best were from Bishop Edward Daly, whom I had contacted, and Cardinal Ó Fiaich. From the start he had managed to get the support of the Tory MP Sir John Farr who worked hard for Paddy Hill from the early days. But it was the reply from Tom Sargant at JUSTICE, the British section of the International Commission of Jurists to whom Paddy Hill had sent one of his bundles that expressed it all:

12 July 1982

Dear Mr Hill,
I am very sorry to have delayed so long in replying to your letter and the material about your case enclosed with it.
　I had of course followed the press accounts of your trial and subsequent proceedings and was satisfied that justice was not seen to have been done to all the issues that were raised.
　I have to say with regret however that there is nothing which Justice can do about it. The Home Office has full powers in such matters and we are unable to persuade it to act even in simple cases when we have produced substantial proof of innocence.
　In a case like yours so many reputations are at stake, that in my view the obstacles to be overcome are insuperable – unless and until some independent review tribunal is set up to deal with petitions.

That letter really infuriated me. I rang Chris Mullin and read him the letter. Shortly afterwards, Chris Mullin, then editor of *The Tribune*, asked for a copy of the letter which he published, and also published an article on the Birmingham Six.

In January 1983 I was approached by another journalist, Chris Oxley, the Panorama producer. He wanted to do a programme on miscarriages of justice and asked about the Maguire family. I gave him the numbers of Mary McCaffery, Mrs Kearney, Fr Murray and Fr Faul. I told Mr Oxley that I spent a lot of time giving interviews that were never used and said I would co-operate further only if he gave me some assurance that the programme would go ahead. He said, 'Sister, if I find these people are innocent, no one will stop me.' I told him I would ring him every Sunday evening to see how he was doing. I impressed upon him that I would pray hard that he did not get cold feet or be stopped in the pursuit of justice.

One day Chris Oxley said he was not sure he would make the programme without key figures. I thought then that he must have been forced to give up on the project so I didn't ring him any more. Several weeks later Mrs Kearney rang to say the BBC needed photographs of Annie Maguire. I told her not to bother with them because I was cross about it all and she told me, 'It's your Mr Oxley that wants them – he's going ahead'. The programme went out in April. It was excellent. I rang Chris Oxley's house, spoke to his wife and thanked him. Sister Bernardine rang me, Mrs Kearney rang me. Everybody was delighted. I rang Hugh Maguire and I went to bed very pleased.

That was the first television programme on the Maguires and it helped to sow the seeds. The media interest was spreading beyond Ireland and England. In March 1983, a Swedish reporter, Elizabeth Lindeborg, contacted me. She had visited Fr Murray previously, knew of Fr Faul, knew Clara Reilly and Chris Mullin. Fr Murray gave her my name. We spoke about the Prevention of Terrorism Act, Irish prisoners and Armagh gaol. I was pleased when Elizabeth wrote a double-page spread for a Swedish newspaper on Irish prisoners.

In the autumn of 1984 Paul Hill's aunt and uncle, Theresa and Errol Smalley, asked for my help with their 'Free the Guildford Four' campaign. Before joining them I told them of my concerns about committees. I said that, in my view, an effective committee had to be a small, tightly knit circle of high-powered people. My second suggestion was to hire an effective solicitor. The Smalleys invited me to be on the committee. The solicitors I recommended were Mike Fisher and Gareth Peirce. The former then began to represent Paul Hill and the latter Gerry Conlon. They worked efficiently and tirelessly until the Guildford Four were free. Two especially effective members of the Smalleys' committee were John McDonnell of the Camden Town Council and Ronan Bennett. This committee appreciated the support of the few MPs like Joan Maynard, Jeremy Corbyn and Chris Mullin who campaigned for the Guildford Four. We contacted officials from the British and Irish governments, members of the Church, embassies and various other organisations and individuals. It was the best committee on which I ever served.

I tried many times to enlist the support and active help of

members of parliament. At that time nobody in the Commons wanted to know – Jock Stallard had become a whip and it was impossible to approach him though in the early years he was excellent. I tried Norman St John Stevas because he is a Catholic; I tried once and was rebuffed. I also approached John Biggs-Davison. There were few Catholic MPs we could turn to – I would have gone to anyone but nobody wanted to know. With a few notable exceptions, I did not get very far with the Lords. Lord Kilbracken asked questions on our behalf and was very helpful. The bishops always go into the House of Lords and start the day with prayers. They're meant to bring a Christian element into parliament but those bishops never opened their mouths with our questions about bringing prisoners to gaols near their families to keep families together – until the 1990s when Bishop Daly started talking about the prisoners needing to be near their families – something Fr Faul, Fr Brady, Fr Murray and I had been saying for twenty years.

I noticed the MPs as they walked past while I waited in the lobby or attended a press conference. I lobbied Shirley Williams to protest about the treatment of women under arrest and in gaol. She was a tough nut – a hard woman. I spoke to Roy Hattersely and Mrs Ewing. She was wonderful. She said she did not like the sound of strip-searching of woman, especially pregnant womem, and was prepared to take the matter up with the European parliament. Another MP whom I always found helpful and concerned was Joan Maynard who was a member of the executive committee of the Labour Party. She was exceptional. Right from the start she would chair meetings for us and ask questions – she and Fenner Brockway participated whether it was popular or not and did what was right and just. She still writes to me. An obvious person to lobby was prison reformer Lord Longford. He'd say he was interested but he was often a damp squib and not usually all that helpful. There was, however, the time when Hugh Feeney could not get communion in Gartree. Lord Longford sorted that out and it emerged that the chaplain said he had not been notified that Hugh was a Catholic.

Clare Short also disappointed me. On 24 July 1984 at a meeting about the Birmingham Six at the House of Commons to which seventy MPs were invited only Clare Short and Joan Maynard came. Joan Maynard chaired the meeting and Clare Short sat in the corner and did not contribute.

As well as lobbying MPs and Lords, I realised the importance of making sure journalists were well-informed. In those early years very few were concerned about these miscarriages of justice. A few were interested but they couldn't interest their editors in the story in the early years. I remember one journalist who came to see me saying: 'I suppose you know the Maguires are locked up to terrify the Irish'.

I said 'Yes! They knew they were innocent when they arrested them'.

Even the Irish papers weren't interested except for the *Irish Post* and the reporter David Brazil of the *Irish Press* was very good right from the start. *Hibernia* magazine also carried some good articles. Campaigning journalist Paul Foot then at the *Daily Mirror* replied when Paddy Hill wrote to him saying how outrageous he found the case against the six to be and asked Paddy Hill to keep in touch with him. Of course Chris Mullin was involved after we approached him. I talked to anyone and everyone, not just those in positions of influence. I remember giving a talk to some pensioners in which I said that the prisoners were not thugs and murderers. Whilst this was not well received by the majority, two people approached me and offered to put up families.

I also kept in contact with organisations that could offer support such as the Howard League for Prison Reform, Pax Christi, Christians Against Torture and Amnesty International. Martin Wright was the director of the Howard League from 1970 to 1980 and he put out statements and gave advice. The Howard League were helpful. I had a love-hate relationship with Pax Christi but they were helpful too. I contacted them at various times – in the case of Ronan Bennett and the Persons Unknown Trial, about the Maguires, the Guildford Four, the Birmingham Six. I used to speak to Mgr Bruce Kent the director of CND; I could rely on him. Sometimes he'd annoy me because he'd get cross with me coming to him with one thing and then another. I always felt it was worth talking to anyone because one could sow the seeds of doubt in the official minds.

Fr Faul and I beat a track to Amnesty International to talk about the woes of Northern Ireland and the miscarriages of justice. They didn't help much in the early years although in the mid 1980s they did take up the case of Patrick Hackett. We also kept in touch with the NCCL. I opened my files on the PTA to them as I was the only one keeping them at the time but they never took up the cases

– that was my big problem. These were threatening years and we needed help. There were individuals who were good, I always remember Catherine Scorer who died very young. She worked for the NCCL. The thing about them was that they'd go so far and no further.

Even as it became increasingly clear that the Birmingham Six, Maguire Seven, Guildford Four and Judith Ward were the casualties of miscarriages of justice, people continued to believe that they were guilty.

On 13 May 1985 I went to Channel 4 for a showing of an RTE film about the Maguires with which I had helped. The Maguires had by then all served their time. Jock Stallard looked uncomfortable but I had a good chat with him. Then Lord Attlee arrived and Gerry Fitt came in with great gusto. Orla O'Hanrahan [first secretary of the embassy] came and the head of the Federation of Irish Associations. I told the head of the Federation how the Federation nearly tarred and feathered me when I tried to say the Maguires were innocent at an AGM of the Federation in 1981. Fr Faul had been invited to speak about the blanket protest by the federation at that AGM. I accompanied Fr Faul to the meeting and I sat in the empty rows at the back of the hall. During a lull I said isn't it an awful pity the Federation doesn't do something about the Maguire family. The delegates jumped and said, 'Who let you in; that's political!' I thought they were going to hit me. I said, 'I'm with Fr Faul.' But the hostility and suspicion we encountered did not stop us from carrying on with our work.

Despite the growing media interest there were still times when the British media ignored elements of the cases which I thought should have been reported on. For example, they ignored a letter sent out to the press which Cardinal Ó Fiaich had sent to Home Secretary William Whitelaw on 14 February 1985 calling for a re-opening of Giuseppe Conlon's case. I rang LBC Radio [London] to put my point across on the phone-ins and continued my calls the next day. On 18 February I phoned Pax Christi, to get them to ask Cardinal Hume to back Cardinal Ó Fiaich.

I always oblige journalists when they want information and often gave extensive interviews. Theresa Hynes rang two Catholic papers in London, *The Universe* and *The Catholic Herald*, asking them to run stories on Giuseppe Conlon. David Browne, *The Catholic Herald*'s editor for Irish affairs, then rang me and asked if he could visit me the following day. After a long session he asked me if I would come with him to Hugh Maguire. I asked Hugh if he would see David Browne as David Browne was leaving for Dublin the next day and was due go up to Belfast, staying with Fr Brady. Hugh agreed.

The number of other television programmes added to the increasing criticism of the convictions. Jenny Morgan, a BBC television producer made a programme about my work. She was doing a series of programmes called 'Surviving'. She came to see me in the convent and I said I'd have to ask Mother Provincial, who said she'd have to discuss it with the other Reverend Mothers. She came back to me and told me I could do it but one of the superiors would have to see it before it went out. I rang Fr Faul who said I shouldn't accept censorship. He suggested I say if I was not trusted I wouldn't do it at all. I rang the Reverend Mother and she said she hadn't meant it to sound like censorship and gave me permission.

A few days before the programme was to be broadcast I was driving back from Ireland and I heard on the news that there had been a lot of arrests in Glasgow under the PTA. On the day of the programme (1 July 1985) they were being brought down to London and there was a ring of steel around the city. One was a suspect in the Brighton bombing. I thought that with the anti-Irish feeling that always arises at such times, I myself would be attacked because in the programme I had criticised the police in their use of the PTA. But there was no backlash. In fact the next day I was in a supermarket and two women hugged and thanked me. They were very pleased that I had been saying the things I had – they said that was what it was like for black people as well.

My diary entry reads:

> After the programme Ed Wright rang to say not to worry because the programme was great. Helen O'Brien rang. The Sisters were delighted. Thank God, it is over at last and everyone is pleased. Padre Pio's help, I am sure. I slept soundly.

After the programme, I received many letters and phonecalls thanking me and expressing admiration for my work. A beautiful letter came from Dolours Price Rea whom I had visited at Brixton in 1973. Dolours wrote on the very evening of the programme. Here is part of her letter:

> I watched the programme you did and felt I must write. So many,

many memories came back to me. Your great kindness. It was a wonderful experience for us all – love, realised. I learned so much then about love of each other, of God. It has stood me in good stead ... Sister, do write if you have time. We must meet; there is so much to say.

There was one very mysterious response to the programme as well. I wrote a detailed account of a bizarre meeting in my diary:

Tea in Cadogan Gardens. I got there without any trouble. I rang the bell and a man with a white jacket and a dicky-bow opened the door and ushered me in through a beautiful hall and drawing-room with small coffee tables. Two men were having tea in a corner. We went into a little orangery where an elderly bearded gentleman sat reading the papers. He had an English accent but said he was of Mayo/Wexford extraction. Then he said he had a group, Information on Europe, and now he was into television and he was prepared to do something that could be useful. He would get lists of all the families and the prisoners and he would want photographs, etc. He could get any information I wanted dispersed with the Euro MPs: just send him the paper heading with information. He would get people to sponsor a family – £1,000 a year. He got me tea – brought in by another young man in a bow-tie and dinner jacket – cucumber sandwiches, etc. I came away after two hours bewildered.

I do not know who this man was but I think the place we met was a club. I told him my work was pastoral and I couldn't send him any information. I thought it was very odd, his asking me for names and addresses and photographs. He was pleasant enough – very upper class English. I don't know what his job was. I don't ask questions. But he had seen my film and must have thought there's a little one I can brainwash. I don't know whether he was an eccentric or an agent. It was very peculiar.

A number of those arrested in Glasgow had connections with Donegal and Pat 'The Cope' Gallagher's constituency. I met him and took him to the gaol several times and I was heartened that someone from Dáil Éireann cared enough to visit the gaol.

Chris Mullin told me he was planning to write a book about the Guildford Four. I advised him not to because there was so much tension and contention between the families at the time. Annie Maguire was always complaining about Gerry Conlon. I thought he would have great difficulty. I advised him to write a book about the Birmingham Six. He asked if I would help him as they wouldn't know who he was and I agreed.

This marked the beginning of Chris Mullin's research which culminated in his influential book *Error of Judgement* published in 1986, and a hard hitting investigation by Granada television. This work contributed to the eventual release of the men. I helped Chris Mullin in any way I could. I took him boxes of the papers that I had on the case and told him all I knew. As Chris Mullin became more and more involved in this case, he asked me to help him by recommending him to people he needed to interview, families and ex-prisoners. I cleared the way for him to meet and interview them. He also asked me if I would make contact with Sinn Féin. He knew that unless and until he found the people who really did the bombing, his efforts to clear the men were futile. He would have to start by contacting Sinn Féin in Dublin. I was going to Ireland for my holidays and he asked me to visit the Sinn Féin offices to ask them to co-operate with him.

On 19 June 1985 I visited Sinn Féin's Parnell Square offices. I said I was looking for Mick Murray, a former prisoner with whom I had corresponded in the past. A man stepped forward and said, 'I am Joe Cahill; you are Sister Sarah'. I knew the name and I had an idea that he was important but that's all I knew. We had a long chat and Mick Murray arrived. I told them about Chris Mullin and that he'd be getting in touch with them and that he wanted me to ask them to co-operate with him.

Chris Mullin was also involved in the Granada television World in Action programme entitled *In the Interests of Justice* which was transmitted on 28 October 1985. When *Error of Judgement* was published in July 1986 I was ill. On 1 July I had gone into hospital and on 2 July Ronan Bennett visited me and brought me flowers. He had a copy of the book that he was reviewing for *Time Out* magazine. It heartened me to see an ex-prisoner, intelligent, committed, helping other prisoners. Ronan later investigated the case against the Guildford Four, co-wrote Paul Hill's book *Stolen Years*, and then wrote *Double Jeopardy. The Retrial of the Guildford Four*. [This book is dedicated to me]. On 11 July I heard, 'Hello, Sister Sarah' and it was Chris Mullin. He had a copy of the book for me. I was very touched by what he had written in it, 'To Sister Sarah but for whom none of this would have been possible'.

The World in Action programme and his book showed conclusively that the Birmingham Six had been wrongfully imprisoned. The six men were finally granted the right to appeal their convictions in November 1987 but the judgement, delivered in January 1988 went against them. I attended this appeal regularly throughout its two month hearing, climbing all 130 steps in the Old Bailey to the highest of the public galleries. My diary is full of snatches of conversation between people involved in the case – Lord Gifford, the barrister, Gareth Peirce, Fr Faul, Senator Pascal Mooney, Fr Murray, Peter Barry, Chris Mullin and many others. Very early on Fr Faul said: 'They will not let the prisoners win but will release them during the year. This is what Chris Mullin heard at Joan Maynard's party; he heard it from somebody in Douglas Hurd's office'. In spite of the new evidence, Lord Lane, the Lord Chief Justice said, 'The longer this hearing has gone on, the more convinced this court has become that the verdict of the jury was correct.' There is an account of the last day of the Appeal in my diary on 28 January 1988:

> The queue to get into the public gallery was very long. The police were everywhere. Then at 9.30 they made us all go round the corner. The police cars, outriders and four prison vans came. Security was very much increased. At 10 a.m. the doors opened. Bags searched and up the steps to several police. A policewoman searched me very thoroughly and took my keys and left them on the table. She said that they were expecting trouble if the verdict was unfavourable. Once in the court, it was so packed that I had difficulty in seeing the six men. Lord Lane began the summing up and before long we all knew there was no hope for the men. It became a nightmare to listen as Judge Brown and then O'Connor brutally dismissed the evidence. I looked round the court room and noticed that Lord Gifford's wig was pushed right back whilst that of another defence barrister was pulled down over this nose. Mike Mansfield [the barrister] was livid.

After the judgement the scenes outside the court were wild. The television cameras had been told to push back and there were hundreds of police. Everyone was interviewed including me. It was a black day and all those campaigning for the men's release were overwhelmed. When I spoke to Fr Faul the next day he put a hopeful spin on the results of the appeal – he felt the judgement was so awful it would do the men's case good.

Before the appeal of the Guildford Four Gareth Peirce, Gerry Conlon's solicitor, found vital evidence given to the police, which had been stored in police archives and which was part of a bundle with orders on it that it should not be given to the defence. She discovered that on 4 October 1974, the night of the bombing, Gerry

Conlon had a cast-iron alibi which the police knew perfectly well. Ten people at the Quex Road hostel had seen him that night. They remembered him being there – ten people including a nun and a priest. That night they were watching the news and the flash came on about the Guildford bombings. Gerry was fooling around and annoyed them, so someone hit him and they put him out of the room. He went upstairs to the room he shared with another young man. This young man was leaving that night and was packing. That is how he remembered which night it was. This was all on record. Fr Carolan who was in charge of the hostel told us that ten people had known that Gerry was there all the time although he himself was not one of them as he was not there that night. But it was in the records and Sr Anne Marie O'Boyle was there that evening. Why hadn't they come forward? They said they were waiting for someone to come and ask them about it. Imagine the difference it could have made; just a word to Cardinal Heenan in 1975 calling attention to this alibi would have thrown the whole case.

Finally on 19 October 1989 the Guildford Four's convictions at the Old Bailey were quashed. I was supporting another prisoner that morning in Lambeth Magistrates Court – a young man who had been arrested on charges that reminded me of Annie Maguire. It was early afternoon before I could leave Lambeth Court and go to the Old Bailey. I got there in time to witness a moment that few who saw it will ever forget. It was a wonderful sight – thousands of people waiting. All around, front and back, down the street police were trying to keep the crowds back. I went to see if I had a place. My name was not on the list. I then went to the public entrance and got as near the door as I could. Chris Mullin called me. I had no ticket to get in court but Ann Conlon said, 'I have your ticket' and she pulled me in and gave me a front seat. At 2.30 p.m., having read from papers, Lord Lane declared them innocent. There was a great roar of rejoicing for several minutes. We went to the front door and waited for ages. Then Gerry Conlon came running out and thrust all his belongings into my arms. Paul Hill was taken out the back door and brought to Belfast. He had been convicted of murdering a British soldier. Subsequently this conviction, too, was quashed. Paddy Armstrong and Carole Richardson left with their solicitor, Alistair Logan.

The taxi driver, who took me and several others to the press conference at the House of Commons afterwards, would not take payment as a gesture to the Irish. The press were there in their hundreds. The world's press was there in hundreds. I seized the opportunity to speak about the case of the young man whose wife I had accompanied to court that morning. I asked reporters to ring the Home Office and include this case in their articles. The young man was later released.

Useful and effective as media allies had been, there were conflicts of interest. I had a major disagreement with 'World in Action' in October 1989. This concerned the 'naming of names' on a programme they were making about the Birmingham pub bombings. The events leading to this conflict between 'World in Action' and myself had begun several months before when Lesley Udwin, an actress and film producer, approached me for help with research into a drama documentary for Granada television on the Birmingham Six. I applauded this project and helped Lesley as much as I could. But there was to be a twist in the tale – the film was to reveal the names of three IRA men who did the Birmingham bombing. I was horrified they were going to have the names on television because it would be trial by television. I felt responsible because I had originally introduced Chris Mullin to the Birmingham Six. I visited Chris Mullin with Gareth Peirce. We put up a great case but Chris did not comment. He rang the producer who agreed to a meeting with us but did not want me present. Chris said, 'No Sister Sarah, no Gareth – no Chris!' The meeting went ahead.

Gareth Peirce and myself did most of the talking. I had prepared my arguments and my notes were written into the 1989 diary:

> This programme is not going to get the men out, only the courts can do that. To name these names would be like putting people on trial by television on the word of an informer hated by all shades of Irish people. People named have no redress and are in grave danger of summary justice as in Gibraltar. It also puts their wives and families in danger. If they name the names and the men are not guilty it will take another fifteen years to clear them, ten or fifteen years before some television producer takes up the case! It will ruin the case. Slander is wrong, morally wrong, unethical.

The names were named.

EXONERATION OF THE GUILDFORD Four had an on-going effect on the Birmingham Six and Maguire Seven. The second appeal of the Birmingham Six began in February 1991 and ended with their vindication on 14 March. The counsel for the crown were laughed at when he said John Walker was guilty. After lunch Mike Mansfield summed up very briefly. The judges said they would give their judgement later – but they pronounced the convictions unsafe and unsatisfactory. The court was in uproar. The judges went out. John Walker shouted. 'God bless you, Sister Sarah'. They shouted to me to come out with their families. When the families all left I gave a few interviews. Bishop Edward Daly and Fr Patrick Hannon ran across the road to me. Bishop Daly just hugged me. I went home by bus. Later in the evening Betsey Power came to my door, looking for Gareth Peirce's house, where Billy was staying. I showed her where it was. A short while later Billy Power himself came to say thank you.

Like a house of cards, one case toppled the next. The Maguire Seven were officially declared innocent in the Court of Appeal in December 1992. I thought of Giuseppe's exhortations, of him saying time and again that he was innocent and so were all the others. I thought of what Lord Denning had said at the Birmingham Six appeal – if the men win it would mean that the police were guilty of perjury, violence and threats, that the evidence was lies, the confessions forced. The Home Secretary would have to pardon them – what an appalling vista indeed: how could we have any faith in the system after this?

10

REPATRIATION

It is necessary to call special attention to those more in need of assistance ...
such as the families of those in prison.
POPE JOHN PAUL, *FAMILIARIS CONSORTIO*

The release of the seventeen wrongfully convicted people didn't
mean an end of my work. Throughout the years, I was also keeping up my letter-writing, parcel-delivering and helping people
picked up under the PTA, phoning solicitors, helping families,
putting them up, providing, protecting. The work never stops.

Since the early 1970s, I have agitated for the repatriation of
Irish prisoners, a campaign that still continues as Irish political
prisoners still remain in British gaols. Until every prisoner is returned or released I have no intention of giving up my effort for
the prisoners and their families. How could I – these prisoners
are singled out for prolonged and harsh treatment within the
gaol system. Yet they cause no trouble, are denied parole and
very rarely taken off the highest grade within the three grades of
Category A. This is not because of the nature of their offences but
because they are Irish political prisoners.

For as long as anyone can remember it has been Home Office
policy to house prisoners as near as possible to their homes.
Where Irish prisoners are concerned this policy was not followed. I'm not talking only about repatriation for political prisoners but their cases are the most urgent because of the length
and harshness of their sentences. Ordinary prisoners should also
be allowed go home if they wish. There are three decisions involved in any transfer. The prisoner must apply, the holding
country must agree and the country to which the prisoner wishes to go must also agree.

The struggle for repatriation goes back to the start of the
troubles when Marian and Dolours Price, Hugh Feeney and
Gerry Kelly, the Old Bailey defendants, mounted their hunger-
strike which ultimately led to their return to Ireland. Two other
prisoners, Michael Gaughan and Frank Stagg, went on hunger-

strike when they were told they could not serve their time in Ireland near their families. Michael Gaughan died in June 1974 and Frank Stagg in Wakefield in February 1976. I knew Frank Stagg's family and I was constantly in touch with them during his hunger-strike. His mother lived in Ireland but she often came over. This was a time of terrible tension for prisoners' families. Hunger-striking is a very Irish form of protesting. Its origins can be traced back to pre-Christian times. If one had a grievance against the head of a clan, one sat on his doorstep. Everyone passing saw this and refusing food brought shame on the head of that clan. It's one of the oldest forms of protest. The list of those who have undertaken hunger-strikes is long and some hunger-strikers won their demands. Apart from the success of the Old Bailey people, in the last twenty-five years hunger-striking has resulted in tragic deaths. I tried to help the Stagg family and comfort them – the anguish of the families was heart-breaking.

Frank Stagg's mother Mary wrote to me in April 1975 just after his first hunger-strike:

> I am Frank Stagg's mother. He is at present in a punishment cell in Wakefield Prison. I came over here from County Mayo a few weeks ago shortly after his father had died. I am 69 years and in poor health and it is with great hardship I made the journey. He was then in the hospital wing and was very ill. He was taken from there 2 weeks ago and placed in a punishment cell. We have applied to have him transferred to N. Ireland as I will not be able to make the journey again, expense-wise and health-wise. I fear very much that he will go on hunger-strike again if he is left in this punishment cell. You might be able to talk to someone on his behalf and I will be thankful. Please do pray for him as I fear very much for him, being in solitary confinement and not in good health from the effects of recent hunger-strikes.

A year later she was back by her son's side as he lay dying, shrunk to four stone and blinded by the illness engendered by his fast. Even after he died, he was still subjected to injustice. His mother and some of his family were waiting at Dublin airport for his body to be returned. The plane carrying his body was ordered to go on to Shannon and the body was brought from Shannon to the church in Ballina by the Irish government. The church was full of police, Mrs Stagg told me. She showed me a photograph and her son was not buried in the Republican plot but in an ordinary plot and then it was filled in with cement. They posted a guard on his grave. Michael Gaughan's funeral had attracted huge crowds on its journey to the west of Ireland and the Irish government ensured that this would not happen in the case of Frank Stagg. They hijacked the coffin which remained, even after the burial, under armed guard for six months. When the police guard was taken off the grave a priest and a group of others exhumed the remains and buried him in the Republican plot.

Not so long ago a chaplain told me that it's part of the system to make the families suffer, that in this way they hurt the prisoner. By tearing the families apart you torture the prisoner and by doing that you torture the families. The miracle is that so many Irish families have stayed together – a tribute to the wives and mothers who suffered terrible hardships for so many years. In the struggle for repatriation it's the families who suffer.

Over the years I have repeatedly done what I could to promote repatriation for Irish prisoners. Early in 1978 I contacted Lord Kilbracken asking him to raise the question in the House of Lords. I went along to hear the debate on 7 February 1978. Lord Brockway sat in front of Lord Kilbracken and supported him with further questions. Lord Longford arrived late and apologised for missing the question time. Three bishops in surplices sat in front of me. Lord Kilbracken's question concerning the transfer of prisoners to near their homes touched a subject at the heart of Christianity – the family. The bishops remained silent during the discussions but then asked, 'When were parking regulations to be enforced?' A subject that had nothing to do with Christainity.

On 29 June 1982 I wrote to Lord Hylton in the House of Lords. I sent him information about the objectives of the campaign to repatriate prisoners started in the early 1980s by the RFPC. Later Lord Hylton asked a question in the House of Lords about the repatriation of prisoners. Mr Darnbrooke, a Belfast probation officer, gave me a copy of his heartening report to them.

I decided not to contact Lord Hylton again having discovered that he was involved in some special projects with prisoners. This came to my notice thanks to a chance visit by a New Zealand nun staying at the convent. She was interested in working for prisoners and came in one day very excited saying she had found some nuns in Camden whose sole work was with prisoners. She gave me the address. I was intrigued as I'd never heard of them. I went down and spoke to them and found they took in prisoners leaving gaol but they didn't work with families. I asked the nun if she had any literature on their work. She gave me a booklet about the conversion of prisoners to Born Again Christianity. I discovered that a prominent government minister was connected to the hostels. Prisoners who became 'Born Again' got early releases. I was aproached and asked would I give the names of Republican prisoners who might be interested in the scheme. I did not co-operate as I did not think early release in return for religious conversion was appropriate. I felt, too, it was open to the accusation, given the involvement of a government minister, that it was politically motivated. I felt it wasn't the Church running it. It was politicians. Had I not found out it was politically motivated I might have become involved because obviously I'd like people to be Christian and do the right thing.

By this time, however, I had lost faith in the British authorities. I realised that the European Courts of Justice and the United Nations held the only hope for repatriation. The prisoners themselves would have to instigate this move, and they were slow to act, perhaps because their solicitors were also reticent to move, believing as many of us once did in the British justice system. Although an unpopular issue with the governments concerned, repatriation was mentioned by a few members of the Church. I was consoled by a statement by Cardinal Ó Fiaich that appeared in three Irish papers in April 1983. On 16 March 1986 Bishop Edward Daly gave a homily in Westminster Cathedral. He said that strip-searching should stop, innocent people should be given a new trial and prisoners sent home to serve sentences – a big change from the time we were made to feel criminals if we mentioned anything like that in the cathedral.

For years I have been lobbying MPs, TDs, government ministers in Ireland and England and high-ranking members of the Church about the repatriation issue. The first big mail-out on this subject by myself and Theresa Hynes through the RFPC occurred during 1982 and this is the letter we sent:

> You will be aware that a Council of Europe Convention on the transfer of sentenced persons was recently concluded at Strasbourg. *The Times* (London) of July 30th '83 reported a British Commons written reply by Mr Leon Brittan, the British Home Secretary, in which he indicated that the British Government intended to sign the Convention in August.

Article 2 of the Convention reads as follows;
General Principles

1. The parties undertake to afford each other the widest measure of co-operation in respect of the transfer of sentenced prisoners in accordance with the provisions of this convention.

2. A person sentenced in the territory of a party may be transferred to the territory of another party, in accordance with the provisions of this Convention, in order to serve the sentence imposed on him. To that end he may express his interest to the sentencing State or to the administrating State in being transferred under this Convention.

3. Transfer may be requested by either the sentencing State or the administering State.

Irish prisoners in Britain fall into various categories – those born in Ireland and serving sentences for different offences, those who are Irish citizens, whether born in Ireland or not, those sentenced for political offences, etc. Not all Irish prisoners would opt to serve their sentences in Ireland, some having stronger family connections in Britain, but obviously some would.

May we draw particular attention to those serving sentences for political offences. These prisoners frequently have little family connections with Britain; they invariably are in Category A – the highest security grading, with all that implies for their freedom of movement and association within the prison community. They are usually serving very long or life sentences in a most hostile prison situation. Although they are regarded by the British Government as ordinary criminals, they are treated quite differently from ordinary criminals as regards visits, constant sudden changes from prison to prison, long periods in solitary confinement, refusal of parole, and the frequent arrest of relatives on their legitimate journeys to and from prison visits, etc., etc., often with drastic consequences for not only the prisoners but especially for their families.

The British Government is admirable in its efforts to obtain not only the transfer but the release of its own subjects from prisons abroad. Mrs Thatcher and her Cabinet have put pressure openly and firmly on foreign governments for the release of heroin pushers and mercenaries while at the same time refusing, so far, to allow Irish prisoners from Northern Ireland to serve their sentences near their families, although in many cases this would be a great improvement from a humanitarian point of view for both the prisoner and his family.

The new Convention is obviously of great importance to those interested in prisoners' welfare and their families. It has been under consideration by the Governments concerned for some years and we presume the Irish Government and Opposition already have a

159

united and open policy about the Irish citizens imprisoned in Britain who wish to serve their sentences in Ireland.

We therefore ask for a firm declaration of policy by the Irish Government that Irish prisoners should be returned to serve their sentences in Ireland if they so wish, and for public support to press the Government to declare this policy. As far as the individual is concerned we ask that he/she ascertain the views of his/her TD and urge repatriation for Irish prisoners in England.

One significant reply was from Garrett Fitzgerald [14 July 1982]:

I think I can understand the difficulties and hardships being faced by the families of Irish prisoners being held in British jails. I would be happy to do whatever I can to help, but I feel this is something that can only be done privately and quietly.

Before I can consider any moves which might be helpful I would need further information on the number of prisoners, how many of them are serving long-term sentences and how many, of those, have their families domiciled in Ireland?

Some of this information may be available as the result of a parliamentary question. I would strongly urge you to approach your local member of parliament and ask him to put down such a question. If that is impossible for you I might be able to help in this regard, but this information would be indispensable to any further action.

We were pleased to get this letter. At least it showed an interest and we had expected to be dismissed.

In September 1991, almost ten years later, myself and Sr Benedict Kelly, a Mercy nun from Liverpool who was working with me for a year, launched a major new campaign for the repatriation of Irish prisoners. In the intervening years I kept up a steady flow of pressure on those with the influence to raise and promote this issue, but received little encouragement. However Sr Benedict and myself decided to increase the pressure and mount a campaign because Britain had signed the Council of Europe Convention on the Transfer of Sentenced Persons. Ireland had not yet done so and it was useless to do anything until Ireland had signed the convention.

Prisoners from countries who signed the treaty were going home and there seemed to be one rule for 'ordinary decent criminals' (ODCs) and another for political prisoners. The headline in *The Sun* of 17 November 1991 reads 'Supercrook is off home to sick mum.' The supercrook in question was Valerio Viccei who got twenty-two years for a £40 million robbery. Viccei was an Italian neo-Fascist who explained in the book he wrote about himself that he had given up bombing left-wing television stations so he could devote himself to bank robberies. He wrote: 'I have abandoned the rarefied pure air of my idealised forest and travelled all the way down to the polluted town'. According to the *Sun*: 'The jailed mastermind of Britain's biggest robbery is being moved to a gaol in his native Italy because his mum and dad miss him'. His parents were too old and sick to visit him, he told the Home Office, and Parkhurst where he was serving his sentence had no Catholic priest or chapel.

It was the European ruling, signed by Italy, that had got him out and home and I'm glad he got home because all prisoners should be near their families. I had a lot of prisoners on my list who were not from Northern Ireland and were not political. After a year or two they would be moved to serve their time nearer their families so there was no problem – some of them were criminals on very serious charges. I'm only sorry that Ireland didn't ratify the treaty until the summer of 1994 when Albert Reynolds was Taoiseach.

I realised for a long time that it was useless writing to the Home Office or MPs or anybody about prisoners going home to the south of Ireland. We always got a *proforma* letter back from the Home Office stating that as the Irish government had not ratified the treaty such transfers could not be considered and so we concentrated on the Irish government and sent personal letters to TDs who had prisoners in their constituencies. When we got an acknowledgement we'd write back and ask them if they were going to do anything or if they had done anything. This barrage of letters went to TDs, government ministers and private secretaries and we kept it up for almost a year.

As part of the on-going campaign Sr Benedict and myself wrote another letter and did a mailing on 28 July 1992. We were so busy that a key point was left out of the letter – that, if the prisoners from the south could go back, then it would also apply to those from the north. Sr Benedict sat by the post box for several hours and managed to retrieve the letters before the postman took them. The following is a copy of the letter after it was retrieved and rewritten. It was sent out to a long list of government ministers and TDs and amended for each TD to include details of prisoners in their constituencies:

Last month we returned from Ireland, having travelled up and down the country visiting the families of Irish prisoners in English jails. We were impressed and edified by the bonds of love between these parents and their imprisoned daughters/sons. We visited eighteen elderly parents and were saddened by their anxiety as to how long more they will be able to undertake gruelling journeys to isolated corners of England. Some of them have been travelling on hazardous, costly journeys for up to nineteen years, obeying Christ's command to visit prisoners. Some of these parents even pleaded with us on their death-beds to bring them to England for a last visit to a son.

On the other hand, for wives and their families to maintain relationships with long-term prisoners is very difficult and consequently marital breakdown is very high. Fifty per cent of the marriages of those on our list have already broken down, in spite of efforts to maintain the relationship. For the families who do manage to keep contact it is a difficult task, demanding great effort financially and consuming great amounts of time. The cost of transport and time off work alone runs into thousands of pounds yearly. This is a lot of money for poor people without any assistance. That so much contact is maintained is a tribute to the strong bonds of the family unit in Ireland. We have known children, now adults, who never saw their fathers except in a prison visiting-room surrounded by prison officers under high security conditions.

All these are good law-abiding families who would never see the inside of a jail but for the political situation. We feel a conciliatory approach to the families and prisoners would be in the interests of peace and justice. There are only twelve political prisoners from the south of Ireland. Many of them have taken degrees and seventy per cent are studying for degrees, so they would not be disruptive in any way. Twenty years is a long time to be dragging children to the remotest corners of England. It was admirable the efforts Ireland made for Brian Keenan's release and likewise what the Church of England has done for Terry Waite. It would be a very Christian gesture to do the same for these innocent suffering families that we have visited.

In 1989 Mr Viccei, an Italian, was convicted and sentenced to twenty-two years for the armed robbery of £40 million. After just two years, he is about to be moved back to Italy near his elderly parents to serve his sentence. Surely those families we have visited deserve to have their children near them also. Justice, mercy and Christian commitment compel us to ask you to use your influence to hasten the return of these prisoners to Ireland to complete their sentence near their families.

When we got a reply from anyone it was usually just an acknowledgement. We also wrote to the Home Office on this issue several times. The replies were always similar, letters that did not serve to further the campaign at all.

There were a few who were very concerned about the repatriation issue, like TD Éamon Ó Cuív. We wrote to him on 12 March 1992 expressing our thanks and telling him of our disappointment with the Minister of Justice Pádraig Flynn. We often corresponded with Éamon Ó Cuív and he did what he could. We also lobbied Peter Barry who replied both sympathetically and constructively. He put down a parliamentary question to the new minister for justice.

We were no strangers to the Minister of Justice Pádraig Flynn as we wrote to him regularly. We were disappointed in his initial replies which were *pro forma* letters offering nothing. But the pressure paid off in a small way in the end. We pulled no punches in our response to these replies. In a letter to Pádraig Flynn we said:

> 11 March 1992
> Thank you for your letter which we received from your secretary re the prisoners in English jails. We find it very disturbing that you and your Department are so reluctant to ratify the European Convention for the transfer of Sentenced Persons. We are getting the very same letter from you as we got from Mr Gerry Collins when he was Minister of Justice. This letter seems to be a standard letter sent out by the Department. For the last four months we are told that the practical and legislative measures are under active consideration. We would be grateful to know how long more this active consideration has to continue and if any further progress has been made since we first received this letter in December.
>
> This issue is very important to many families and to us. Please do your best to bring it to a successful end. We think that there is an oral question down for 18 March in the Dáil. Will you please back it if there is such a question?

At last a month later we were getting closer to something more satisfactory and received a letter from Pádraig Flynn's secretary. We immediately wrote back. Finally on 13 July Pádraig Flynn replied. It was our first breakthrough and, despite the half measures suggested in the letter and Pádraig Flynn's proposals being short of what the campaigners demanded, we were pleased. We may not have been promised what we wanted but at least the government were committed to signing the treaty.

IN NOVEMBER 1992 I HAD A TERRIBLE ACCIDENT. I often went early on a Saturday to 8 o'clock Mass at Westminster Cathedral to take in Confession as well. It was near Christmas and I needed wrapping-paper so I crossed the road outside the cathedral to go to Paperchase. It was so early that Paperchase wasn't open so I came back out and went back towards the cathedral. I crossed the road. There were bollards in the middle. I got to the traffic island and looked up and down and saw a green car but it wasn't moving – or so I thought and I crossed. I woke up late that night in hospital with my legs in plaster from the hips to the ankles, a broken shoulder and concussion. I was terrified. I kept wondering would I ever walk again. The doctor came and said I would. I had a huge black eye but strangely enough, although the bridge of my nose was broken, my glasses were not only intact, they weren't even scratched.

A priest was passing the scene of the accident and recognised me and gave me the Last Sacrament. I received three sacraments that morning – Holy Communion, Confession and then the Sacrament of the Sick out there on the road. The policeman came in the ambulance with me and he came to see me a few times. He wanted a statement from me but at the time I couldn't remember anything. I still don't. I lost track of night and day. I was in hospital for four months and had to recuperate for as many months afterwards.

THE PROCESS STARTED BY Sr Benedict, Sr Imelda and myself worked its way through the red tape. I reminded the minister who succeeded Pádraig Flynn, Máire Geoghegan-Quinn, of Pádraig Flynn's letter and the possibility of a limited ratification of this treaty by the Irish government. The British Home Office meanwhile pursued an investigation of inter-prison transfers under the direction of Lord Ferrers, who submitted a report in November 1992. He recommended that Irish prisoners in English gaols be moved to Northern Ireland gaols to facilitate family visits. The Home Office accepted these recommendations.

The following month ten Irish prisoners requested transfers. Having waited sixteen months, they had not received a reply so they asked the Belfast solicitors, Madden and Finucane, to represent their case to the Centre for Human Rights at the United Nations. This was done on 28 April and 19 May 1994. On 7 June the United Nations official informed the solicitors that contacts were under way with British authorities and the appropriate United Nations commissions. In early July the gaol service began informing the prisoners involved of imminent transfers.

A copy of the solicitors' requests echoed and reflected the things we had been saying for years: the difficulties and expense elderly parents experience in long journeys, disruptions to family life and the breakdown of relationships which prisoners' rehabilitation jeopardise. For years I had been saying there was no use in appealing to the British authorities. The United Nations provided the prisoners' only way home.

At the time of going to press most of the prisoners from the south of Ireland are still in English gaols, some having served over twenty-one years.

11

SOLICITORS AND BARRISTERS

Then addressing the people and his disciples, Jesus said, 'The Scribes and Pharisees occupy the chair of Moses ... but do not be guided by what they do: since they do not practice what they preach. They tie up heavy burdens and lay them on men's shoulders, but will they lift a finger to move them? Not they! Everything they do is done to attract attention like wearing broader phylacteries and longer tassels ... Alas for you, Scribes and Pharisees, you hypocrites. You pay your tithes of mint and dill and cumin and have neglected the weightier matters of the Law – justice, mercy, good faith.'
MATTHEW 23:1–23

All those who challenge the establishment on the subject of the six counties of Northern Ireland find themselves pitted against prejudice and ignorance. When it comes to the attitudes of the judiciary and many of those who work in it, the quotation from Matthew always comes to mind. I remember the opening ceremony of the legal year – they all parade in their knickerbockers with an air of official solemnity and dignity and then in their every day working lives many of them negate it by their bias and prejudice when faced with either a black or an Irish defendant. They fail in their duty by not being guardians of the law and justice – something that shocked and appalled me and became very clear to me after the trial of the Guildford Four and the subsequent revelations of the conspiracy to obstruct the course of justice. I recognise how crucial it is to have a blameless judicial system.

In the years since I have worked with prisoners and their families I have come across many people who work within the British legal establishment. There were those, the wearers of knickerbockers, the hypocrites and Pharisees in phylacteries and tassels who really let their clients down. But there were others, the good ones, who were brave and who fought for their clients in difficult and controversial cases.

In Robert Bolt's play *A Man for All Seasons*, Thomas More

says, 'Whoever hunts for me will find me hiding in the thickets of the law'. Later in the play, although his situation is more dangerous, More still trusts the law, calling it 'a causeway upon which, so long as he keeps to it, a citizen may walk safely'. But neither the 'thickets' nor the 'causeway' provided him with a refuge from injustice. I am reminded of these images when I think of how badly prisoners and their families have been served by the legal establishment, those 'thickets' lined with traps and snares from which some have never extricated themselves. The 'causeway' people have followed in good faith – as Giuseppe Conlon did for example, and this has led to unjust imprisonment. Until Guildford and Birmingham, I had the average person's knowledge of courts and lawyers. I thought, here were indeed refuges where citizens would find safety. I soon learned of the traps.

It became clear to me very early on as I accompanied families to courts and met them at police stations, that to prevent injustices being perpetrated against those arrested by the police, the services of an effective solicitor were essential. At first I was like all the families and believed that as long as someone was a solicitor they must be competent and capable. Like many others I soon realised that several solicitors were very careless and incompetent and went through the motions – they didn't really fight because it's very time-consuming to do so. Many of them didn't seem willing to take on the extra work of getting to grips with legislation brought in to deal with the Irish political situation. I had made it my business to become acquainted with the workings of the Prevention of Terrorism Act and it didn't take me long to work out that most solicitors knew very little about it. In defending Irish people, it is essential that they be familiar with the PTA, interested in the client and his or her family, be good and sensitive communicators who are willing to act quickly. Finding solicitors to fit this description involved a process of trial and error. I learned that solicitors' skills ranged from excellent to hopeless and I built up a long list of effective solicitors throughout Britain. The first two I found were Mike Fisher [Christian, Fisher & Co.] and Brian Rose-Smyth. I discovered who won cases for people and made a note of the names. The first barristers I came across who were effective were, at the time, newly qualified and are now household names – Rock Tansey and Mike Mansfield. They were competent and keen. In the 1980s Gareth Peirce and Neil O'May [Bindman & Company] joined this group. All are experts in criminal law and understand the PTA thoroughly. I'm sure there are many other good solicitors but, once I had the list of those I knew and trusted, I always contacted them for families because I felt the responsibility of the prisoner's life in my hands. If I took a risk and got them a solicitor I knew nothing about and that solicitor failed, I too would have failed and the consequences for the prisoner and family could have been very serious.

Most of those arrested under the PTA were innocent and uninvolved in any political or criminal activity. They had no idea how to assess a solicitor's ability. They were under arrest and terrified and they would accept the services of a duty solicitor. These duty solicitors would, by and large, be competent and experienced in giving advice on ordinary, everyday, criminal matters but, in my experience, very often they were not familiar with the workings of the PTA which they would not encounter in day-to-day practice. Frequently this could result in wrong advice to clients. When the client wanted to exercise the right to change solicitor, the duty solicitor sometimes was reluctant to hand over the case.

Several years later as the Guildford Four were preparing for their appeal, Errol and Theresa Smalley, Paul Hill's aunt and uncle, asked me which solicitor would be best for Paul. Paul, Carol Richardson and Paddy Armstrong had all been represented by a Guildford-based solicitor, Alistair Logan, who kept their case alive in the minds of the public by very effective radio and television programmes and several hard-hitting newspaper articles. We thought all were being represented by one solicitor at the time. I don't believe a group of prisoners on the same charges should have just one solicitor representing them. Two or three heads are better than one and you need some competition between the lawyers, something that can only benefit the prisoners. Paul Hill changed to Mike Fisher and Alistair Logan continued to represent Carol Richardson and Paddy Armstrong.

I knew it was crucial to the appeal to have solicitors like Mike Fisher and Gareth Peirce who would leave no stone unturned. It was material unearthed by Gareth Peirce – and by Alistair Logan and Mike Fisher – which ultimately forced the Court of Appeal to vindicate the four and release them. The material unearthed by Gareth Peirce and Mike Fisher, whilst it must have greatly influenced the judges, was kept from open court and not made public until the time of Paul Hill's trial in Belfast – and Gerry's film *In the Name of the Father* came out.

Gerry Conlon was always sure about one thing – like his father he would not accept half measures. Gerry wrote to me in December 1986 and told me he had heard that Paul Hill would be prepared to accept a pardon from the Home Secretary. Gerry was asked would he be prepared to accept the same. He said absolutely not: never, never! He said he was an innocent man, 'I came into prison an innocent man and I will only go out of prison an innocent man, with no lurking doubts. My father would turn in his grave. He'd never have accepted anything less than complete vindication and most importantly he would never forgive me. My father died hoping that his death would be the key to opening the case and our names being cleared. He died hoping to prove our innocence and if need be I'll stay in prison till I die unless they admit we are innocent.' Gerry was relieved that the news given to him by his visitor had been wrong and that Paul Hill was not going to accept a pardon.

I admired Gerry Conlon's passion and determination but knew that his only hope of achieving his goals was through a good solicitor. I had a battle with him to get him to instruct someone of on my list. In January 1987 he wrote to me again saying:

> You seem very concerned about the decisions that I will have to make regarding the legal representation that I will have to get sooner or later. Please, dear Sister Sarah, tell me what you believe I should do about getting a solicitor, you obviously don't want me to be misrepresented ... Please give me what advice you can, also your own suggestions as a possible solicitor, I would be so grateful for your advice. I would hate to lose the case again ... I wish with all my heart that I could have you as my solicitor as I know no stone would be left unturned. I have the same faith in you that my dear father had. I know he was able to turn to you for comfort and advice and how much he respected your views.

I wrote back and tried to persuade him to take Gareth Peirce but he was stubborn. He wrote a sharp but good-humoured letter to me at the end of September 1987. He started by saying how surprised he was to hear from me after so long and goes on:

> I know you are a busy woman for sure, but I don't think you

stopped writing to me because you were too busy. Oh no, I think you stopped writing because of my refusing at the time to get a solicitor of your choice. I've no doubts that you have my best interests at heart and only want to help me as much as possible. So now that I've finally got a solicitor who you approve of, could you please answer me a question or two...Well, now that I've got that off my chest Sister Sarah, I must tell you that I'm very impressed by Gareth. I've only met her twice but she seems to be very interested in helping us and has certainly seems to know her job. I feel she is going to be a big help to us.

I had never stopped corresponding with Gerry Conlon, sending him the same cards and postal orders as the other prisoners. But lots of post goes missing and never get to prisoners!

IN DECEMBER 1987 I was asked by Mary Nelis, a prominent member of the Creggan community in Derry, if I would try to help two young boys who got into trouble. It was not serious and I felt they should have got bail at the very least. I went to the hearing in the magistrate's court and was impatient with the solicitor. He had no sureties lined up. Another solicitor whom I criticised retaliated by telling a prisoner that I had had a bust-up with him, that he was friendly with Cardinal Hume and he would get him to put the boot into me. I said, let him do his worst, I am doing nothing wrong.

When I get a call from a family distressed about one of their relatives, I always ask if they want me to find a solicitor. If they do, then I turn to my file of solicitors. Mike Fisher is one I'd ring often; throughout our association from 1973 he never let me down, not even when I called him at midnight.

I can think of one prisoner who might have been out years ago if he had had the right lawyer. The family had decided on a solicitor and were very stubborn about him. They told me who it was and I advised them against it, I suggested they get Brian Rose-Smyth as the solicitor and Rock Tansy or Mike Mansfield as the barrister. They would not change and he lost. I know of many examples like this. When things go very wrong they realise their mistake and appeal to Neil O'May, Mike Fisher, Brian Rose-Smyth or Gareth Peirce, expecting them to work miracles.

Another problem I have come across is that of prisoners who have retained solicitors who shelve cases, delay court action, or appeal, and even lie about registering their cases in Europe.

170

Sometimes I persuaded these prisoners to engage a solicitor from my list. A prisoner changing solicitors can often have difficulty retrieving his legal papers even though technically they are his property.

Some solicitors, unfortunately, have faith in the law and will not allow any publicity before the trial. I believe if people are innocent then the time to get them out is before the trial. After conviction a prisoner could wait seventeen years for freedom, as was the case with the Guildford Four and Birmingham Six.

Since people can be held for seven days in police stations under the PTA, it is imperative that an effective solicitor be available as soon as possible. The police know this and can make access to a good solicitor difficult at this crucial time. Irreparable damage can occur. Police sometimes make access to a good solicitor difficult by lying: they might say that the arrested person is not in the police station or that he or she has rejected the effective solicitor's offer of help. It may be discovered later that the person was advised by the police that they would be better off without a solicitor or that they would get out sooner if they did not have a certain solicitor. Suspects are often advised that solicitors will have a financial interest in keeping them in longer.

As already stated, not all solicitors are familiar with the workings of the PTA. I know some cases where they told suspects that under the PTA they have to talk – failing to warn them of their right to silence. I have also known situations where it was suggested to suspects that they talk 'off the record' and make 'admissions' or 'confessions'; they need never have made them and with good legal advice they wouldn't have made them. Gradually over the years I noticed a change in the attitude of the police towards the choice of solicitors. In the early days of the PTA I could contact a solicitor and send him to a police station. Later the police would only admit solicitors who had been requested by the suspect or his family. Now the request must come from the suspect himself. There have been people held under the PTA who have told me, after their release, that requesting certain lawyers is met with the response that merely by asking for someone who has successfully represented Irish people means that the suspect must belong to the IRA. This insinuation is intended to discourage suspects from requesting these good solicitors – a back-handed compliment to competent lawyers. Others have told me that they have told the police they wanted certain solicitors to represent them, only to be told by the police that they'd never heard of them. The same police station would tell me that the prisoner had not requested the services of that person.

It is ironic that I should have to help protect people from the law when the law itself should protect them. Finding the solicitors is the first step. If a case goes to court, the defendant needs an equally good barrister. I knew very little at the beginning but soon worked out that a barrister who is going to be any good to a defendant must have not only an excellent grounding in the law but must be a good advocate in court, present the legal argument well, cross-examine skilfully, sum up the case properly and have a positive rapport with the solicitor. Very few barristers excel in all areas, but the good ones excel in several. I'm sure there were others who would have been as good as those I came to respect and admire but, as with the solicitors, I recommended people I had tried and trusted. I was wary of those with too many strings to their bow – lectures, conferences, etc. I noticed they came to court tired or unprepared. Others would be so successful that they were overbooked and left cases to junior barristers. Some barristers were also affected by serious family problems. I feel these barristers should not take serious cases where people's lives are at stake. I have also seen clients who were left without their solicitors or barristers in court. The accused should never forget that the barristers and solicitors are their servants.

There were exceptions, people who would fight hard for their clients, even when the clients were not in the dock. I remember the day the Maguire Seven asked leave of the court to appeal their convictions. By this time Giuseppe Conlon was long dead, but the defence wished to appeal his conviction to clear his name. Giuseppe was the client not in the dock. Legally, dead people do not exist, so Giuseppe, being absent, could not appeal. Mr Butterfield, QC, argued for the prosecution that Giuseppe be denied the right to appeal, as the law prescribed. After part of Mr Butterfield's plea, the judge recessed briefly. I rushed from my seat to Mr Butterfield as he waited for the case to continue. 'Mr Butterfield,' I said, 'please don't oppose Giuseppe's appeal'. The prosecutor drew himself up and snapped, 'Point of law, point of law'. Undaunted, I continued, 'It may be a point of law to you, but it's a human being to me, and I promised that human being that I would clear his name'. At that moment the judges returned. Mr Butterfield resumed his prosecution of Giuseppe's appeal.

172

And then a wondrous thing happened. Just as he launched forth into his argument, one of the longest and loudest peals of thunder I have ever heard interrupted his speech. Patrick O'Connor, barrister for the deceased, remarked that perhaps the Almighty was speaking on Giuseppe's behalf. Maybe he was because Patrick O'Connor, won the right to appeal for Giuseppe.

In February 1988, just after the Birmingham Six had their appeal rejected, Gerry Conlon wrote to me saying:

> We are up against a powerful firm, the courts, the cops and the government, i.e. the Establishment ... we are not going to go away, we will clear our names and we will expose British justice for what it is – corrupt.

Gerry Conlon's words were very prophetic. After the release of the Guildford Four Lord 'Appalling Vista' Denning said, 'British justice is in ruins'.

Even in 1994, twenty years after the PTA became law, I am still coming across cases of people who had been ill-advised by their solicitors. These solicitors didn't know how the PTA worked. I remember the cases of two women who had relatives who were suspects. Neither women had any experience of the law, the police or solicitors. When they were arrested they were given duty solicitors who did not know the PTA and who advised them to answer the questions put to them. They did not know they had a right to silence and were not told of this by their solicitors. (The right to silence was not abolished until 1995.) They were held for seven days and both were manipulated into unwittingly giving answers that could be interpreted as incriminating them on a charge of withholding information. There was no other evidence against them. As a result they answered the police questions, refusing to speak about relatives the police wished to arrest or charge, and these refusals were the only evidence against them.

One was interrogated for two days and then became ill with an appendicitis and was taken to hospital for two days. She was immediately returned to custody and interrogated for a further five days. So distressed was she by this experience and the subsequent postponement of her trial that she attempted suicide. When her case came to trial she was acquitted. The other spent eighteen months on remand before she too was acquitted. During her remand her husband who was released from gaol on bail died of a heart attack. He too was awaiting trial for withholding information. The day before his trial was to be heard – by which time he was dead – the charges were dropped. Had these people been properly advised of their rights they would never have been charged.

12

JUDGES AND COURTS

There are a sort of men whose visages
Do cream and mantle like a standing pond,
And do a wilful stillness entertain,
With purpose to be adress'd in an opinion
Of wisdom, gravity, profound conceit,
As who should say, 'I am Sir Oracle,
And when I 'ope my lips, let no dog bark!'
THE MERCHANT OF VENICE. I. 1. 88–92

I spent many days accompanying families to courts and attending trials. Everything about the judicial process, starting with the walk along the street approaching the courthouse itself and ending with the behaviour of many of the judges, confirmed my suspicion that the British legal system was not what I believed it to be. Cases against Irish defendants are held amidst very heavy and ostentatious security. Even for cases in magistrates' courts roads are sealed off, there are van-loads of policemen and police marksmen on roofs of building. Having run the gauntlet of getting into the building, one faces the further humiliation of a thorough search in front of other people. Hundreds of families have to endure this. I used to dread it.

Sometimes fear got the better of me. It happened to me on one occasion when Tommy Quigley's mother was visiting him and tried to get a visit on the day of his court appearance. She was not allowed a visit. I tried to discourage her from going to the hearing itself because he'd only be up for a few minutes for his remand to be renewed. Without telling me she went alone. I never forgave myself for having that fear. She said it was all worth it, just to wave at him to let him know she was there. That was one time I failed a family.

Most families coming over for trials had never been inside a courtroom before, let alone been confronted by the intimidating security. I was surprised to find that the big cases are a spectator sport. Most of the Irish cases are heard at the Old Bailey. Often I've been there with a family. You queue outside the door to the public gallery and you look at the people in the queue and wonder what their interest is in these maximum security trials. At first I assumed they must be connected – family or police for example – but I found that for many people it's a hobby; they go there to watch trials. I think it's macabre. One gets to know the faces – it's always the same people. They probably thought I was like them! Once inside the police immediately search your bag, then starts the 130-step climb. There's no lift or if there is it is unavailable for visitors. Upstairs there's an area with screens. Women are searched one side, men on the other. The women are much slower although men have far more pockets than we do. They'd feel all around my veil and I remember one saying to me, 'I never thought I'd search a nun'. She must have been convent educated. Some are very nice, others paw you. The men get through quicker and get the best seats. If it's an Irish trial you get into the corridor and opposite the entrance to the public gallery. The next hurdle is the point where identification is required. A policeman sits at a table outside the court and asks for a driver's licence or an official document with your name and address on it. They write down your name and address in a big book and give you a number. Sometimes the next day they accept your number, sometimes they don't. They make a note of your connection to the trial and then you walk past another policeman standing at the door. Very often they would tie ribbon round the first three rows to cordon them off and people are forced to sit at the back, limiting both space and vision and the ability to hear – all in the name of security. The whole process, which is repeated every time you go in and out, is extremely distressing.

I often looked at the judges and thought of Solomon in all his wisdom having to decide which of the two women was the rightful mother of the child. Judges should, like Solomon, have wisdom and compassion. Theirs is a very difficult job. I believed them to be objective but I soon revised this idea after a trial or two when they seemed more in sympathy with the prosecution than the defence, treating the prosecution's case with care and respect and the defence with bias and prejudice. Even on occasion being rude to defence lawyers and barristers. I often wondered how the defence lawyers could endure this treatment. I sometimes thought that judges will have to face another judge at the end of their lives and account for their judgements here on earth. The one individual in a trial who cannot be hired or fired is the judge (or in an appeal the three judges). A judge is power personified and how a judge uses that authority can mean the difference between 'the thickets of the law' as refuge or trap.

The most infamous example of this judgemental bias came with Lord Denning's summing up in the appeal of the West Midlands police against the charges of assault brought against them by the Birmingham Six. I nearly know it off by heart:

> If the six men win, it will mean that the police were guilty of perjury, that they were guilty of violence and threats, that the confessions were involuntary and were improperly admitted in evidence and that the convictions were erroneous. That would mean the Home Secretary would either have to recommend they be pardoned or he would have to remit the case to the Court of Appeal. This is such an appalling vista that every sensible person in the land would say: it cannot be right that these actions should go any further.

These words testify to the judge's greater concern about results for government officials and police than for observance of law by all citizens. I might say here: 'I rest my case'.

I did not however rest my case then but went with Fr Faul to visit Brian Rose-Smyth and Rock Tansy, the lawyers dealing with the case Judge Denning dismissed with such drastic consequences for the six men. We were dumbfounded! This was such a set-back. It gave me a sense of hopelessness, if the police were found guilty it would be an appalling vista – in other words the police can never be charged and can do what they like with impunity.

I recall another extraordinary comment made by another judge, Lord Lane, who said in 1988 in the appeal hearing for Liam Quinn that although the police had broken every rule in the way they had identified the defendant (the only evidence in the case) he would uphold the conviction because they broke the rules outside the realm. The identification, crucial to the case, took place as the defendant stood between two prison officers in a Dublin courtroom. The rules had been broken. All suspects are entitled to a properly conducted identification parade. There was no such parade. Similarly the law says there should be no trial if there has been an unfair delay that prejudices the defendant. In Liam Quinn's case the British police delayed for six years before arresting him in the USA in the hope that he might have strayed into England meanwhile and it was thirteen years before he stood trial at the Old Bailey. Despite this fundamental flouting of the rules and conventions, Liam Quinn's appeal was not successful and he remains in gaol today, serving a life sentence.

This incident confirmed my feeling that Irish prisoners are more harshly treated and have suffered particularly from being given longer sentences than others accused of similar offences. Animal-rights activists who bomb facilities where experiments are conducted on animals often receive short or even suspended sentences and are given bail while awaiting trial. Political prisoners from other foreign countries who engage in violent crimes in Britain are often given shorter sentences and are allowed to serve them in open gaols. They also receive parole. Sentences of twenty-five to thirty-five years are usual for Irish prisoners, though Paul Kavanagh, Pat Magee and Tommy Quigley had their sentences of thirty-five years raised to fifty years by the Home Secretary.

On one very rare occasion the family of an Irish defendant and myself emerged from the Old Bailey smiling and laughing. An amazed policeman asked me if the prisoner had won his case and I replied that he had lost it but had received a sentence of only twenty years – much shorter than expected.

Judges in English courts are permitted to give opinions on crucial matters, something I regard as inappropriate. They use body language as well – huff, puff and roll the eyes during the defence summing up. It's reasonable to assume that juries are influenced by judges' behaviour.

I think that the judges' tendency to bias towards the prosecution, particularly in cases involving Irish political offences and black defendants, stem from their class background. The bar is a moneyed profession; there are no grants to study for it and most who do manage to fulfil the rigorous studies and pass the exams are financially supported through their studies by their families. This automatically excludes almost all working-class people, very few of whom make it to become barristers, let alone QCs. It remains an overwhelmingly white, upper middle-class preserve. Barristers have very little contact with ordinary people, and tend to become pompous and arrogant.

I observed Ivor Judge, leading crown counsel in the Birmingham Six appeal, in action. When Mr Baldock [the scientist who contested the original forensic evidence for Granada Television] was back on the witness stand for the defence he was attacked by Ivor Judge QC and by the judges. It was appalling. Mike Mansfield [defence barrister] was furious. Then the judge told him it was up to the court, not him, to say what was to be done. Sparks really were flying.

Lord Gifford [defence barrister] asked to call a new witness. The witness was a taxi driver who spoke to a policeman on the night the Birmingham Six were arrested. He said when the six were sent to Winson Green gaol the officers would beat them up and that would cover the bruises they received from the police. The judges would not allow the witness to be called.

The defence had, as the court knew, been scrupulous in following the letter of the law in summoning this witness. The defence lawyer went first to the Irish police to report that he believed he had relevant evidence. The Irish police notified the British authorities but there was a delay of three weeks before the defence was informed – by this time it was the middle of the appeal hearing. By 3 December 1987 Chris Mullin knew the men would lose the appeal. He said to me, 'Now everything is down on record and we can go international'.

Every suspicion and criticism I had of the bias and prejudice of judges in English courts when faced with Irish defendants in political trials was confirmed during the judges' summing up at the Birmingham Six appeal. Lord Lane began the summing up and before long we all knew there was no hope for the men. It became a nightmare to listen as Judge Brown and then Judge O'Connor dismissed the evidence. The harsh judgement was read out in an equally harsh voice. Mike Mansfield was livid. The hardest thing of all was the justification of the evidence of Dr Skuse. [The prosecution scientist on whose nitroglycerine tests the original convictions depended and whose evidence was later proved to be extremely unreliable.]

These three judges presided over a cruel injustice and it must have haunted them in March 1991 when the Six were at last declared innocent.

Fr Patrick Hannon, an Irish barrister and professor, asked in an article in *The Furrow*:

Were the judges biased? Not wittingly, not with malice; but yet inevitably. A man who is driven to his work is not likely to know how natural it is to change your mind about a departure time if your purposes are as well served by a later train. An Englishman, even if

Catholic, is probably unable to see the outright ineptitude of the suggestion to an Irishman that money collected with the aim of travelling to a funeral ought instead to be given to the widow. And in Ireland you can go to a funeral without thereby endorsing all or any of the beliefs of the deceased.

Judges could also be affected by the social standing of visitors in the public gallery. I attended the appeal of three Irish prisoners at which many TDs and senators were present. On this occasion the judges were friendlier to the defence than any judge had been in any of the other Irish cases I attended. They were catering for class bonds, they were snobs. It reminds me again of what Jesus said about the least of our brothers and sisters: 'As long as you do it for one of these, the least of my brethren, you do it to me'.

The establishment and its agents, such as judges and barristers, seems to have even less understanding of black people and their culture. There are many black people in gaol waiting-rooms and in the courts. The Irish and black people are a minority in the community but a disproportionately high number in gaol waiting-rooms. Surely they do not have a monopoly on violence! It's just prejudice. It seems as far as many judges are concerned that they have even less understanding of black people than they do of Irish people.

Besides the right to freedom and justice, accused and convicted people who are subsequently proved innocent have a right to their good name. Although all seventeen of the Birmingham Six, Guildford Four and Maguires are now out of gaol, they do not all enjoy freedom from suspicion. The judiciary has not acquitted itself with the dignity expected of its profession in this context. Even after the seventeen had been released and their convictions quashed, some of its leading names were casting doubt on the latterly proved innocence of all concerned. No apology was given to any of the defendants.

The May Enquiry was set up on 26 October 1989 one week after the quashing of the Guildford Four convictions. The enquiry's task was to look into the circumstances surrounding the convictions of the Guildford Four and Maguire Seven. May's final report came into public circulation on 1 July 1994. I spent a lot of time at the enquiry. There was an extraordinary moment on 23 May 1990 when I was approached by the former government scientist Douglas Higgs. Mr Higgs was head of the Royal Armaments Research and Development Establishment (RARDE) at the time of Judith Ward's arrest in 1974. It was Mr Higgs who said traces of nitroglycerine had been found in her caravan. Along with two other scientists from RARDE he was accused at Judith Ward's appeal of being 'economical' in his statement and misleading prosecution counsel. But it was the judges who levelled the most stinging criticism at the three scientists:

> They took the law into their own hands and concealed from the prosecution the defence and the court matters which might have changed the course of the trial.

This evidence had knock-on effects on the trials of the Birmingham Six and the Maguire Seven.

At the lunch-break Mr Higgs, who had been giving evidence, at the May Enquiry, came over to me to ask why I was taking copious notes. He said he was a seventy-year-old and a Catholic. He wanted to know what connection I had with the case and I told him. He said of course as a scientist he was neutral.

He was bluffing at the May Enquiry, spouting out chemical formulae, and yet he was the one who said that only nitroglycerine would give the results that were used as proof both in the Judith Ward trial, the Maguire trial and the Birmingham Six trial. It came out eventually that for the Judith Ward he had done tests which showed that other substances could produce the same results!

I met him again at the Courts of Appeal during the Maguire appeal. At first I didn't see who it was and then I said, 'Is that Mr Higgs?' He said he thought I wasn't going to speak to him. I told him that I just hadn't recognised him at first because of my deteriorating eyesight. I was with Sarah Conlon and she shook hands with him. He said he had felt so guilty about what happened he had not been to Communion. I thought of all Sarah had been through and yet she shook his hand. He was the one that had been so important in the evidence against Giuseppe! It was extraordinary – the whole cycle of events. I thought the wrath of the establishment would fall on Mr Higgs because of what he had done – but nothing happened. The thickets of the law effectively protected Mr Higgs.

The May Enquiry settled nothing. It stretched over four years and was a waste of time and public money. The convictions were eventually quashed, but they are all flawed with the judgement which found only that the convictions might not have been proved beyond reasonable doubt. Annie Maguire invited me to the pub to celebrate, but I declined. Sarah Conlon, Giuseppe's widow, had little, if anything, to celebrate either.

As far as I was concerned the first real moment of celebration came in June 1992 at Judith Ward's appeal and vindication. The Ward appeal proved at long last that scientists had been lying to the courts since Judith Ward's original trial in 1974 by saying that only nitroglycerine reacted to the thin layer chromatography test, the test that was responsible for an unknown number of sentences but certainly more than twenty. At last there was evidence in court that proved that tests conducted before Judith Ward's original trial had shown that other substances, such as shoe polish and cigarettes, produce the same results as nitroglycerine. The judges had never used such strong condemnation. They strongly condemned the scientists and the Director of Public Prosecutions. Judith Ward, it must be remembered, is an Englishwoman. Nevertheless the scientists, the police, the representatives of the Director of Public Prosecutions and the prosecution barristers who were exposed by the Ward appeal, were never punished for violations of law. What good can even the most excellent lawyers do when they are up against the fabrications of the combined forces of the prosecution, the scientists employed by them and the police? How can the public trust the police and their witnesses or juries believe them ever again? Though these same courts cleared Giuseppe Conlon's name, they smeared it in the process.

The 1993 acquittal of all the police officers accused of assault in the Guildford Four arrests is a case in point. This acquittal seemed to imply that, although the Guildford convictions had been quashed, perhaps, since the police had been declared innocent of assault, the four really were guilty and their forced confessions valid. Thus began a whispering campaign that continues in some circles and causes the cloud still hovering over their reputations.

ON 13 FEBRUARY 1992 THE jury was out discussing the verdict in the trial of William, an Irish defendant, charged with conspiracy to cause explosions. The members had been out for a day and a night. The second day they were in discussion until midday when the judge called for them and gave them a majority direction of ten to two. They sent a message out to the judge at about 2.15 saying they were split and couldn't resolve the situation to achieve the majority as directed. They asked the judge if he would accept less. He refused. They went back out. When the jury goes out the court is cleared until the jury returns. I was with Siobhán, William's wife, and I had given relics of Padre Pio to Helena Kennedy, QC, who was William's barrister, to put in her pocket. There were about ten of us in the seating area all with our faces to the wall praying fervently. I'm sure the police thought we were crazy. Siobhán had a rosary blessed by Padre Pio and we passed it along the line and each said a rosary on it. When the jury had not reached a verdict the judge suggested that it return and he would disband the members with a view to calling a re-trial. Helena Kennedy begged for more time, saying the trial had lasted several weeks and the jury should be given longer. The judge told the jury it had until 4.00 p.m. We went back to our praying positions. Four o'clock came and we went into the court. When asked if they had reached a verdict, the foreman said, yes. The defendant was found not guilty on all counts.

I remember the excitement and relief that swept through the public gallery after the weeks of tension and the hours waiting for the jury to come back. After that we all went back to my flat and celebrated with champagne – such victories were so rare. I said to Helena, 'Don't imagine it was you that won the case – it was thanks to Padre Pio!'

When Sir James Miskin, the senior judge at the Old Bailey, retired he gave a press conference and television interview in which he spoke of the release of the Guildford Four on a technicality, suggesting that they were guilty. He said their release had been a 'mad decision'. It was only the threat of a libel action, which caused him to retract this statement. Similarly, Lord Denning said that if the Birmingham Six had all been hanged, there wouldn't have been all this fuss afterward. When asked by a television journalist what he should do in response to a prisoner's claim of innocence, he replied, 'Oh walk away and ignore him. I have a lot of letters from people in prison who say they have been wrongly convicted'. Lord Donaldson, the trial judge of the Guildford defendants, received great prominence in The Mail on Sunday, when he suggested that it would be better to have a verdict of 'not proven'. This would link the verdict with the Home Secretary's references to the Court of Appeal, suggesting that those who are acquitted are not always innocent.

Neil Butterfield, QC, told the May Enquiry that the reputations of many professional people were at stake, indicating, I think, a greater concern for their status than for justice, truth and the good name of every citizen, regardless of class or status.

Paul Hill successfully appealed against his conviction in the Brian Shaw murder case in 1994. Until then, the wrong-doing by police had not been publicly exposed in the case of the Guildford Four either in the Appeal Court or the May Enquiry. Paul Hill's defence presented evidence, at the Shaw appeal, that police officers had performed a mock execution and off-the-record interviews in police stations. Defence counsel also cited documents proving police interference with interviews.

My old friend and tutor from Chelsea Art School Mr Edward Wright designed the mobile sculpture that is still outside Scotland Yard. Mr Wright explained the significance of its symbolism to me. It is made of stainless steel and rotates so that it symbolises alertness, stainlessness, brightness suggesting that the police should be like that – blameless, alert and always moving to meet the needs of justice. Of course we need a police force but they should live up to the ideals Edward Wright had in mind.

13

PRISONERS

Until all are free, we are all imprisoned.

GRAFFITO

I have communicated with hundreds of prisoners and their families since beginning my work in the early 1970s. Even now, blind, frail and unwell, I use the last glimmer of my sight to squint through an extremely strong magnifying glass making out the addresses of the prisoners on my list and sending them all cards and postal orders for Christmas, St Patrick's Day, Easter, birthdays. Their families still come and stay with me. Former prisoners visit me regularly in my North London flat and I still keep in contact with several prisoners who have been transferred to Ireland.

Gaol conditions were appalling in the 1970s – prisoners were moved around the country to make it difficult for the families to visit – and visits were behind glass with warders writing down everything said. Visits were cut short for no reason – some people were told visits would be terminated if 'English' was not spoken [because the warders did not understand the Irish accents]. The ways of breaking sad news were sometimes inhuman. Prisoners were sometimes denied medical treatment and held for long periods in solitary confinement. Families and visitors were insulted and were subjected sometimes to strip-searches and, occasionally, body searches. Prisoners are allowed visits only from people who knew them before they were convicted, etc.

Bit by bit Kate Akaster and Edward FitzGerald, QC, chipped away at the prison rules – going to Europe and the UN – until the harshest restrictions were lifted.

However in the 1990s government policy reverted to the severe régime and conditions – visits behind glass, hand-cuffing, being chained, etc. – are as bad as in the 1970s.

Irish political prisoners are serving very long sentences and are denied parole. The harsh conditions are aimed at breaking the prisoners' spirit – but political prisoners expect very little from the system and they are never disappointed.

The first prisoners I met, some of the only ones I was ever permitted to visit, were the Old Bailey defendants. It was a rude and brutal baptism for me as I embarked on what became my life's work. I have kept in touch with several of them since they were arrested in 1973.

On 3 December 1973 Gerry Kelly, during his hunger-strike, wrote:

> My ninetieth day of hunger-strike. Well, they force-fed me today, I barricaded myself in but they just used a scaffolding extension leg to open the door. When the screws and medical officers surrounded my bed, I knew it was futile to struggle but I resisted as best I could. My head was held back by the hair ... and about six to eight men helped hold me. One held my arm in a wrist lock and didn't ease any of the pressure the whole time. They forced a clamp into my mouth and then the rubber tube. I can still taste it, and it was quite sickening. My throat is still sore. Something looking like milk was poured down, but I brought a lot of it up again. The way it is done is pretty brutal and very degrading especially since I was struggling naked in front of female nurses. I was feeling pretty sorry for myself just after it was over and truthfully nearly crying ...

Gerry Kelly, Hugh Feeney and Marian and Dolours Price survived. One who did not was Frank Stagg who died in Wakefield gaol on 12 February 1976 – on hunger-strike because he was protesting against the Home Office's refusal to transfer Irish prisoners back to Northern Ireland. Frank Stagg suffered terribly, not only was he suffering all a prisoner does on hunger-strike, but he was denied the last sacraments as he lay dying. Frank Stagg's sister visited him in Wakefield. She was shocked at his appearance and phoned me to say she was eager to get him the last sacraments but she was refused. She asked me could I help. I was afraid to ring the bishop so I rang Mr Micklewright, a fighter for justice – I met him in the early 1970s during civil rights efforts and he continued to support my work for prisoners.

Amphlett Micklewright, a lawyer and former Anglican clergyman, was very interested in Irish affairs and worked with us on the RFPC. I remember Mr Micklewright told me to ring Dr Wheeler, the Bishop of Leeds, but he was away. I asked to speak to whoever replaced him and I rang him. I told him my name convent, etc. and I also said I was a friend of the Stagg family and we were worrying about him not getting the last sacraments. He said that he had his eye on Wakefield and was quite abrupt. He put the phone down on me.

Mr Micklewright rang me to see how I had got on. He then rang and I recorded Mr Mickelwright's account of the conversation he had with this bishop:

X: Why am I being tormented over this Frank Stagg?
Mr Micklewright: He is dying and happens to be in your spiritual care.
X: He is only a bus driver from Coventry.
Mr Micklewright: Jesus Christ was only a carpenter from Nazareth.
X: Are you a member of a terrorist organisation?
Mr Micklewright: I am only a member of the Bar.

He became more civil and Mr Micklewright went into the theological aspect of the hunger-strike and the sacraments and threatened to publish this in the *Yorkshire Times*. He asked if he could tell the press that he had spoken to a person of responsibility in the Church and that he had promised that Frank Stagg would receive the last sacraments. This was agreed and he said he would see to it himself. Next day Frank Stagg was anointed.

I was a bit upset about that conversation. I was afraid that Mr Micklewright would think terrible things about the Catholic Church and I used to pray about it. My prayers were answered as some months later Mr Micklewright rang to say he was receiving instruction in the Catholic faith. He was eventually received into the Church but he was more useful to me as a Socialist! The Church would listen to him quicker! Dr Micklewright died on 14 January 1992 and I attended his funeral. By 1992 I was no longer driving a car because of serious eye problems. The journey to Dr Micklewright's funeral was not an easy one, but fidelity to friends is very important to me.

IN 1987 I WENT TO see Gerry Kelly who by then was in Belfast's Crumlin Road gaol. He had escaped from gaol and been recaptured in Holland from where he was extradited back to Ireland. That wasn't Gerry Kelly's only escape – he had broken out from St Patrick's, Belfast, and Mountjoy, Dublin and attempted escapes from Wormwood Scrubs, Long Kesh and Musgrave Military Hospital as well as the big successful escape from Long Kesh. Such strength of spirit may amaze most people, but I was not the least bit surprised by Gerry's tenacity.

On the day of my visit to Gerry Kelly, Sarah Feeney and I left for Crumlin Road gaol after breakfast. It was a dull day and inclined to drizzle. We queued and queued and paid in £5 for Gerry. The gaol is medieval. The searchers were very polite, asked me if they could search me, tied my shoes after the search, etc. The waiting-room was like something from the seventeenth century. When we eventually got to Gerry he was delighted to see us. He 'loved' the Dutch gaols and the Dutch prison officers were wonderful. He had television and electrical switches in his cell. No bars on the windows – but he was fourteen floors up. He was interesting, and the half hour was too short.

Besides keeping a positive attitude Irish prisoners used their gaol time to pursue education when opportunities became available in the 1980s. The great irony is that after Gerry Kelly's release, in spite of or perhaps because of all that he had experienced, he should have been involved in the early stages of the secret peace talks between Sinn Féin and the British government.

I have gone to Long Kesh gaol in the company of many families visiting their relatives. It was never a pleasant experience: – into a waiting-room which was usually quite full. After about fifteen minutes wait we were usually called and would enter the steel van – like a mobile room. There were no windows, no door handles – and yellow plastic chairs. We then started on a very bumpy ride, shaking and swaying and then the horn would hoot and we would stop. There would be a long delay during which we would hear voices outside. On again, stopping again. More talking. The van door would open and a prison officer enter to count us. The door would close again. Again bumping and bouncing. Then another halt. Doors would open and we would go through two or three gates, with plenty of prison officers around. We would get to a hut that is a waiting-room, full of wives, mothers and children. And after about twenty minutes we would finally be called for the visit.

SOON AFTER THE REMANDING OF the Old Bailey defendants, I found that I was being forbidden to visit Irish political prisoners or even correspond with them. Although I have always worked with any prisoner who needed my help, I have worked mainly with

Republican prisoners because they are the ones whose families are most abused, harassed and frightened. What has always been clear to me is that most English people do not realise that none of the Irish political prisoners and their families whom I have helped would have set foot in police stations let alone courtrooms or gaols if political freedom and equality had existed in the six counties. This does not mean my work was political; far from it, it has always been Christian and humanitarian. If the political situation in the six counties were just and democratic, there would have been no need for my prison ministry in the first place.

Shortly after Prime Minister Jim Callaghan sent British troops into Ireland in August 1969 as peace-keepers, Dr Patrick J. Hillery, Minister for Foreign Affairs, explained the real cause of Ireland's problems to the United Nations Security Council:

> Partition was accomplished by the British government as a concession to an intransigent minority within the Irish nation. Ireland was divided as a result of an act of the British parliament in 1920, an act in favour of which not one Irish vote, either north or south, was cast.

To understand my work with families and prisoners, people require some understanding of the situations that generated the problems. The Irish prisoners I helped, both Loyalist and Republican, were in gaol because of political upheavals not of their making. It's dreadful to see the sorrow, wave after wave of sorrow.

I was always happy to visit prisoners but the authorities would not let me. I have a file full of refusals from the Home Office explaining in the cold language of officialdom that nobody may visit Category A prisoners who is not either a family member, or whose friendship began after the date of imprisonment. This ruling was changed in the mid-1980s with some people allowed to visit prisoners – but not I! All Irish political prisoners have been Category A. Their visitors must be vetted and approved but exceptions can be made when the governor or chaplain of a gaol think it 'necessary or desirable'. Such exceptions have only been made for me twice that I can recall – once when Giuseppe Conlon was dying and a second time in 1995 when the prisoners were refusing to take visits because they were again forced to take them behind glass [closed visits]. It has crossed my

189

mind that perhaps the prison chaplains themselves were not happy with having me in as a visitor. The problems I experienced with prison chaplains and the Irish Chaplaincy are much harder to understand than the obstructiveness of state authorities who perceived themselves as embattled and acted accordingly in ways that were not pleasant. The obstructiveness of the chaplains shocked and surprised me. I could not work out whether I represented a threat to their control of all matters religious within the gaols or whether the difficulties they caused me stemmed from the Catholic tradition of male authority and female subservience.

MY EXPERIENCES AT BRIXTON GAOL were always problematic. When I cooked a meal for Ronan Bennett and went to Brixton with it the prison officer at the food counter was very nice to me. When I turned to go up to the visiting-room, I was confronted by a huge senior prison officer covered in gold braid who said that I could not have a visit with Ronan Bennett. I asked why and he said he was not allowed to tell me why. I asked if Ronan was punished and he repeated that he was not allowed to tell me. I left. Two days later I rang a friend of Ronan's who told me that Ronan had wondered why I had not visited him when I brought the dinner, as he was expecting me. No explanation was ever given. This was the way prisoners and their families were treated, and this is a mild example.

I had heard about Ronan Bennett being on remand in Brixton from his mother. My first visit with him was on 27 February 1979 and I liked Ronan immediately I met him. He was easy to talk to and remains a friend to this day. When I first went, he couldn't understand why a nun had come to see him. One day when I went to see him he was behind glass – I don't know why. Another sister, Sr Emmanuel, had come with me and she was very shocked. She thought it very cruel and when she saw young Ronan like that it made her think of a caged bird and she wept. He spent twenty months on remand. When the case came to court he and his co-defendants were found not guilty of the conspiracy charges. I went to Ronan's trial in November 1979 during which he defended himself. He spoke long and in detail. At about 11.30 the judge said something about a break and Ronan said he did not need a break but would the judge like one. Of all the prisoners I've known he is the one most regularly in touch. He has achieved great things since his release from gaol and is still very loyal to the other prisoners. In 1984 he climbed the spire of St Mary Le Strand in London with a banner. Some of his friends in the six counties had been held on remand for three years on the word of an informer. He too had been imprisoned in Long Kesh and was released after the Court of Appeal had quashed the convictions against him in 1975. Ronan is a writer now. He has written novels and film scripts and items for radio and the newspapers.

It was not only gaol visits that were difficult. Letters were often returned unopened to the sender as I was to experience for myself. After a number of cases were taken both to courts in England and to the European Court of Human Rights, the prisoners' rights regarding correspondence improved. For years the prison authorities had been able to withhold any letter they took objection to whether from a prisoner writing to someone outside or vice versa. I have a copy of a letter I wrote to Paul Holmes in 1973 sent back to me with this explanation:

> I enclose a letter from you addressed to Mr Paul Holmes which was opened in the course of routine censorship.
>
> Convicted prisoners in this prison may write three letters a week to relatives and friends known to them before they came into custody, and may receive a reply to each letter they send out. Letters received in excess of this number or written by persons who are not relatives or friends as described above, must be returned to the sender unless there are grounds for exceptional treatment, e.g., if a prisoner is not using his full allowance of letters.
>
> Mr Paul Holmes is taking up his full allowance, and so far as I can ascertain you are not a relative and were not personally known to him before he came into custody. I am afraid that I must therefore return this letter.

This kind of censorship continued until 1983. The change had a knock-on effect on all prisoners and I found found that the prisoners could again correspond with me.

For all the years of the war in Ireland, people supporting the prisoners and their families have been seen as pariahs by certain sections of society and by those in authority. A sinister atmosphere was engendered by covert actions by police and intelligence services. On 19 January 1980 I was trying to help a young man who had been arrested and I rang my local MP Jock Stallard. This young man had been released from gaol and was re-arrested by the police inside the gaol as he was coming out. His sister and I were waiting for him but he was driven away between two policemen. The gaol officials and the police said they didn't know where he was. Jock Stallard said that he did not want to have a conversation on a tapped phone. It is sad that one cannot discuss the rights of individuals on the phone. I had Charles Haughey's private number so I rang him and then things started to happen. We soon found out where he was being held. They tried to make him join the IRA and become an informer. He said he had never been a member of the IRA and refused.

My life was touched by sinister events many times. An example that springs to mind was something that happened in 1980. Little did I know that because I had taken a weekly parcel to Gerry Tuite in Brixton gaol, I would end up being an object of interest to the Special Branch. On 16 December I prepared Gerry Tuite's meal and was driving to Brixton gaol when I heard over the car radio that he and two other non-Irish high security prisoners had escaped. I turned at the first opportunity and took the parcel back to the convent. The authorities launched a massive effort to recapture the prisoners. Two days later the police called on me. I was unwell at the time and waiting to go into hospital with TB. Sr Rita, the superior, came in to say that two policemen were there. She said they were very nice. I went in to the two 'nice' gentlemen. I told them I brought parcels to Gerry Tuite. They knew that I did not visit him. I told them I looked after Gerry's mother when she was in London. When the policemen told me that the three escapees had used tools to make holes in cell walls to facilitate their escape I reminded my visitors that tools would not fit into a dinner and that besides the food was all chopped up by the warders before it got to the prisoners. Apparently the other two Category A prisoners with whom Gerry Tuite had escaped were not under the same close surveillance as Irish prisoners. The police accepted my explanation but I had a feeling that I would see these policemen again somehow.

Five days later, in the afternoon, police surrounded the convent. I thought they were coming to take me away but they said they were chasing a burglar who jumped over our wall. Maybe it was a dress rehearsal. Fortunately, all the other nuns were away.

I was stopped by policemen on several occasions for very flimsy reasons and my car was searched. These events may sound minor but I had every reason to be genuinely afraid that the police would find some way of linking me with Gerry's escape. I had seen too many people convicted on fabricated evidence and I knew that my status as a nun did not necessarily provide protection. My harassment was minimal compared to what prisoners and their families went through. One who lived in fear, having served his time, went to university in London but it was almost impossible to get on with his studies as within a few weeks he had been attacked half a dozen times near the university. He also received death threats over the telephone and had no choice but to hide away in his flat. I think it was organised by the Special Branch; they used to follow him everywhere. This man became a good friend and, after the party thrown for me by Helena Kennedy on 17 September 1989 to celebrate my golden jubilee as a nun, it was the solicitor Mike Fisher and this former prisoner who took me home and stayed talking late into the night.

Over the years I have received hundreds of visiting orders from prisoners asking me come in and see them but almost every one of those VOs was rejected by the authorities. The Home Office has often explained this away as being a routine security measure but it is one that has never extended to the gaols of Northern Ireland. Other people, even members of left wing political groups and parties have been allowed in on compassionate grounds, and other members of the Church have been permitted to make visits on the grounds of pastoral care. For years I suspected they considered me a security risk and then I got the proof. The process of getting in to visit a prisoner begins with the VO sent out by the prisoner. One then has to fill in a form and enclose two snapshots of yourself which are then returned to the gaol and vetted by the Home Office. I have a file full of rejections. One day a prisoner wrote to me asking me to visit and I wrote back saying I would be refused but to send me the VO as I was collecting the rejection letters. The authorities stopped sending me the forms after that! Then in 1985 a Category A prisoner in Long Lartin gaol who had asked for me to be on his visitors' list got hold of a document from a junior Home Office minister. It said, 'The Home Secretary has fully considered your petition. The decision not to allow Sister Sarah Clarke to become an approved visitor was on the grounds of security. The Secretary of State is not prepared to give detailed reasons for the decision.'

Nor was any reason given when Paul Hill invited me to his

wedding in February 1988 in Long Lartin to Marion Serravalli. Others were allowed in – amongst them Jeremy Corbyn and John McDonnell – but not me. I was the only one excluded. The names had to be approved by the Home Office. I wonder if it was because I had persisted in highlighting miscarriages of justice down through the years. In his book *Stolen Years* Paul Hill records:

> I had to submit to the Home Office the names of the guests for vetting. Among those I wanted to invite was Sister Sarah Clarke, the Irish nun who had worked so hard for us. The Home Office refused to approve her for unexplained 'security reasons'.

When Jeremy Corbyn put a parliamentary question to Douglas Hogg on 15 February 1988 as to why I was not allowed to go to the wedding, the reply stated that I was not on the approved list of visitors for Paul Hill. Nor were some of the other people who were permitted to go to the wedding!

I was in the Strangers' Gallery at the House of Commons with Gareth Peirce late at night on 16 June 1988. We had gone there for the launch of Clare Short's 'Time To Go' initiative and later went to listen to a debate on the Criminal Justice Bill, when much to my surprise my name cropped up. At about ten Sir John Farr introduced his amendment and quoted the Luton, Guildford and Birmingham cases. Then Roy Hattersley and Clare Short joined in. Merlyn Rees spoke about the Guildford Four then Chris Mullin spoke for one hour about the Birmingham Six and Guildford Four. After 11.20p.m. I began to wonder would I miss the last bus but Gareth said she had the car. I heard Jeremy Corbyn asking the minister (Chris Patten) as he was speaking if he knew that Billy Armstrong had a nervous breakdown, that Paul Hill had been moved forty-four times from prison to prison, that Gerry Conlon was in solitary confinement in Full Sutton (which he wasn't) and that Carol Richardson was under heavy sedation and not allowed visitors. Then to my complete surprise he asked why it was that Sr Sarah, a Catholic nun, was not allowed to visit these prisoners on purely humanitarian grounds? It was so strange that I was actually there to hear it. The question about me was not answered by the minister.

Apart from my regular brushes with prison officers, I have had little direct contact with the forces of law and order, something I regard as a merciful escape. I might have been a bit scared a few times but it was nothing when you think of what prisoners and their families were going through. Imagine what the women were suffering in the gaols. Strip-searching was used against prisoners and families on a regular basis.

Between 1982 and 1985 the women in Armagh gaol, particularly the Nationalists, were strip-searched, according to one survey, thirty times each. Many were strip-searched not only before and after court appearances and visits, but randomly, a tactic brought in, it was claimed in the House of Commons, after two keys were found in the possession of remand prisoners. But the use of strip-searching was not confined to Northern Irish gaols as a letter from Martina Anderson makes clear. She and her co-defendant Ella O'Dwyer were strip-searched hundreds of times during their period of remand. Martina Anderson wrote to me in November 1985 from Brixton gaol:

> As for strip-searches they are still continuing regularly, sometimes up to three a day. It used to be we would have had four on a Thursday but our solicitor got the two stopped at the court. Needless to say the police denied giving us any! Suppose they will say the same about the five we were given at [the police] station, three on Saturday and two on Sunday and not one of them carried out in a dignified manner, in fact the one I got after refusing to put my pants right down, I got dressed and then a plain clothes policeman came into the cell and threatened to pull the clothes off me. He did the same to Ella when she was first stripped.

Out of the blue and for no apparent reason in the 1980s I got a letter from the authorities saying I was cleared to visit Paul Norney in Wormwood Scrubs. I couldn't believe it. I was sitting in my room looking at the letter, about to ring the gaol to check up on this when the phone rang. It was the prison chaplain and he had rung to tell me it was a mistake, that I wasn't cleared.

In spite of the confusion or perhaps because of it, I was again visited by the police. On 9 February 1990 they arrived at 3.30 p.m. and started not just simple questions but a form of interrogation. They asked me all about the Walsh family. Why I was applying after seventeen years to visit Roy? Why I was stopped from visiting? Had I identification as to who I was? I showed them an old driving licence and said I had not renewed it. They asked me if I still drove, if I lived alone. Did I keep people? I asked them why they asked so many questions. They replied that they wanted a fuller record. Then they asked for LSU Croft Lodge address and I gave them Mother Provincial's name as well. I rang her when they left and she said not to worry.

I rang the Home Office regularly to remind them that I was not a security risk and that I had never done anything to warrant their suspicion. Once a Home Office official, I can't remember who, told me to try again. I got in touch with Roy Walsh who was then still in gaol and went through the motions yet again. I rang the Home Office to find out about it just before Christmas, and to my shock they said I'd been cleared. I was delighted and after Christmas rang Gartree to ask them to get a message to Roy to send out a VO. But then the security people at Gartree said I was not cleared! I rang the Home Office and got a young woman who said my request had gone upstairs, whatever that meant. She told me to ring back in a week. When I did she said 'You're not cleared'. I asked her what it said on the file and she told me it said I was a security risk.

AMONGST THE MANY I helped was a man (whose family were from Armagh) that Fr Murray had asked me to visit. His family came over and I looked after them. I didn't ask why he was in gaol because I never do and his mother asked if I would go and visit him after they had gone. I said of course I would. He wasn't Category A so there was no problem. I'd take a parcel up to him and visit him but he used to disturb me by describing the murder he'd committed. He killed a homosexual and he gave lurid descriptions of this terrible murder telling the people on either side of where we were sitting. I didn't like it but I wasn't there to preach to people but to pray for them and to worry about them. When they moved him from Brixton to Wakefield he was always writing to me asking for things – saucepans, watches, holy pictures! I thought he had no one else but then I found out he had visits from priests and other nuns and was giving them lists of things he wanted!

In visitors' queues I met many different people. I got to know Sonia Sutcliffe through staying in the visitors' hostel in Parkhurst on the Isle of Wight. People in her situation want to talk to somebody. She didn't want to talk about the case so we talked about other things. I have stood in line with members of the Kray family and the families of Chinese Triads. On a visit to Annie Maguire in Cookham Wood, the women's gaol in Essex, I reconised a woman at a nearby table as Myra Hindley. Sometimes I met people who seemed richer than others. A woman in mink smiled wanly at me one day and remarked that she had never expected to be in such a queue but her son had become involved in drugs. I wanted to console her and said the real offenders were the drug pushers. The woman replied sadly, 'My son was a drug pusher'. She had French books for her son who was at university but they told her she couldn't hand in French books. I had the same trouble with some Irish language books. The authorities said they were political and stopped them going in.

On 25 April 1980 I was in the tea-room outside the gate at Brixton gaol. There was a woman weeping there. I spoke to her – she was an ex-nun and she was weeping because her husband was in gaol for shoplifting. I took her with me and found she had no home. She asked me to take her to Euston Station. Another who often approached me in the queue was, I think, a lawyer acting for an man who had allegedly injected a Nigerian politician to knock him out and then put him in a crate. I'm not sure who the man was, possibly the family's lawyer. He always spoke to me, often about Mass and religious things.

I became friendly with Sheila Heather-Hayes, the mother of a young prisoner in Ashford, a remand gaol in Middlesex where I went to see young people when their families asked me to visit. Sheila's son Jim was only eighteen. At that time the gaol had a bad reputation because of the number of young people who committed suicide there. Sheila's son killed himself. It was heartbreaking. She sent me a little book she had made of poems he had written, and this is one of them:

> Hanging from the rafters on a greasy rope,
> When they read your note they said he couldn't cope.
> Life ain't a game, they reckon, for the weak,
> Corpse on a rope, 'twas just another freak.
> You might have been a Hitler, you might have caused a war,
> Or just another nobody, priest or whore.
> You wouldn't take the chance, didn't have no hope,
> You're hanging from the rafters on a greasy rope.

In March 1983 I made two visits to Ashford gaol to see two young Irish boys, whom I will call Michael and Robert. They were held there on remand for a minor offence. On 27 April 1983 Michael had gone to court and got two years. We saw Robert with a prison officer beside him who kept butting in to our conversation. Robert said he was punished for staying too long in the shower. The prison officer said that was not true – he was punished for having to be told twice to get out of the shower. The punishment was that he had his radio removed for three days, pay lost for three days, put in solitary – terrible punishment for such a minor offence. All I could do was try to cheer him up.

My contact with some prisoners went on after their release; sometimes because they were harassed by the police even after serving their time. One such was a man I will call John, a burglar who had served several periods of imprisonment. John frequently called to see me after one of his releases. On one occasion, his eyes dancing in his head, he admired the furniture in the convent and remarked, 'If you weren't here we'd clear the place out'.

I am often asked how as a Catholic and a nun can I fail to condemn what prisoners have done – be they Irish political prisoners or others. I have learned to love these people who break the law because, innocent or guilty, they're human beings. We are not meant to judge or condemn. There is far too much condemning; it is my role to give a helping hand. Christ identified with the sinner and condemned the sin.

I have always felt I should focus not only on the prisoners but also on their families. It is easier, of course, to be the mother of a victim than of a murderer because people are sympathetic to the first but regard the murderer's mother as criminal too. I saw the Irish prisoners' families in Britain shunned and spurned and the doors shut on them at lowly bed and breakfast guest houses, on entering the gaol gates or visiting the House of Commons.

Two cases I recall from more recent years are those of Tommy Quigley sentenced to life imprisonment in 1985 and Liam Quinn similarly sentenced in 1988. I believe the two prisoners were not guilty of the offences for which they were sentenced. Had their cases come to court post-Guildford, Birmingham, Maguire and Ward, the outcome might have been different.

I tried to expose the injustices of these cases. It seemed obvious to me to raise Liam Quinn's case with Paul Hill and his partner Courtney Kennedy when they were in London in 1989. Liam's mother and aunt were with me in the flat and I asked Paul and Courtney to call. I could sense that as they were telling them about Liam, Courtney Kennedy wasn't interested. She was obviously uncomfortable and didn't say anything. I thought she would be sympathetic because Liam was an American citizen.

When I saw the Kennedys at Paul Hill's appeal against the Brian Shaw murder in Belfast in early 1994 I gave documents to Ethel Kennedy and explained what I was giving her and why. There were also a number of important lawyers at the trial as observers and I gave them copies of the documents. A couple of the lawyers wrote back saying they were unable to do anything. The papers was also given to Joe Kennedy. Liam Quinn is still in gaol.

EVERYTHING ABOUT A PRISONER'S life except the absence of freedom is uncertain and subject to change according to the whim of the Home Office, politicians, the governor, or the prison officer on duty.

The Home Secretary Leon Brittan announced at the Tory Party conference in 1983 that all people who had a mandatory life sentence had to serve twenty years before a date would be considered for their release. A mandatory life sentence is one in which a judge must give a life sentence when the prisoner has been convicted. A discretionary life sentence is one in which the judge decides what sentence a prisoner gets at his own discretion. In either case, the Home Secretary can set a tariff – the actual number of years a prisoner will serve. These tariffs are ostensibly designed to reflect the requirements of retribution and deterrence. The trial judge files a report to the Home Secretary outlining the case and the degrees of danger represented by the defendants. The Home Secretary then sets a tariff – the time a prisoner will serve before being considered for release.

In a written reply to Michael Mates in the House of Commons in November 1983, Leon Brittan confirmed what he had said at the Tory conference about those serving mandatory life sentences. He said that those who had been convicted of murders resulting from terrorist acts, the murder of police or prison officers, the sexual or sadistic murders of children, or murders as a result of armed robbery, would not be considered for a release date until they had served twenty years regardless of the sentence handed down at their trial.

A case was taken by a prisoner who won the right to know what the tariff was that was set for his sentence, the number of years he would actually have to serve as opposed to the number stipulated by the judge at the trial. As a result of this case, it transpired that up until then this could be done but the prisoners were not informed. This meant that lifers were effectively in the dark about the number of years they could expect to serve. Roy Walsh, Paul Holmes and Billy Armstrong, the three still in gaol for the Old Bailey bombing whose sentences were discretionary not mandatory because nobody was killed in the bombing, made a breakthrough at a judicial review. The court said they had the right to know what their tariffs had been set at. They discovered these had been secretly set at the time of their trial by the Home Office at twenty-five years. When they won the case they were told of this and the court said the number of years they actually served had to be in line with defendants who had been involved in the same kind of offence and had to be comparable to theirs. Hugh Feeney, Marian and Dolours Price and Gerry Kelly were already out by then. The three men were transferred to Northern Ireland and released soon afterwards.

It is in this context that Paul Kavanagh, Pat Magee and Tommy Quigley have discovered that a previous Home Secretary had set their tariff at fifty years despite the judges recommended sentence of thirty-five in open court. Paul Kavanagh has questioned the Home Secretary's right to impose this extended tariff on him, outlining the facts of the case against him which relied heavily on extremely questionable evidence. There was nothing but the flimsiest suggestion that Kavanagh had been involved in the offence for which he was convicted. In a clear and compelling statement to the Home Secretary, he outlines the case against him, the dubious nature of the evidence used to convict him, and questions the Home Secretary's right to have imposed such a high tariff on him. These cases are examples of politicians interfering with the judiciary which should be independent. They are dragging British justice into the gutter.

As I keep saying, the blow is not only to the prisoner but also to the family. It is good to discover that I am by no means alone in my views on this. I found an ally in an unexpected quarter, Andrew Coyle, a former prison governor whose publication *The Prisons We Deserve* (1994) stressed the need for families and prisoners to maintain relationships.

I am glad to see that now at the time of writing, the Irish government, including Fine Gael politicians, are aware of the situation of prisoners and their families. For twenty years we were trying, unsuccessfully, to make them take up the issues and I can't remember how many times I went to see TDs and ministers and they just sat and looked at me or accused me, as one did on Radio Éireann, of exaggeration. When Peter Barry TD became Minister for Foreign Affairs in the late 1980s he gave me an hour and a half of careful attention. He heard me out about the plight of the prisoners and their families and was the first major Irish politician to discuss the PTA against which he spoke publicly. On 19 October 1987 Peter Barry was one of a number of TDs and dignitaries attending a meeting at the Irish embassy in London. This meeting was ostensibly to discuss miscarriages of justice but I kept trying to broaden out the issues to include prison conditions. Later there was a social gathering at the Tara Hotel where I felt I was treated flippantly, dismissively and patronisingly. I gave them all an envelope in which there was a letter from a prisoner explaining why he wanted to be repatriated. With the exception of Peter Barry who asked questions, the others made me angry.

My eyesight was more or less gone by 1990 but I tried to keep on at my work. I still kept my diary, which people say is remarkably legible for someone who can see so little. In November of that year, soon after being told I would never be able to read again, I went to the Old Bailey as I had done so many times before. I was still subjected to taunts and insults as my diary entry records:

A large group of police inside the door. The usual policeman started to jeer and deride: Was the cloth genuine? I said nothing. I continued on into the court room and when the midday break came went out approached a policeman and asked him: 'Am I breaking the law by coming? Do I have to endure insults when I come to the Old Bailey?' I said I had been going there since 1976.

Abuse has been a constant part of any work I have done as friend and adviser to prisoners and their families.

14

SUMMING-UP

Be ready at all times to answer anyone who asks you to explain the hope you have in you, but do it with gentleness and respect. Keep your conscience clear, so that when you are insulted, those who speak evil of your good conduct as followers of Christ will be ashamed of what they say. For it is better to suffer for doing good ...

1 PETER 3

London's Tate Gallery, with its fine collection of modern art, is one of my favourite places. It always renewed my spirits when I was discouraged. The ingenious technique pointillism, of creating a picture by blending hundreds of small dots, has always fascinated me. My own life resembles an impressionist's work. So many dots, people, events, relationships, situations, have mingled on the canvas of my life. This chapter has borrowed the legal term 'summing-up' to try to convey some aspects of my life, dots that seem particularly significant. I recognise the miracles by which eighteen innocent prisoners have been proved guiltless but I also feel that the situations which allowed their original imprisonment remain unchanged. The terms of the unjust treaty of 1920 keep Ireland divided, the Prevention of Terrorism Act remains in force and the current Criminal Justice Act will strengthen its powers, strip-searching continues, etc. The May Enquiry really achieved nothing. In spite of twenty-five years of work for justice, I feel I have little to celebrate in terms of clear-cut improvements.

Besides these political difficulties, I have suffered various personal slurs on my character and ministry. The painful episodes with prison chaplains have left their scars. Were they the reasons I was denied visits with Category A prisoners? Although members of Sinn Féin and revolutionary Communist parties have been allowed visits, they were denied to me. I have never knowingly broken the law or a prison rule, yet to the Home Office I am a security risk. When I learned that in August 1985, I asked my superior's permission to do again what I had done with adverse publicity since my Civil Rights days – go public. I sent the information and a copy of my rejection slip to various newspapers including the *Observer*. I regard these slurs as back-handed compliments by the authorities – am I such a thorn in their sides?

In 1986 the prisoner's cause suffered a major loss in the sudden death of Fr Brian Brady. Mrs Kathleen Feeney rang me from Belfast on 29 September to share the painful news which shattered all who knew Fr Brady. I wrote my feelings:

> It is such a sad bit of news – a great man, a friend of Ireland, a holy man, a brilliant man. May he rest in peace. I will have a good friend in heaven. I rang Fr Faul. He had not heard about Fr Brady's death. What a loss Fr Brady will be ... No wonder God took him away. I just must go to Fr Brady's funeral. Fr Murray rang when he heard the news of Fr Brady's death.

When Fr Brian Brady was buried on 3 October, I joined the throng that mourned him:

> We left Feeney's at 4.30 p.m. for Drumbo. The coffin had arrived in the church. We got in and it was crowded. The coffin was large but unadorned. It took ten or twelve men to carry it. Fr Kelly said the Mass and preached. Two bishops were there. It was a very sad occasion. After Mass the coffin was opened. I went by and placed my hand on Fr Brady's ... Why has God taken the best friend the poor have?

Indeed, this death was a major loss. Perhaps, though, like the death of Giuseppe Conlon, Fr Brady's ultimately helped the vindication of the innocent. Almost exactly three years later, on 19 October 1989 the convictions of the Guildford Four were quashed and the vindication of the other fourteen for whom Fr Brady had campaigned followed in the early 1990s.

These grey 'dots' on my canvas are relieved by bright ones: a number of sisters are now doing pastoral ministry in gaols. These women, both Anglican and Catholic, are dedicated to prisoners' needs. Unlike some chaplains, the sisters do not sit on punishment boards nor do they as some chaplains do carry a bundle of keys like prison officers. They do not veto prisoners' mail and visitors, a power some chaplains exercise. They are part of the pastoral service in a gaol but their role is not mixed with administration. This situation provides the freedom from official responsibilities which good pastoral work requires. It now remains for other sisters to answer Pope John Paul II's call to work for prisoners' families, a need not yet fully met. So firm is my belief in this work for families that I have tired to continue doing it despite increasing health problems.

IN 1988 MY SUPERIOR SUGGESTED that I move into a flat in order to accommodate prisoners' relatives during visits to England. After fifty years in convents, I had to face shopping, cooking and worst of all, ironing. This new housekeeping began for me on 6 January 1989. Many people were very helpful, but my niece Frances Cahill was one of the most supportive. Frances' visit of 25 March 1989 was memorable day for aunt and niece:

> Up at 8.00 a.m. when Frances rang to say that they were coming to London today – nothing in the flat. I went to the freezer and took out chops and put them in the microwave on auto freeze for five minutes. Then I washed. Came back. The auto freeze melted the plastic stand, the chops burned, and the microwave was in a mess. Cleaned it up, salvaged what meat there was. Dressed and went to the shops, got more meat and vegetables. Came back and got a casserole ready and into the oven. Then I put out the milk bottles and the door locked behind me. I asked Mr Wardle [neighbour] to ring Joan [a friend] who has a set of keys. She was out. He kept ringing but no Joan. Frances and family came, so I told them to go down the town and come back later. The man at the top of the house tried a ladder, but the windows were locked. In the end they smelled the casserole burning, so they rang the Council. With that Joan came and the Council man together. The dinner was ruined, so they had nothing. They brought piles to me – a lovely little teapot with roses on it. Coffee, salmon, a coverlet, etc. etc. They had a cup of tea.

Fortunately, only the dinner was burned, and the family had an unforgettable day!

There have been moments of joy such as the day Hugh Feeney was released from Long Kesh on 9 March 1990. Mary Feeney rang from a call-box near the gaol breathless to say they got a call at 2.20 to say Hugh was getting out. She was outside the gaol. After 4.30 she rang again from her brother-in-law's shop on her way back. Hugh came on the phone. He did not seem to realise what was happening.

My rewards also consist of the affection of the prisoners and their families. On 30 April 1990 I was staying with the Feeneys in Belfast. I wasn't feeling well after a long day visiting prisoners and families. (I was in my seventy-first year.) I said to the Feeneys, 'Thanks be to God, now I'll be able to go to bed'. There was terrible consternation: 'No you can't do that!' they said. I understood their dismay shortly afterwards when I was taken to the venue in West Belfast for a surprise party organised by some of the families I knew. I'll let my diary finish the story:

> We got there at 9 p.m. and when we went in I got a standing ovation. There was lovely Irish music and then Fr McCloskey sang Danny Boy. Mairéad Farrell's father came up to sing the third verse. Gerry Kelly gave a speech: I was given a beautiful silver cross from the prisoners in England, a hand-knitted black cardigan, a beautiful black cardigan, a beautiful clock, an engraved crystal plate and two huge bouquets of flowers. I gave a bouquet to Mrs Farrell for Mairéad's grave ... It was a splendid evening.

Another bright dot also appeared in 1990 when London's office of *Pax Christi* asked me to allow my photograph and a statement about my work to appear on one of its Peace Sunday posters. I felt honoured by this request, as other posters for the occasion paid tribute to Archbishop Oscar Romero, Rigoberta Menchu, Thomas Merton, Franz Jägerstätter, and a number of other distinguished activists for peace and justice.

Serious eye problems have, perhaps, been my heaviest burden. The prospect of retirement to Ireland was an inviting possibility but after consideration I stayed in London to continue my work. I forsook my car and readjusted to using public transport. I continued going to the airport to meet families and work for prisoners.

IN THE SPRING OF 1993 as I was recovering from my accident, a Belgian friend, a former pupil dating back many years to my school-teaching days, visited me. When she returned to Belgium her car was pulled to pieces by customs officers and a week later she was visited and questioned by the Belgian police. They wanted to know if I had asked her to do anything and about her friendship with me. She was reluctant to tell me about this which makes me wonder whether other people have been similarly questioned, people I have never heard from again.

In January 1995, my doorbell rang unexpectedly one afternoon. I pressed my intercom buzzer but nobody answered so I foolishly opened the door of my flat which leads to a small hallway leading to the front door. This, to my surprise, was already open. My neighbour from the flat upstairs had opened it. I could make out the shapes of two large men whom I didn't recognise. They put a card in my hand. I explained that I was blind and could not read it. They said they were police officers from Cambridgeshire. They failed to warn me of my statutory right that I was under no obligation to speak to them and unless I actually invited them in they had no power of entry. The merest nod of acquiescence can be interpreted as an invitation, something I only discovered afterwards and out of a mixture of panic and good manners I invited them in. I should have known better.

This visit left me very shaken. They questioned me about my contact with prisoners at Whitemoor gaol in Cambridgeshire some of who had escaped five months earlier. I had never met any of them since I was not permitted to visit Category A prisoners but I had corresponded with them and had spoken to them on the phone. I told them I was never at Whitemoor gaol, nor had I sent any parcels, etc. The police told me that they knew that anyway because they had transcripts of the conversations I had had with the prisoners. I told the police I knew I was being taped; it was obvious the prison authorities would do that. They took a statement from me which they asked me to sign. I couldn't read but I felt so intimidated by them that I signed it. They then took my finger-prints. I kept asking them why they were taking my finger-prints. When other prisoners with whom I'd corresponded and to whom I'd taken parcels had escaped, my finger-prints weren't taken. They said different forces had different methods.

They looked at the picture of Padre Pio on the wall and asked me who he was. They said he looked like he was going places. I said no, he'd arrived – he was in Heaven. They looked at another picture on my wall – one by my old friend and former tutor, the late, Paul Piech featuring the John Donne poem in which he wrote 'No man is an island', and they said 'Who is John Donne?' I said he was a metaphysical poet and they said Terry Waite had written about him. I said I too had read Terry Waite's book (on an audio tape). I resented them taking the statement and my finger-prints. It was as though they were criminalising me but then perhaps I shouldn't object – Christ himself was criminalised.

I am ashamed that after all these years – and all my experience – I didn't know my rights. I didn't know I could refuse to speak to them, which I would have done politely, nor did I know that I could refuse to have my finger-prints taken. Surely they should have told me that as a matter of courtesy? But it has taught me something. I know now how the innocent can be made to feel threatened and even guilty. I wouldn't have minded talking to them had it been done properly. It is the manner in which it was done that I object to. I was made to feel so defenceless!

Complaints were sent to the Cambridgeshire Police by the Irish embassy, my Mother Provincial, my Irish societies and Gareth Peirce, and I received an apology. When an unemployed man read about me he sent £5 to assist me.

A few months later prisoners from Full Sutton were told that if they wanted to speak to people on the telephone, all those they wished to call must first be approved. They had asked for me to be on their approved list. I followed the same procedures as with permission to visit or write to prisoners, filling in the same forms and supplying snapshots of myself after which a Scotland Yard prison's security official made an appointment to visit me to verify that I was who I said I was.

He was a perfectly polite gentleman but I found the whole visit very curious as did a friend of mine who was there with me. The man came in and started talking about Irish history. He said, amongst other things, that Field Marshal Montgomery had been ashamed to be British because he had seen what the Black and Tans had done and knew of the atrocities the English committed against the Irish. He said he knew all about me because he had seen the film about me made by the BBC ten years previously. Then he started to talk to me about visiting prisoners at Belmarsh and Full Sutton. I explained that really I had got in touch so the prisoners could phone me. I told him that my old friend and former tutor Mr Edward Wright had designed the revolving sculpture outside Scotland Yard because it occurred to me that I had not pointed this out to any other police officers who had visited me. That seemed to throw him. He asked my friend if she was foreign – goodness knows why since she had spoken several times and was quite clearly English. On his way out he started to talk to her about me, asking oblique questions and implying that if I did my kind of work I must expect to be harassed. However I have now been cleared to visit three Category A prisoners.

MY DIARIES VIBRATE WITH hundreds of lives related to the struggle for justice and my quarter-century commitment to Irish prisoners and their families. People who have known me might express my work in the single line from Matthew's Gospel, 'I was in prison and you visited me'. That would be the greatest highlight on the canvas of my life.

> *The wilderness I understand is the one that doesn't entail being remote from people. Being with God, yes; but taking others with you.*
>
> DOM HELDER CAMARA

INDEX

Drumm, Máire, 47
Drury, Bishop Thomas, 66, 68, 99, 137, 138
Duffy, Annie, 83
Duggan, Harry, 50
Duignan, Bishop, 14
Duignan, Sr Kostka, 14
Dunne, Mrs, 55
Durham, 48, 124

Emmanuel, Sr, 190
Ennis, Fr, 128
Error of Judgement, 150
Esler, Gavin, 140
European Commission of Human Rights, 34, 80, 89,
European Convention of Human Rights, 80
European Court of Human Rights, 76, 91, 191
European Courts of Justice, 158
Evans, Fr, 63
Ewing, Mrs, 145

Fairgreen Infant School, 19
Familiaris Consortio, 113, 115
Farr, Sir John, 143, 194
Farrell, Mairéad, 103, 104, 205
Farrell, Mr, 104, 205
Faul, Fr Denis, 33, 37, 38, 62, 63, 65, 68, 75, 76, 83, 86, 87, 90, 94, 100, 103, 107, 108, 109, 110, 113, 115, 116, 118, 119, 124, 126, 128, 131, 133, 135, 139, 141, 142, 143, 144, 145, 146, 147, 148, 151, 177, 203
Faulkner, Brian, 46
Federation of Irish Associations, 147
Feeney, Hugh, 39, 42, 43, 44, 45, 47, 48, 50, 51, 97, 145, 155, 186, 200, 204
Feeney, Mary, 48, 96, 97, 103, 204
Feeney, Mrs Kathleen, 48, 97, 203
Feeney, Sarah, 45, 48, 188

Fell, Fr, 85–90, 91, 98, 99
Fell, Harry, 86-90, 98, 99
Fell, Mrs, 86
Ferrers, Lord, 164
Finnegan, Eileen, 31, 32, 34
Fish, Hamilton, 138, 139
Fisher, Mike, 62, 63, 65, 66, 67, 100, 144, 167, 168, 170, 193
Fitt, Gerry, 122, 128, 129, 147
Fitzgerald, Edward, 185
Fitzgerald, Garrett, 160
Flynn, Pádraig, 163, 164
Foot, Paul, 146
Fouts, Nancy, 23
Fraser, Hugh, 94
Full Sutton, 194, 207
Furrow, The, 179

Gallagher, Pat 'The Cope', 149
Gartree, 145, 196
Gaughan, Michael, 47, 48, 91, 92, 155, 156, 157
Gemma, Sr, 68
Geoghegan-Quinn, Máire, 107, 164
Gertrude, Sr, 14
Gibson, Mrs, 95
Gibson, Noel, 95
Gifford, Lord, 142, 151, 179
Gillespie, Mr, 95
Gilmore, Fr Bobby, 116, 117, 118
Glenholmes, Richard, 112
Goldring, Maurice, 23
Gone with the Wind, 14
Great Hunger, 92
Griffith, Fr Michael, 12
Guardian, The, 79, 80, 140
Guildford Four, 38, 49, 50, 51, 83, 121, 122, 127, 132, 133, 134, 140, 144, 146, 147, 149, 150, 151, 152, 153, 166, 167, 168, 171, 173, 180, 182, 183, 184, 194, 198, 203
Gutierrez, Gustavo, 39

Hackett, Mrs, 92